'He does what no other scholar I know of can do in presenting the full range of global military history.'

Peter Lorge, Vanderbilt University, USA

The seventeenth century has long been seen as a period of 'crisis' or transition from the pre-modern to the modern world. This book offers a chance to explore this crisis from the perspective of war and military institutions in a way that should appeal to those studying global history.

By placing seventeenth-century warfare in a global context, Black challenges conventional chronologies and permits a reappraisal of the debate over what has been seen as the Military Revolution of the early-modern period. The book discusses war with regard to strategic cultures, assesses military capability in terms of tasks and challenges faced and attaches styles of warfare to their social and political contexts. Genuinely global in range, this up-to-date and wide-ranging account provides fresh historiographical insights into this crucial period in world history.

Jeremy Black is Professor of History at the University of Exeter, UK. He is a leading authority on early-modern British and continental European history, with special interest in international relations, military history, the press, and historical atlases. His recent publications include *The English Seaborne Empire*, *Rethinking Military History*, *The Age of Total War*, *Using History* and *Naval Power*.

Beyond the Military Revolution

War in the Seventeenth-Century World

Jeremy Black

palgrave
macmillan

First published 2011 by
PALGRAVE MACMILLAN

Palgrave Macmillan in the UK is an imprint of Macmillan Publishers Limited, registered in England, company number 785998, of Houndmills, Basingstoke, Hampshire RG21 6XS.

Palgrave Macmillan in the US is a division of St Martin's Press LLC, 175 Fifth Avenue, New York, NY 10010.

Palgrave Macmillan is the global academic imprint of the above companies and has companies and representatives throughout the world.

Palgrave® and Macmillan® are registered trademarks in the United States, the United Kingdom, Europe and other countries.

ISBN 978–0–230–25155–7   hardback
ISBN 978–0–230–25156–4   paperback

This book is printed on paper suitable for recycling and made from fully managed and sustained forest sources. Logging, pulping and manufacturing processes are expected to conform to the environmental regulations of the country of origin.

A catalogue record for this book is available from the British Library.

A catalog record for this book is available from the Library of Congress.

10   9   8   7   6   5   4   3   2   1
20   19   18   17   16   15   14   13   12   11

Printed in China

For Tony Kelly

Contents

Preface

'This victorious action drew to a close with the day itself; it was as though the sun decided not to set until it could see and cast its rays on the triumph of Your Majesty's armies.' Prince Eugene's dispatch to the Emperor Leopold I from his overwhelming triumph over an Ottoman (Turkish) army at Zenta in Hungary in 1697 was one of the more memorable lines I encountered as a student. This book is fired by the same interest, an interest in the global nature of conflict and the importance of warfare in human development. The seventeenth century has long been seen as a period of 'crisis' or transition from the pre-modern to the modern world. This book offers a chance to explore this crisis from the perspective of war and military institutions in a way that should appeal to those doing global history. In doing so, picking the seventeenth century permits a reappraisal of the debate over what has been seen as the Military Revolution of the early-modern period. The original account of this supposed transformation highlighted 1560–1660 as the key period of change, and looking at this subject again permits a re-examination of both the thesis and its chronology. Moreover, discarding 1660 as an end date for this study both permits a reconsideration of the conventional account and also opens up an integration of post-1660 *ancien régime* armies, navies and warfare with that of the preceding period. As such, this approach to military history is of wider historiographical significance. In this book, I also discuss war with regard to strategic cultures (and élite culture specifically), assess military capability in terms of tasks and challenges faced, which, in turn, brings issues of variety and flexibility to the fore, and attach styles of warfare to their social and political contexts.

In thinking about and writing this book, I have benefited greatly from teaching the period since 1980 and also from reading the works of others. There is always the danger that new work will be presented as a critique of what has come before. That is not my intention, as I see historical study, like the subject it describes, as a relationship between generations and among colleagues. Indeed, I would like to record my gratitude for the friendship and work of other scholars on the period, notably Brian Davies, Peter Lorge, John Lynn, Geoffrey Parker, David Parrott and Peter Wilson: if there is not always agreement, there is always respect and affection, and that is an important part of my world. Given my criticism of the Military Revolution thesis which Geoffrey has so ably pursued on the European and world scales, I would like to record my enormous respect for his wide-ranging and perceptive scholarship and my gratitude for his friendship and support over the years.

It is a great pleasure to thank Pradeep Barua, Guy Chet, John France, Greg Hanlon, Harald Kleinschmidt, Peter Lorge, John Lynn, Tim May, Stephen Morillo, Olaf van Nimwegen, Ciro Paoletti, Kenneth Swope, John Thornton, David Trim and Erbin Xu for commenting on an earlier draft. None is responsible for any errors that remain. I have also benefited from the opportunity to give lectures at Columbus Ohio, High Point, North Carolina, the National Maritime Museum, London, and Oxford, and from hearing a characteristically thoughtful lecture by David Parrott. Kate Haines has proved a most helpful editor and Caroline Richards a very supportive copy-editor. It is a great pleasure to dedicate this book to a good friend and fellow scholar and to note a decade of friendship and many good walks and pleasant lunches that have brought me much enjoyment.

1 Introduction

War played a key role in the history of the seventeenth century. It was a prime means by which empires, states and peoples expanded and resisted expansion, and the way in which ministers, rulers, dynasties, indeed systems of control, were overthrown in particular states. War thus linked the Europeans establishing their position in North America to the Manchu taking over the most populous empire in the world, Ming China.

Method

There is a danger, however, that military history on the global scale can become a blizzard of names and dates. That is not the intention here, but neither is it the plan to reduce this fascinating and complex century to the simplicity of a clear-cut pattern with allegedly exemplary battles or leaders that apparently provide guidance to an obvious schema. No such schema existed and, however attractive, the idea of exemplary battles or leaders is highly questionable. Moreover, I reject the idea that discussion should be related to a thesis of military change based on stages established by ideal forms of conduct and paradigmatic powers providing a clear model for conduct,[1] not least because this problematic thesis leads in practice to a focus on a small number of powers, with much of the world ignored or discussed largely in terms of these powers, for example with reference to the idea of the diffusion of best practice through the emulation of their methods.

The Military Revolution

Such an approach is seen in the most influential book on the subject, Geoffrey Parker's impressive and groundbreaking *The Military Revolution: Military Innovation and the Rise of the West, 1500–1800* (1988). He argued that 'all the evidence for radical military change, whether in army size, fortifications, or firearms, comes from the lands of the Habsburgs or of their neighbours … That was the heartland of the military revolution', and, as is normal with historians seeking to establish significance, it was the area

1

of Parker's expertise. The Spanish branch of the Habsburg family ruled not only Spain but also much of Italy as well as the Spanish Netherlands (modern Belgium). Elsewhere in Europe, where the changes of the Military Revolution do not take place or not to the same extent, this situation is presented as failure.[2] This approach is replicated by Parker at the global scale, which is highly instructive as far as linking developments across the world is concerned, notably those in Japan with those in Europe. Yet, the global approach is also unhelpful as it assumes or implies that there was a clear pattern of appropriate development predicated on an obvious best practice.

In practice, the principal modern analytical framework and device for the period, the Military Revolution, has been applied with a number of different emphases, and there is not always a ready relationship and correspondence between these. Michael Roberts, who famously advanced the idea, was particularly interested in combined arms tactics and governmental development.[3] Tactics were discussed in terms of infantry volley fire, with the view that there was only one doctrine concerning the effective use of muskets in the field, and that the drill and discipline necessary to provide this became crucial to a distinctive Western way of war.[4] Moreover, the new-model tactics presented as necessary to make best use of the pike–musket combination were regarded by those who advanced and deployed the thesis of the Military Revolution as requiring larger forces, and as both needing, and making possible, a stronger government able to support such forces.

Yet, in discussing those states, peoples and groups who acted other than in terms of this Revolution largely in terms of failure, or with that assumption at least implicit, this argument is methodologically questionable, not least as it is normal to adopt practices that seem appropriate, and past societies generally had a better idea of this than scholars writing with the confidence of posterity. Furthermore, the approach is empirically problematic as the variety of military systems and methods were fit for purpose within the constraints of the relevant social systems, the latter an insight noted by eighteenth-century writers discussing, at least *en passant*, historical sociology, most obviously Edward Gibbon and Adam Smith. The caveat of social constraints is instructive, and is frequently employed to criticise societies that did not adopt firearms, or did not use them successfully, but that simple model has to be handled with care as it makes the adoption of the gun the prime narrative and analysis of military development when the situation, in fact, was more complex.

This complexity reflects the number of routes of development, a situation that arose from the great variations in the cultural and environmental contexts of warfare. Thus, a nomadic society in Central Asia (or Central Eurasia as it is sometimes now termed) operated in a very different fashion to urban northern Italy, an area in which states were numerous and state boundaries relatively well defined. It is also misleading to adopt a determinist approach to environmentalism and to assume that all nomadic (or urban) societies acted alike, or even were likely to do so, an approach that, in particular, can lead to the inaccurate primitivisation of the former, as in some of the writing on China's steppe opponents, those who lived on the plains to its north and north-west. As a related point, fitness for purpose, the classic definition of fighting and organisational capability, had differing meanings and consequences across the world. It is terribly tempting to search for comparisons as a means of explanation, but such comparisons have to be grounded in these understandings of contexts and meanings, rather than being used as a basis for statements about a relative capability that is wrenched out of context.

An instance of this problem is provided by the central concept employed when discussing warfare in Europe and then, by extension, the world, the Military Revolution already referred to. As originally advanced and applied, notably in the 1950s by Michael Roberts, a specialist on seventeenth-century Sweden,[5] this thesis was an account of change within Europe (understood throughout as Christian Europe). Roberts saw the Swedish army under Gustavus Adolphus (r. 1611–32) as bringing to fruition tactical innovations developed by the Dutch in order to increase infantry firepower. The Dutch introduced broader and shallower troop formations which permitted more soldiers to fire at once, and in the 1590s they developed continuous fire by using a volley technique, so that one rank of soldiers fired simultaneously and then reloaded while other ranks fired in turn. This method produced continuous fire, and thus offered a protection against attack separate to that provided by pikemen. The method was also developed in Japan from the 1560s, but was advanced in Europe by William Lodewijk of Nassau, Governor of the Dutch province of Friesland and a scholar of Classical literature. The *Tactica* of Aelian written in about 100 CE (AD) provided the key text, and in 1594 William wrote about it to his cousin, Count Maurice of Nassau, the commanding general of the United Provinces (modern Netherlands). Aelian provided much detail in matters of drill, and this detail proved of great value to the army organisers of the period, as did his critical account of earlier works on the art of war. Editions of Aelian included a Leiden one in 1613 and *The Tactics of Aelian or art of embattailing an army after the Grecian manner* (London, 1616).[6] Reference to Aelian reflected the authority of Antiquity and the habit of comparison with Classical methods, which were well established in the literature on war, as with Imperiale Cinuzzi's *La Vera Militar Disciplina Antica e*

Moderna (Siena, 1604), Hermannus Hugo's *De Militia Equestri Antiqua et Nova* (Antwerp, 1630) and Jacques Ozanam's *Traité de Fortification, contenant les methodes anciennes et modernes pour la construction et la deffense des places* (Paris, 1694). Authors who wrote on modern military history, such as Johann Jacobi, also published on Classical warfare, in his case *La Milice Romaine* (Frankfurt, 1616).

Maurice was impressed by Aelian's account of the drill of Classical pikemen and slingers, and he took steps to improve and standardise the drill and the army. Maurice also increased the firepower of each company and encouraged the standardisation of weapons, although this was a difficult process because the company commanders were responsible for buying the weapons themselves. Real standardisation began only after 1627 when the captains were obliged to procure their equipment from provincial arsenals.

The importance of mercenaries, which included the majority of Gustavus's troops in Germany in the 1630s, and the hiring of foreign officers helped ensure a spread in tactical innovations, as did publications such as Henry Hexham's *The Principles of the Art of Militarie; practised in the wars of the United Netherlands* (3 vols, 1635–40); but, as new methods spread, they were also changed. Whereas the Dutch had earlier tended to use the rotation of ranks of musketeers defensively, so that, having fired, they retired to reload while colleagues behind took their place, Gustavus employed rotation offensively, the other ranks moving forward through stationary reloaders. He also equipped his infantry units with mobile small cannon and trained his cavalry in a shock charge pressed home with swords in the manner of the Polish cavalry, rather than with pistol fire at short range. The latter inflicted casualties but lacked impact and decisiveness.

Roberts's concentration on the Dutch and Swedish was refocused by Parker to include Spain but was also broadened out fruitfully to consider the world scale: first, the role of the Military Revolution in giving Europeans greater relative capability, and thus aiding their expansion, and, secondly, parallel and contrasting developments across the globe. The Military Revolution therefore came to stand for the discussion of military activity and change both in a period of time – the early-modern period, generally understood as 1450–1790 – and also in terms of a particular response, that to the ready availability on a large scale of gunpowder weaponry.

In turn, the period of time takes on reality in a European narrative of history that is structured in military terms with reference to this weaponry and related infantry tactics, and thus fails to give due weight to differing trajectories of development.[7] It is not immediately clear, for example, why so much more attention is devoted to the military history of Western Europe, the centre of the Military Revolution, rather than Eastern Europe, other than as a result of a misleading primitivisation of the latter that underplays the extent to which there were important developments in both regions. Indeed, in terms of the consolidation of states that were to be important to subsequent European history, the seventeenth century was significant in Eastern Europe, notably with the survival of Russia from the 'Time of Troubles' in its early years, and that of Austria from Ottoman (Turkish) assault in 1683. More generally, the close-order tactics used in battle in Western Europe and considered by the protagonists of the Military Revolution were not very serviceable in many contexts around the world. Even in Western Europe, the combined armed tactics of the Military Revolution were (as ever) far easier to discuss in training manuals, which emphasised drill, and to attempt in combat, than they were to execute successfully under the strain of battle. Moreover, the contrasting fighting characteristics of the individual arms – muskets, pike, cavalry, cannon – operated very differently in particular circumstances, and this situation posed added problems for co-ordination. So also did the limited extent to which many generals and officers understood these characteristics and problems.

Military adaptation is a more appropriate term than revolution, not least because the latter carries with it a meaning of clear intention and direction, and a teleology linked to that of a comparable presentation of government development. In practice, the major characteristic, in both warfare and government, was that of expedients, such that the pursuit of successful expediency became more than solely a method of response and, instead, frequently was also the goal of change. Both on campaign and on the battlefield, far from war being won by planned action, it was often the side that was less prevented from pursuing goals by its weaknesses that was successful; and coping with these weaknesses was the major skill of command. On campaign, providing supplies was both difficult and vital,[8] while, amid the uncertainty of battle, the retention and use of reserves was often crucial.

Aside from the historical focus on the Military Revolution, the 1990s and early 2000s saw a revived interest in the concept of military revolution,[9] as work on the contemporary 'Revolution in Military Affairs' (RMA) led to consideration of supposed antecedents.[10] This, however, was a somewhat dubious proposition, not least because the self-conscious character of the RMA as a revolutionary, new development was not widely matched in the early-modern period. Instead, there was also then a strong, continued and, in many respects, new belief in the value of Classical exemplars, and therefore a looking back to the ancient world which was still strong in the seventeenth century; indeed, aspects of the work on military tactics drew directly on Roman examples. Whether or not there is an effective modern RMA, as opposed to a discourse to that end, that offers no proof of a similar situation in the early-modern period. The case for a military revolution then remains not proven at best and dubious at worst. The relevant literature is of great value, but the increased looseness of categories (and chronological extension) for discussion of the early-modern Military Revolution is such that there is no longer the analytical clarity that was once the case.

Instead, the concept has become widely used despite, or maybe because, it can be employed with a variety of meanings as to definition and dating, causes and consequences. Moreover, the phrase Military Revolution combines a noun with an adjective such that, in grammatical terms, it should be understood as signifying a revolution that is military in kind, whereas it has been used to denote a revolution concerning the military, with the revolution understood as concerning core aspects of war making affected by weapons technology and its consequences on the conduct of war. Thus, a phrase such as 'revolution in the conduct of war' might best describe the standard thesis, although in practice there was no revolutionary change in this conduct during the period 1450–1790, at least on land. In lieu of such a revolution, the demand for maintaining the stability of the world prevailed, and the modifications in weapons technology, tactics, operations and strategy that occurred were adapted to the overall demand for this stability.

The variety of meanings can make overall assessment difficult, but there is also often insufficient attention to process when discussing the early-modern Military Revolution. Indeed, the idea of a military revolution rests essentially on a 'push' theory of warfare, which interprets war in terms of the material culture of conflict, specifically the weaponry, such that tactical factors linked to the use of weapons tend to drive the analysis. This approach devotes insufficient attention to operational 'push' factors, but even more to 'pull' factors in terms of demands on the military, in other words the purposes of military capability, use, and related force structures and doctrines. There is scant sign of a full-fledged revolution in these purposes in Europe, certainly on land, in the seventeenth century or, indeed, in the early-modern period as a whole; although, at sea, there was a new interest in Europe from the late sixteenth century in protecting or attacking transoceanic maritime links. Moreover, maritime capability required detailed planning, logistical support, political commitment, administrative competence, leadership and training, as well as an ability to overcome the challenges posed by technological innovation. The maritime expeditionary warfare of the Mediterranean, Baltic and Atlantic was an important aspect of the conflicts of the period between European states.

Yet, despite the enhanced capability of the major European naval powers, the use of the concept of a military revolution, even at sea, and, certainly, more generally, can carry with it misleading teleological connotations. On land, military adaptation, particularly to the opportunities and problems for co-ordination of individual arms, is a more appropriate term, while the timescale of the adaptation does not anyway accord with understandings of revolution as occurring over a relatively short period. As another qualification of the concept of a military revolution, far from war being necessarily won by planned action, it was frequently the side that was less handicapped by deficiencies that was successful: coping with problems was the major skill of command, both on campaign and on the battlefield. However, in making these and other assessments, there is always the problem that operational and tactical details for many of the wars, including the deployment of forces on the battlefield and the course of engagements, are less than complete, and, for many campaign engagements, were limited.

The intention here is to consider the seventeenth century not in terms of the Military Revolution, a concept that can readily shift meaning and context, but rather to focus on capability, change and continuity, and only at the close to consider whether the Military Revolution is still a relevant concept.[11] Here the global reach of the Military Revolution thesis is matched with discussions of local military histories from all over the globe, discussions that undermine the single-cause determinism of that thesis. The start and end dates chosen to frame the investigation are primarily stages in Christian chronology, but they are also chosen precisely because they do not appear as turning points, and thus their choice indicates a theme of continuity that is significant. This theme links to a wider critique of a misleading tendency in work by some early-modernists to treat medieval warfare as primitive in comparison with what was to come, and also to present it in teleological terms with an emphasis on the development of infantry and, in particular, on archers, notably longbowmen, as progenitors of the subsequent introduction of hand-held gunpowder weaponry. This approach has led to a slighting of the variety of medieval warfare and to a misleading account of its development.[12]

Nevertheless, at the same time, changes did occur around the world. Aside from those of the fifteenth and sixteenth centuries, and their continuing consequences for developments in the seventeenth century, the contexts and uses of force in 1700 were not identical with those in 1600. That situation highlights the need to consider changes during the century, albeit again without overloading any particular chosen turning point. For example, although warships in 1700 were still wooden vessels dependent on wind power or that of human rowers, the organisation and firepower of European warships changed greatly during the century and there has been discussion of an early-modern naval revolution.[13] However, the 'although' phrase captures the difficulty of deciding where to place the emphasis, a perennial issue for historians, and one that is of particular note for a century generally discussed for Europe in terms, first, of the supposed revolutionary character of its early decades and, secondly, of a more conservative, or at least non-revolutionary, second half.

Ironically, in so far as significant European changes can be discerned, these, indeed, should be dated to the period 1660–1760, rather than the previous century, the period of the classic Military Revolution as advanced by Roberts. In particular, to consider the period from 1660, the tactical innovations focused on line-ahead tactics at sea and the development of the bayonet on land, both measures that enhanced firepower and mobility, can be set alongside the significant development in British and Russian military power, as well as the growth of what have been termed fiscal-military states. In the sense of 'beyond', it is also necessary to ask how the relationship between the seventeenth century and the following century is to be considered. In particular, there is the question of whether the closing decades of the seventeenth century established a pattern, of change and/or continuity, that was the key element for most of the eighteenth, the approach taken for example both by those who discern Europe in terms of fiscal-military states and by scholars who focus on the concept of Absolutism. This topic relates to how the period of the alleged early-modern Military Revolution links with that beginning with the French Revolutionary Wars.[14] In doing so, it is appropriate to address these issues at the world scale as this approach provides a way to gauge their wider significance.

Linked to the standard chronological approach, with its emphasis on the early decades of the seventeenth century, as well as to the idea of an early-modern Military Revolution that imposed heavy burdens on states and societies, comes the concept of a general seventeenth-century crisis, which has been held to be the consequence and cause of political and military events and developments around the world. This concept has been applied both specifically to the mid-century and, more generally, to the century as a whole with its varied and related demographic, economic, social and political problems. The crisis may have been triggered by a sudden change in global temperature which had drastic effects on the food supply and stability of peoples across the world.[15] As such it is a reminder that human agencies, whether or not in warfare, were not necessarily the drivers of change.

Suggesting that discussion can, indeed should, move beyond the idea of an early-modern military revolution raises questions that are both latent throughout the text and that can guide the response to it. In particular, there is the question of whether there is an overarching thesis to replace that of the early-modern Military Revolution and, if so, what its relationship with that concept will be. Alternatively, can the concept of the Military Revolution be adapted to make sense of developments around the world during the seventeenth century? The concept has been used thus, notably by Parker and, for Morocco, by Weston Cook, and also, for example, to discuss West Africa in the 1690s.[16] Nevertheless, there is room to ask whether the very concept of the early-modern Military Revolution can be employed, even transformed, to respond to the variety of developments, particularly in China and India as well as Europe; or whether the challenge is too great, such that a new concept is required. Peter Lorge's argument that a military revolution, in the shape of the ability to produce and sustain effective gun-using forces, occurred in Asia and then spread to Europe is valuable, but may also indicate an overloading of the term.[17]

The interrelated nature of wars in different regions certainly represented a form of transmission between events and developments in particular areas. Thus, the Ottoman empire's ability to respond to challenges from Safavid Persia to its east was, at least in part, dependent on the state of its relations with Christian Europe to its west and north. Yet, there was also more separateness than was allowed for by those who suggested that such relationships could readily be affected. In February 1676, a British envoy in The Hague, the capital of the United Provinces (Netherlands), noted the talk there that the hostile Louis XIV of France would ensure peace between Poland and the Ottomans, so as to enable Poland to attack Brandenburg-Prussia, which would weaken the coalition opposed to France in the Dutch War that had started in 1672. Meredith added, 'yet they do not seem to think the influence of that king [of Poland] upon his nation to be such as can bring that design to pass without great opposition and on the other side they seem very confidently to build upon the Muscovites [Russians] engaging for them against the Swedes',[18] who, in turn, were allied with Louis XIV and opposed to Brandenburg-Prussia and the Dutch. In the event, Poland and Russia did not attack Brandenburg-Prussia and Sweden respectively.

Themes

The tension between the specific and the general, and between research and theorisation, is a common one in history, and military history is no exception. Thus, for example, the sweeping statements frequently made about the Military Revolution or concerning European *ancien régime* warfare (that of 1648–1789), and their 'location' in terms of general theories of military development, appear misleading, if not glib, as any consideration of the excellent detailed work available suggests. Notably, *ancien régime* European warfare can be dismissed as rigid and anachronistic, as is frequently done from the generalists' perspective, only if a very narrow and misleading view of it is taken. Instead, this warfare displayed both dynamism and flexibility, although, at the same time, its dynamism and flexibility should not detract attention from the variety of military systems and conflict elsewhere in the world. This comparative dimension is an important topic for research and discussion, and must not be reduced to a consideration only of warfare between Europeans and non-Europeans.

More generally, models of military development that assume some mechanistic search for efficiency and a maximisation of force do violence to the complex process by which interests in new methods interacted with powerful elements of continuity. For example, a stress on the value of morale and the importance of honour came naturally to the aristocratic order that dominated war making, and traditional assumptions about appropriate conduct were important in force structure and tactics. Across the world, notions of best practice and effectiveness were framed and applied in terms of dominant cultural and social patterns. Thus, although gunpowder-armed forces pressed hard in the seventeenth century on those who lacked such armaments,[19] bellicosity, capability and sophistication were far from restricted to the world of gunpowder empires.

The cost of war

Lastly, a simple point that is always pertinent for military historians. In writing and reading about the subject, it is all too easy to forget the pain and suffering involved in conflict and warfare, for soldiers and civilians alike. Given both personal experience and accounts of atrocities, for example Christian Loper's *Laniena Paswalcensis: that is, a tragical relation of the plundering, butchering, ravishing of the women and firing of the town of Pasewalke in Pomerland [Pomerania]* (1631), that was not a mistake made by contemporaries, and is not the case here. The killing of civilians and rape of women was commonplace[20] and in Western Europe was not limited to the barbarities of the Thirty Years' War (1618–48), as is sometimes implied. It is arresting to note in the archives accounts of episodes such as that at Maastricht (in the Netherlands), a fortress captured by the French from the Dutch in 1673. In September 1676, the French sent out a raiding party that burned down houses, took prisoners and extorted contributions of supplies to support their garrison. The Dutch, however, forbade their subjects to pay these contributions, and, as a result of the non-payment, the French executed their hostages in May 1677.[21] The military themselves suffered terrible casualties. Visiting the Dutch camp before besieged Maastricht in July 1676, John Ellis found many wounded 'maimed many of them as if they had been in a sea-fight, such scarcity of legs and arms there is amongst them'.[22] Thus, read about war, but also be aware of what you read.

2 Sixteenth-Century Background

Introduction

An understanding of the sixteenth century is important to that of the following period, important in order to understand events but also so as to provide a background for analysis. The latter conventionally rests in large part on the reading of the seventeenth century as part of a distinct early-modern period that began in the late fifteenth century. For the outset of this period, the fall of Constantinople, the capital of Byzantium, the Eastern Roman Empire, the city now called Istanbul, to the Ottomans in 1453, as well as Christopher Columbus's arrival in what became to the Europeans the New World in 1492, and the beginning of the Italian Wars in 1494, are classically seen as (alternative) turning points, although each of course had little direct relevance for the regions in which the bulk of the world's population lived, East and South Asia. At any rate, the reading of the seventeenth century within the early-modern period is as part of a treatment that looks at the idea of a transforming 'long sixteenth century'. The idea of such a transforming long sixteenth century rests on a number of factors, specific both to military developments and events, and those in which warfare was located. These specific factors focus on the spread of gunpowder weaponry and the absolute and relative capability advantages to which it led, both on land and at sea. The 'location' of warfare is related to these factors in terms of the many needs and opportunities created by powerful states and far-flung geographical connections and ambitions.

Gunpowder

None of these factors began promptly at 1500. Indeed, the Mongol empire of the early thirteenth century created by Chinggis Khan had more far-flung connections and ambitions than those of the Eurasian empires of the fifteenth century. Moreover, gunpowder, so often seen as the key turning point into and/or of military modernity, or, at least, modernisation, had a much longer genesis than might be suggested by any focus on the late fifteenth century. Instead, gunpowder weaponry developed first in China, where the correct formula for manufacturing gunpowder was discovered in the ninth century, and effective metal-barrelled weapons were produced in the twelfth. Each of these processes involved many stages. With gunpowder, it was essential to find a rapidly-burning mixture with a high propellant force, while, for effective cannon, it was necessary to increase the calibre and to move from pieces made of rolled sheet iron, reinforced with iron bands, to proper castings. Gunpowder was used at sea as well as on land, but even when gunpowder weapons had developed, their use was still restricted by their limitations and by the need to decide how best to employ them in battle and siegecraft, as well as by a preference for already-established arms. Nevertheless, by the beginning of the sixteenth century, restrictions on the use of gunpowder weaponry had been overcome in a number of important areas, and, despite serious problems in ensuring the availability of the raw materials both for gunpowder and for firearms, this usage was to spread during the century. At the same time, not all dynamic powers made much or, in some cases, any use of gunpowder. It was not used by native societies in the Americas, nor in Australasia, Oceania or sub-Saharan Africa. Focus in the sixteenth century, however, centres on the 'gunpowder empires', imperial powers that used gunpowder weaponry.

The Ottoman empire

On land, the most notable 'gunpowder empire' was the Ottoman (Turkish) empire, which expanded to make major gains on three continents, Asia, Africa and Europe, and which, from 1453, had its capital at Constantinople. The Ottomans initially relied on mounted archers, but, in the second half of the fourteenth century, they developed an infantry that became a centrally paid standing army, eventually armed with handguns and supported by field cannon. By the late fifteenth century, the Ottomans were successfully using their firepower to create and exploit a capability gap. Muslim rivals suffered as much, or even more, than Christian ones from the rise of the Ottomans, and under Selim I 'the Grim' (r. 1512–20), the greatest challenges and opportunities for the Ottomans came in Asia; although he only achieved so much. Selim defeated the Safavids who had conquered Persia (Iran) and Iraq in the 1500s, but he was unable to impose his own protégé on the country. Indeed, at one level, there was an essential geopolitical stability on land in early-modern Eurasia, and certainly in contrast with the earlier situation under the Mongols. Nevertheless, the Ottomans were able to create a far-flung empire, as were the Safavids. Yet, a comparison of the two indicated that there was no one route to success in terms of force structure and tactics, a point that remained the case in the seventeenth century. Whereas the Ottomans had made the transition to a mixed force, combining their *janissary* infantry with cavalry, the Safavid army was of the traditional Central Asian nomadic type: archers on horseback who provided both mobility and firepower, the ability to control vast spaces and effective conflict on the battlefield. Cultural factors were important, as the Safavids thought firearms cowardly and, initially, adopted cannon with reluctance. Similarly, the Egyptian-based Mamluk empire of Egypt, Palestine and Syria, which was rapidly overthrown by the Ottomans in 1516–17 in one of the most successful wars of the century, put a premium on cavalry and did not associate the use of firearms with acceptable warrior conduct. Like a number of other warrior cultures, such as the Aztecs of Mexico, conquered by Spain in the early 1520s, the Mamluks stressed individual prowess and hand-to-hand, one-to-one combat with a matched opponent, and this commitment made them vulnerable to forces that put an emphasis on more concerted manoeuvres and on anonymous combat, particularly those forces employing firepower.

The major military states of the sixteenth, like the seventeenth, century fought in a variety of contexts, and this variety posed a challenge to their strength and capability, a challenge that underlined the usual risk of overreach. For example, the range of physical and military environments in which the Ottomans had to operate was striking. In the sixteenth century, aside from attacking the Mamluks and, repeatedly, the Safavids, with their large cavalry armies, the Ottomans fought the (Christian) Europeans on land in Europe, North Africa and Abyssinia (Ethiopia), each very different military and political environments, and fought them at sea in the Mediterranean, Red Sea, Persian Gulf and Indian Ocean, as well as fighting a series of less powerful polities, ranging from Bedouin Arabs to opponents in the Caucasus. With differing emphases, this variety still pertained in the seventeenth century, and if the emphasis was more clearly then on conflict on land, there were still contrasts at sea between conflict with Cossacks in the Black Sea, Venetians in the Mediterranean, and Habsburg boats on the rivers of Central Europe.

Ottoman capability drew on a military that required a considerable measure of organisation, especially in logistics, which, indeed, was a characteristic of the major military powers as they had to operate across a considerable range. The Ottoman military combined the strengths of different systems – organisational, bureaucratic and fiscal – alongside tribal forces, notably allies and tributaries, especially the Crimean Tatars, but also local allies in Algiers, the Horn of Africa and elsewhere.[1] The diversity of the Ottoman military system was an inherent source of power, one that was linked to the breadth and depth of its recruitment pool, a characteristic also true of the contemporary Habsburg military, notably the armies of Spain, as well as of that of Manchu China in the seventeenth century. Thus, rather than uniformity being a key to success, it was the combined arms capability derived from the nature of composite empires that was crucial. This factor may seem to be at marked variance with the standard account of modernisation, which puts an emphasis on such uniformity, but the current emphasis on combined arms capabilities in the modern world serves to underline the extent to which uniformity is not, in fact, a key factor. At any rate, Ottoman success led other states to imitate aspects of their military organisation and methods. The *janissaries* served as a model for infantry forces developed in Poland and, more notably, for the musketeer force established by Ivan IV (Ivan the Terrible) of Muscovy in 1550.

South Asia

Further east, another major power of the seventeenth century, the Mughal empire of India, was established in the early sixteenth. Babur, the founder of the empire, was an instance of the extraordinary military potency of Central Asia, and, yet again, cavalry forces from there had a major impact. This was partly a matter of numbers, with the Mughal cavalry more numerous than that of many individual opponents, but also of the vigour with which they were employed. Using tactics similar to those of the Mongols under Chinggis Khan, Mughal mounted archers fired volleys repeatedly in order to disorientate their opponents and make them vulnerable to a more direct attack. As a result of the value of their cavalry, control over the horse trade from Central Asia was important to the later position of the Mughals in India.[2]

Akbar (r. 1556–1605), the grandson of Babur, who rebuilt and extended the Mughal empire in India, took great interest in the improvement of muskets, maintaining a special collection that he tested himself. His artillery was superior to that of rivals and was instrumental in the capture of well-fortified positions, but, in 1581, Akbar's massive field army still only included 28 cannon in a force of 50,000 cavalry and 500 war elephants. Firearms helped Akbar, but the great extension of Mughal territory during his reign, which provided the basis for Mughal power in the seventeenth century, reflected his energy and determination, the divisions among his opponents, the impressive demographic, economic and financial resources of Hindustan and the regions already gained by conquest, and the strength of the Mughal military system. Aside from firearms, the Mughals also used heavy cavalry armed with swords and lances, horse archers, and war elephants; and the successful combination of a number of military traditions was important, as also for the Ottomans and, later, for the Manchu in China.

Less striking or well known are other Central Asian military forces of the sixteenth century each of which continued to put an emphasis on cavalry: the Uzbeks, Kazaks and Mongols. Yet their success invites critical attention to the customary stress on firepower seen with the phrase 'gunpowder empires'. This question is directly pertinent to the seventeenth century, both because the major political forces then were in place by the late sixteenth century and because this issue raises the question of whether the situation was different in the seventeenth century. The Manchu who conquered Ming China in mid-century were not a Central Asian people and had a mixed economy of which only part was similar to that of the steppe, but their emphasis was on cavalry and their army was the most successful of the century.

In many cases, firepower did produce a very valuable capability advantage in the sixteenth century, as in the seventeenth.[3] At the First Battle of Panipat in 1526, when the Mughals decisively defeated the predominant power of northern India, the Lodi sultanate of Delhi, Babur, alongside his horse archers, employed both matchlockmen and field artillery successfully against the cavalry of the Lodis, whose armies did not use firearms. In 1528, Safavid artillery played a role in Tahmasp I of Persia's victory over the Uzbeks at Jam. Tactics were similar at Panipat, Jam, and the Ottoman victories of Chaldiran (1514) and Mohacs (1526), over the Persians and Hungarians respectively. The winning side employed a deployment known in Turkish as *tábúr cengi*: a row of carts linked by chains was arranged across the centre to block the advance of the opposing force and, behind it, both artillery and infantry were deployed, transforming with firepower the traditional idea of a wagon fort. To complete the combined arms approach, mounted archers were placed on the wings.

Firearms helped relatively small forces to beat far more numerous opponents at Kanua in 1527, when the Mughals defeated Rajput cavalry and armoured war elephants, as well as at Jam, and at Tondibi (1591) when a Moroccan force crushed the army of the Songhay empire of the Niger Valley. Thus, firearms altered the balance of military advantage between states, peoples and areas, and possession of, and expertise in, firearms became a priority in the struggle for predominance, or even survival. Persia, for example, obtained cannon from the Portuguese Persian Gulf base of Hormuz and from Russia, and by 1600 had about 500. In turn, as rivals of the Persians and the Portuguese, the Ottomans provided firearms, or soldiers armed with firearms, to the Uzbeks, the Khan of the Crimean Tatars, the sultanate of Aceh in Sumatra (an Islamic opponent of the Portuguese), and to supporters in the Caucasus. The Ottomans also sent military advisers to the Mughals, assisting them in incorporating firearms and infantry into their armies. The Ottoman attempt to build a canal to link the Black Sea and the Caspian was not only intended to influence developments in the Volga valley but also to improve connections with the Uzbeks.

The new weaponry spread elsewhere in Asia and Africa. The rise of the Mughals was not the sole narrative in India, and in southern India the Hindu state of Vijayanagara, under its dynamic ruler Rama Raja (r. 1542–65), maintained its position by deploying armies equipped with artillery manned by Portuguese or Muslim gunners. In turn, Ibrahim Qutab, Sultan of Golconda (r. 1530–80), who played a major role in overthrowing Rama Raja, relied upon both heavy cavalry led by his nobility and a European artillery corps. Yet, as a reminder of the role of environmental constraints, the situation in southern India was not typical of that further north, as the land was more forested (although not to the extent of South-East Asia), and more mountainous. The climatic and disease environments of southern India were also poorly suited to the breeding and health of sound horses, and such environmental constraints continued to be very important throughout the seventeenth century.

Firepower

Environmental differences were important to the role of cavalry and also, by extension, to the situation as far as firepower was concerned. Areas suited for light cavalry, and where mounted (horse) archery was frequently used, were not particularly conducive for infantry musketry, because the loading and firing processes for the latter were far slower, and the infantry were therefore vulnerable to the mounted archers. In this contrast, experience was the key factor, although weapon and weather were also very important, and, therefore, rates of fire varied greatly. Nevertheless, it was estimated that in seventeenth-century India, a mounted archer could fire six arrows in the time it took a musketeer armed with a matchlock musket to fire one shot.[4] Just as mounted archers continued to play a major role in India, so Mongol pressure on China in the sixteenth century, and Manchu success there in the seventeenth, reflected their effectiveness. Infantry's lack of mobility increased its vulnerability to mounted archers, and this vulnerability helps explain why pikes played scant role in the areas under the sway of these archers, as pikemen were particularly slow and also operated in dense formations which increased their vulnerability to fire. Pikemen were not important in India, Persia or China, although hand-held stabbing and slashing weapons were used by infantry there. Too close a focus on gunpowder weapons and, more generally, on firepower, makes it overly easy to overlook the continued importance of cutting, stabbing, slashing and hitting weapons that could be wielded by both cavalry and infantry. Alongside javelins, such weapons played the central role in sub-Saharan conflict; while, used by disciplined troops in massed formations, the pike remained important on the European battlefield until the late seventeenth century, although the Russians tended to rely not on pikemen but on mobile field fortifications and their own cavalry to protect their musketeers from cavalry attack. Offering defensive strength, the long pikes protected both pikemen and the musketeers from cavalry and pike attacks, for the pike was also an offensive weapon. The squares of pikemen helped structure battlefield formations, while the pike was the last of the major weapons in European warfare that focused on stabbing or slashing, rather than firepower, although, in contrast, the spear was still used extensively in Africa in the nineteenth century. The pike also underlined the traditional nature of much warfare, for the pikemen looked back to their most famous exemplar, the phalanxes of the Macedonian army under Alexander the Great in the 330s BCE.

The sway of the environment was more complex and allowed for more variations in practice than broad-brush interpretations might suggest. Thus, in the Deccan, the plateau in central-south India, the Mughals were resisted in the seventeenth century not only by the light cavalry of the Marathas but also by the infantry of the Qutab Shahi Sultans of Golconda who were armed with impressive muskets that reflected the quality of Indian metallurgy. Moreover, although the Marathas focused on cavalry, they also recruited infantry which were armed, variously, with swords, bows and firearms.[5]

It would be a mistake to assume that infantry armed with firearms was the default position in the absence of mounted archers, a position that arose from the capability advantage of such infantry in this absence. In practice, aside from the comparative advantages of mounted archers, there were many disadvantages attached to the use and provision of gunpowder weaponry, for example, not simply issues of accuracy and speed of fire, but also the supply of gunpowder, as well as the availability of shot and the provision of muskets. Moreover, other weapons offered much in particular environments. Thus, in Bengal in the lower Ganges valley area of India, *paiks*, light infantry armed with spears, proved effective in the often waterlogged terrain.

More generally, it is also clear that not all sieges and battles were decided by firepower. Sieges were frequently determined not by the presence of wall-breaching artillery, but by the availability of sufficient light cavalry to blockade a fortress and ravage the surrounding country. This challenge was best resisted by coastal positions when they could be resupplied by sea, such as Ottoman-held Azov when besieged by the Russians in 1695. Moreover, the demonstration of force could be more important than its usefulness in action. Thus, many sieges ended with a surrender in the face of a larger besieging army, a relationship that could be almost ritualistic in its conventions; although surrender might also involve the betrayal of the position by part of the garrison.

Indeed, alongside the customary stress on firepower, however much this is changed by adding non-gunpowder weapons (archery, slings, and the javelins much used in Africa) to the usual emphasis on firearms, it is clear that other factors played a major role in conquest. The ability to benefit from divisions among opponents was very important, not least for the Spaniards in the New World and the Mughals in India. In East Africa, moreover, the Portuguese benefited from the help of the rulers of Malindi in attacking those of Mombasa: in 1591, they co-operated in capturing Mombasa, the ruler of Malindi becoming Sheikh there while the Portuguese built a powerful fortress, Fort Jesus. In the Hijaz (west Saudi Arabia), the Ottomans took over the position of the Mamluk rulers of Egypt, but this 'conquest' involved co-operation with those already in control locally. Thus, Selim I issued a *firman* confirming Sharif Barakat, the Amir of Mecca, in his position, and the Ottomans subsequently ruled the region for four centuries through the Sharifian family. This situation was the reality underlining the appointment of Ottoman governors in Jeddah and Medina. The ability to win local allies was important to the transition from invasions to successful conquests, and is therefore a major qualification to the standard emphasis on firepower.

The limited role for firearms was not restricted to India, where, indeed, there was no major change in their character or use until the spread of the flintlock musket in the eighteenth century. This limited role could also be seen in Africa, China and Persia, in all of which gunpowder weaponry was known, let alone in areas where it was unknown, such as Oceania (the Pacific) and Amazonia.

China

In China, the military strength of the Ming empire in the sixteenth century lay primarily in the size of its army and, to a lesser extent, in fortifications, rather than in firearms. In 1569, according to the Deputy Minister of War, the army had an authorised strength of 3,138,000 men, but the real strength was only 845,000. Of this, the majority, about half a million, served along the northern frontier where there was a series of major garrisons. This provision became increasingly important as Mongol attacks became more serious in mid-century, and contrasted with the lesser attention which the Ming devoted to Japan and, even more, their southern borders. In a pointed qualification of the idea of strong and expansionist gunpowder empires, the Chinese sought to cope with the Mongols by relying on walls and on garrisons at strategic passes – just as Muscovy developed the 1000 kilometre Abatis Line of fortifications against the Crimean Tatars between the 1520s and early 1600s, providing a basis for successive southward movements of fortified positions and lines over the following century. Steps were also taken to accommodate the Mongols: in 1571, the year in which Khan Devlet Girei of the Crimean Tatars was able to launch a devastating raid on Muscovy (later Russia), the Chinese signed a treaty with the Altan Khan. More generally, alongside force, trade and gifts were used as effective means of defence by powers, especially the Chinese.

European expansion

An emphasis on conflict elsewhere and on other expanding powers acts as a corrective to any tendency to see military history largely in terms of Europe, specifically of (Christian) European initiatives, with the addition of the Ottoman pressure on Christian Europe. This addition appears to make relative capability in Europe, notably between the Ottomans and their European opponents, the key indicator of military proficiency, but this approach is misleading. Instead, on a world scale, the Europeans appear as distinctive because of their range and naval power, rather than their strength on land, although in Europe the latter also was in some cases dependent on maritime support, and the English and Venetians in particular had developed ways of war in which amphibious capability was important.[6] With the exception of Russian expansion – the conquest of the Islamic khanates of Kazan and Astrakhan in the 1550s, and expansion in Siberia from the 1580s – maritime power was crucial to the range of European activity and it was through the projection of this power that the 'Old World' and the 'New' were connected. Moreover, this power was not contested in American waters, for neither the Incas nor the Aztecs had naval capability, the numerous Aztec canoes being used on lakes. In the Indian Ocean, the Portuguese fleet defeated Egyptian and Indian rivals, and was able to check or defeat Ottoman naval advances or to limit them by relying on fortified ports.

Thanks to the profits brought by overseas territories and trade, as well as to demographic and economic expansion, the European powers also displayed greater military force within Europe. The ability of European states to finance military activity increased in the late fifteenth and early sixteenth century with greater political consolidation and administrative development. The process of consolidation was challenged, however, from the 1520s, as the impact of the Protestant Reformation increased domestic divisions within Europe, and the resulting geopolitics of disunity underlined comparisons with early Chinese history rather than with the large, consolidated state of sixteenth-century China,[7] a contrast that remained pertinent for the seventeenth century.

Fortifications

Nevertheless, alongside anxieties about potential attack stemming from this disunity, the availability of resources that could be directed by governments was obvious in the ambitious European fortification programmes of the sixteenth century, programmes that were also seen in the seventeenth century, most prominently in its last third. Fortifications designed to cope with artillery were first constructed in large numbers in Italy, and were then spread across Europe in the sixteenth century, in particular by Italian architects, although the largest new fortifications in Europe, those at Smolensk in Russia built between 1595 and 1602, were built in the traditional fashion with a stone wall 6.5 kilometres long and 13–19 metres high, strengthened by 49 towers. Such fortifications, however, were regarded as anachronistic in most of Europe because cannon were most effective against the stationary target of high stone walls. Indeed, Smolensk's walls were breached by the besieging Poles in 1611 and by the Russians in 1633.

In general, fortifications were redesigned to provide lower, denser and more complex targets. In the new system, known as the *trace italienne*, bastions, generally quadrilateral, angled and at regular intervals along all walls, were introduced to provide gun platforms able to launch effective flanking fire against attackers, creating killing zones in front of the walls, while defences were lowered and strengthened with earth in order to reduce their vulnerability to attack. These improvements lessened the decisiveness of artillery in siegecraft, restoring to the defensive some of the advantage lost with the development of artillery. Furthermore, the new fortresses were defended by cannon, and states were able and willing to deploy large numbers of them.[8]

Developments in siegecraft simply encouraged the opposing process of strengthening fortifications, and the application of relevant knowledge was fostered by publications. In 1626, Honorat de Meynier, a retired French military engineer, published *Les Nouvelles Inventions de Fortifier Les Places* which, the title page announced, had been presented to Louis XIII (r. 1610–43), a presentation that reflected both credit on the book and also a sense of what was appropriate patronage by a king of France. The year 1683 saw the publication of Michael Mieth's *Artilleriae Recentior Praxis* (Frankfurt) and also Mieth taking a major role in the successful defence of Vienna against Ottoman siege; his work was reprinted in 1684, at the start of a major process of reconquest from the Ottomans that involved numerous sieges.

The weaknesses of states

Yet, alongside administrative development and greater military capability came a pressure on available resources and borrowing possibilities that would have led most monarchs and ministers to smile at any remark that there were more resources to tap. This pressure was particularly, although not only, the case with civil wars. For example, in France during the Wars of Religion from 1562 to 1598, lack of finance resulted in the steady decline in effectiveness of the royal army, and in a reduction in the size of forces deployed by the combatants[9] that prefigured the situation for the combatants across much of Europe in the Thirty Years' War (1618–48). When the Huguenot (French Protestant) stronghold of La Rochelle was besieged by the royal army in 1572–3, it was impossible to constitute a naval force that could effectively blockade the fort, and this helped ensure the failure of the siege, which proved a contrast to the successful siege of 1627–8. The problems associated with raising sufficient funding to sustain high levels of operational warfare were faced by all the major European combatants during this period, and were probably managed best by the Ottomans.[10] The frequency of mutinies reflected these problems, as, although political factors could play a significant role, as in the case of the Ottoman *janissaries*, for example in 1622, mutinies generally arose when pay was not forthcoming and when credit with the local communities was withdrawn. The prevalence of desertion was another consequence of the general situation, and this prevalence encouraged the punitive punishment regime that characterised the armed forces of the period, both on land and at sea.

Variety of military environments

Problems associated with funding could take precedence over the variety of force structures and military environments, but, in turn, not all forces relied on pay nor on sophisticated administrative organisations. Indeed, the tension between settled societies and nomadic or semi-nomadic peoples, whose organisational systems were very different, remained a major factor, and linked the period to earlier centuries. This distinction did not exhaust the diversity of arrangements that was relevant to the purposes and contexts of conflict. As a result, the varied response to firearms should be understood not in terms of military progress, administrative sophistication or cultural superiority, but rather as a response to the different tasks and possibilities facing the armies of the period, within a context in which it was far from clear which weaponry, force structure, tactics, or operational method were better. Within the gunpowder world, armies were usually mixed infantry/cavalry forces, and both infantry and cavalry involved troops that used firearms as well as those that did not. Infantry played the leading role in Western Europe, coastal West Africa, Amazonia, Sri Lanka, the Himalayas and South-East Asia, but cavalry dominated warfare in much of Central and South-West Asia, northern and central India, the savannah belt of Africa, and Eastern Europe, while cavalry warfare became more important on the world scale with the spread of the use of the horse in North America. In the early seventeenth century, Native Americans living near Spanish ranches in New Mexico acquired the horse and, by trade and theft, the animal spread northward, reaching the Kiowa, Comanche, Shoshoni, Nez-Percés and Flathead tribes by the end of the century. This was a very different spatial pattern of diffusion to that seen with the spread of firearms in North America in the seventeenth century, as that was largely from the European colonies on and near the Atlantic coast.

As a reminder of the diversity of military arrangements around the world, in New Zealand, where there were no firearms, *pā* settlements, fortified with wooden palisades (as opposed to *kāinga* or open settlements), spread, particularly on the North Island. Their number suggests serious competition for the resources of land and sea. Although they are difficult to date, and many would not have been occupied at the same time, over 6000 *pā* sites have been found, and it has been suggested that there may have been about twice that number.[11] To underline the variety of military activity even in common circumstances, the nature of combat in Polynesia was different even when there was a common cultural thread as in preliminary rituals and the role of champion warriors. Thus, whereas the Maori used *pā*, the Samoans adopted forts with high stone walls and a protective ditch or moat, while Hawai'ians did not build fortified villages, but relied mostly on natural features for defence. In Hawai'i and Tahiti, there was a preference for fighting in the open, whereas Samoans and Maori relied on surprise attacks. In Hawai'i, units could be 400 strong, but the Maori preferred smaller units that rarely exceeded 140 men. The Hawai'ians used projectile weapons, such as sling and stones, while the Maori made little use of projectiles. The preferred Maori weapon was a smooth greenstone truncheon, while the Samoans relied on lapalapa, clubs with sharp teeth.[12] Firearms also had no role in many other areas, including Australia and much of southern Africa. They were also absent across much of the Indonesian Archipelago, where headhunting was important, as was the capture of prisoners for sale.[13]

The theme of variety can also be seen in naval capability, which may appear surprising, as the focus on what became ships of the line in the literature for the seventeenth century appears to suggest a similarity. Nevertheless, there were other naval forces that need consideration. In shallow waters, such as the Gulf of Finland or the coastal waters of South Asia, galleys proved more useful, and warships of the type of ships of the line were similarly of little value in rivers. River gunboats are generally ignored by naval (and military) historians, both of this period and of others, but they were important, particularly on the rivers of the Balkans and southern Russia, such as the Danube and the Don, in conflicts between the Ottomans and their neighbours, and in China.

Even if the focus is solely on ships of the line, which were, indeed, the most important type of warship in the late seventeenth century, it is necessary to note a parallel with land warfare in which the form, like that of the musket–pike–cavalry co-operation of the period, could include important variations. As with land forces, these focused on specifications, particularly firepower, defensive strength, speed and manoeuvrability. These specifications arose in large part in response to particular taskings. Thus, for warships, there were different emphases in the seventeenth century, including the extent to which ships were expected to cruise to the Indies and to take part in line-of-battle artillery exchanges in European waters. Command skills on both land and sea involved understanding, and taking advantage of, the capabilities arising from specifications, and these are lost from sight if only a uniform account of weaponry and tactics is offered.

This argument about differing taskings and specifications can be extended to the equations of defensive strength and offensive firepower that helped determine the potency of fortifications and the success of sieges. Rather than assuming a perfect state of fortification, it is necessary to evaluate systems not only with reference to the specifications that led to these equations, but also within the constraints of manpower and cost, each of which were also important in judging fitness for purpose. This returns attention from the theoretical and systemic to the particular. At the crudest level, the fortifications deemed necessary to withstand a major siege in Western Europe were generally more than were necessary for Eastern Europe, and far more than were required to defeat a rebellion. Thus, while fitness for purpose is a crucial concept when judging the applicability of weaponry and fortifications, such fitness is frequently misunderstood by putting the stress on the capacity for employing force, rather than the ends or goals that are sought.

Strategic cultures

In considering these ends, the framing and execution of what was subsequently termed 'strategic culture' are relevant, as this concept offers a possible synergy in our understanding of war, linking it to relevant political dimensions. Thus, the pressures arising from international relations are important to the setting of goals and the tasking that, in turn, helps determine military doctrine and force structure and that drives strategy. There has not been a systematic study of strategic culture in this period, and indeed work on strategy is often limited. In particular, it is unclear how best to address the role of *gloire*, loosely translated as the pursuit of glory, in military objectives. An emphasis on *gloire* appears to offer a non-rational account of strategy and policy, one in keeping with the dominant role of rulers and the prevalence of dynastic considerations, but this emphasis, role and prevalence were certainly rational as far as the political purpose, ethos and structure of states were concerned. Thus, Murad IV (r. 1623–40) gained a reputation as the Sultan who had both revived Ottoman military glory through success over the Safavids of Persia, especially regaining Baghdad in 1638, and restored stability to the empire. His reputation was enhanced by the weakness and failure of his predecessors, Osman (r. 1618–22) who was overthrown and killed, and Mustafa (r. 1617–18, 1622–3) who, mentally defective, was deposed twice.

If the point about *gloire* provides the wider context for strategic culture, it leaves more specific choices unclear. In particular, although war and territorial expansion brought exemplary purpose and glory to rulers and aristocracy, while success acted as a lubricant of obedience in crown–élite relations, there were many occasions in which international crises did not lead to war. The reasons for the avoidance of war require investigation from the perspectives of strategic culture and causes of war including the impact of *gloire*, while the war plans drawn up in such crises also need investigation in so far as sources permit. The extent to which 'the military' made a contribution to strategic cultures can be appreciated when it is realised that the military was not separate from political and social hierarchies, but intermixed with them. Particular socio-political groups clearly had distinctive goals, but the extent to which these could be advanced through the overlapping worlds of court, ministerial, aristocratic and military factions, and the consequences for military planning, are unclear, and largely unstudied. Yet, there were choices, most obviously when powers (i.e., rulers or ruling groups) engaged militarily, or considered engaging, on several fronts at the same time and had to decide how best to prioritise between commitments. In such cases, politics were clearly often involved. This was true, for example, of France in the Thirty Years', Dutch and Nine Years' wars, and of successive Austrian Habsburg attempts to reconcile competing commitments in Italy, the Empire (Germany) and the Balkans. The operational history of these conflicts needs to be related to the strategic dimension in this fashion. Thus, in France, the political struggle at the royal court between Cardinal Richelieu and the *dévots* in the 1620s was closely linked to foreign policy and military commitments.[14]

Different strategic cultures also affected the perception of other states, and thus the dynamics of alliance diplomacy, both pre-war and wartime, and this diplomacy, in turn, had an influence on policies and on particular military goals, underlining the extent to which there was a dynamic and changing character to strategic culture, so that contemporaries were faced by uncertainty. Moreover, action–reaction cycles, in which one power sought to counter the advances made by another, as when the French responded to John, Duke of Marlborough's battlefield tactics in the 1700s, indicated the dynamic nature of the challenges facing generals. The dynamic nature of challenges was also true of the variety of environments in which generals and their troops found themselves. The diversity and unpredictability of military tasks, and thus the difficulty, both for contemporaries and subsequently, of judging capability and establishing a clear hierarchy of military proficiency, are underlined.

Three decades ago, meta-narratives of military history were written in terms of a teleology of military progress, administrative sophistication and cultural superiority, specifically the move towards total war capability and doctrine, especially with the maximisation of destructiveness through the enhancement of firepower.[15] At that time, a conclusion in terms of contrasting responses to different circumstances and tasks would have appeared lame, and indeed as a recognition of irrelevance. Now, as the multiple character of modern warfare can be better understood, so the very process of modernisation can be seen to involve far more continuity as well as non-linear development than was hitherto appreciated.[16] In addition, modern interest in limited warfare makes aspects of the doctrine and practice of seventeenth-century warfare – for example the negotiations alongside fighting in India, as well as *ancien régime* conflict in Europe – appear important. However, in practice, their limited character (within the parameters of what was judged possible) should not be misunderstood. The traditional equation of indecisive and limited, both applied to the late seventeenth century in Europe, is not an adequate description of the goals, means and results of this warfare, and, to a great extent, the same is true of India. This book will indicate the decisiveness of much seventeenth-century conflict.

3 Conflict, 1590–1615

There is no clear break to separate the sixteenth and seventeenth centuries. Instead, there were wars in progress in 1600, while, in addition, the events of the early years of the seventeenth century frequently reflected conflicts in the preceding decades. As advanced by Michael Roberts, the Military Revolution spans the century divide, but the wars of 1590–1615 revealed the difficulties of attaining decisive outcomes, difficulties that sit uneasily alongside the implication that greater proficiency arose from the adoption of particular methods.

An instructive instance was provided at the outset, and it is one that also serves as a reminder of the degree to which, as in the 2000s, notably in Afghanistan and Iraq, power projection and victory in battle did not achieve the automatic responses that might be anticipated. Only about half of the 5000 men sent in 1590 across the vast, dry expanse of the Sahara Desert by Sultan Mawláy Ahmad al Mansur of Morocco survived the crossing, but their victory at Tondibi on the River Niger in 1591 made a decisive difference to the politics of the middle Niger valley, as it led to the collapse of the Songhay empire. The Sultan wanted to secure gold, as well as recognition for his claim to be Caliph, the Muslim chief civil and spiritual ruler. As an instance of the porosity of barriers between military cultures, many of the troops sent were renegades: Christians who had become Muslim. Such porosity was widespread and a means for obtaining military skills and also for the transmission of military methods. As an example, however, in 1591 of the different styles and very varied success of attacking Islamic armies, the Moroccan expedition proved a marked contrast to the defeat outside Moscow that year of an invasion by Crimean Tatars. Yet, although, in 1591 after Tondibi, the Moroccans overran territory they then organised as the Pashalik of Timbuktu, strong resistance in southern Songhay prevented further expansion. Campaigning there in 1593–4, the Moroccans suffered the effects of both guerrilla resistance and humidity, while, in 1594, the Pasha of Timbuktu was killed in battle by the animists of the region of Hombori, who were effective despite the absence of firearms. Moreover, in 1609, a Moroccan army was defeated by a Songhay force at the town of Jenne. Songhay, indeed, continued to be a fairly extensive state down the Niger from Timbuktu. Moreover, Mali remained a powerful state upriver until around 1660. Thus, the arrival of Moroccan power did not lead to a long-term transformation in the regional system; the contrary, indeed, as the trans-Saharan empire could not be expanded, nor, in the end, sustained.

Moreover, as an instance of the difficulties of assessing relative military capability, although the Moroccans under Abd al-Malik had crushed a Portuguese invasion at the battle of Alcazarquivir in 1578,[1] and this military verdict against European invasion lasted until the 1840s, there was no comparable Moroccan success across the Sahara; whereas, in contrast, European powers using maritime links, notably Portugal, were able to sustain distant presences, including in West and East – but not, to any extent, in North – Africa.

It is necessary to emphasise the obscure clashes in the Niger region after 1591 because, all too often, warfare there is discussed solely in terms of the battle of Tondibi, which is then employed to provide an instance of the effectiveness of gunpowder technology and the diffusion of the Military Revolution. This method is a parallel to the misleading treatment of eighteenth-century warfare in India in terms of the victory of the forces of the English East India Company over those of Siraj-ud-daula, the Nawab of Bengal, at Plassey in 1757. The emphasis on Tondibi also reflects a frequently misleading preference for supposedly decisive battles that underrates the often lengthy and difficult process of conquest, while pressures of space in books also lead to a focus on particular battles, but these can provide a misleading impression of weak societies that apparently succumbed readily.

The significance of the neglected: the case of the Uzbeks

Pressures of space can also lead to the neglect of military powers that do not appear to 'lead anywhere', resulting in an analysis by omission that can be highly misleading. Thus, the Uzbeks are generally ignored in works on global and military history, although they provide an impressive instance of the continued vitality of the military power of the societies of Central Asia. The Uzbeks tend only to be mentioned in general works when listing the many successes of Shah Abbas I of Persia, for he inflicted a major defeat on them in 1598. Yet, the Uzbeks were an important force. Invading Khurasan (north-east Persia) on a number of occasions in the sixteenth century, they were long at war with the Safavids, while, to the east, the Uzbeks pressed the Dörben Oirats of Mongolia hard, although, from the west, the Uzbeks were under pressure from the Kazaks, another steppe people.

Politics was as significant as relative capability in their story: the Uzbek nomadic system was politically fissiparous and much energy was spent on warfare among the tribes. Unable to manufacture their own, the Uzbeks had few firearms, and requests for them from the Ottomans yielded few. Nevertheless, in the late sixteenth century, Abd Allah Sultan made the last real attempt to unite Transoxiana, seizing Balkh, Samarkand, Turkestan, Badakshshan and Herat, areas covering much of Central Asia and northern and west Afghanistan. This attempt, however, failed in 1598 because of attacks by Abbas I and the Kazaks, and the death of Abd Allah, and the Uzbeks then divided. However, under the Janid dynasty, especially Shaybani Khan, the Uzbeks remained a major force with wide-ranging territories, and they succeeded in undermining Mughal expansion beyond the Hindu Kush mountains in 1647, and only lost control of their territories south of the River Amu (Oxus) in about 1660. To write of the Uzbeks therefore simply in terms of Abbas's victory in 1598, or of Mughal failure in 1647 as an instance solely of the limitations of imperial powers, is unhelpful as it neglects the extent to which peoples and states that did not wield imperial power, for example the Uzbek khanate of Bukhara, could still retain considerable vitality. Moreover, it is problematic to read back from the later Russian conquest of the Crimean Tatars, Kazakhs and Uzbeks, a process that only began in the late eighteenth century and largely took place in the nineteenth. A stress on regions such as Central Asia and on peoples such as the Uzbeks suggests that a narrative and analysis of world military history set in terms of the familiar cast of topics have to be at least qualified.

Japan, Korea and China

The difficulty of conquest emerged clearly in another context, that of Eurasia, as it is now sometimes called. From the late fifteenth century, as the pace of warfare within Japan accelerated, there were a series of major changes in Japanese warfare including larger armies, a greater preponderance of infantry, sophisticated tactics and command structures, and changes in weaponry, especially the spear and armour. Moreover, from the first half of the sixteenth century, effective guns were introduced in Japan as a result of trade. As an instance of the degree to which the diffusion of new technology was dependent on more than receptivity, these guns were widely copied, and rapidly, as Japan's metallurgical industry could produce muskets in large numbers.[2]

The ambition of a key figure played a crucial role in the conflict of the 1590s, just as it did in many other instances. Toyotomi Hideyoshi united Japan by fighting his way into dominance over other *daimyō* (well-known persons/feudal lords), culminating with his defeat of the Hōjō in the eastern part of the main island of Honshu in 1590, in a campaign in which he deployed at least 200,000 troops. Hideyoshi then decided to conquer China, an invasion that would provide new lands for his warriors and enable him to keep his control over them. Continual success had led Hideyoshi to lose a sense of limits while the cult of the warrior in any case discouraged an interest in limits. He planned to advance via Korea, a Chinese client state, and to rule the world from the Chinese city of Ningpo. From there, Hideyoshi intended to conquer India. He also demanded that Taiwan and the Philippines submit to him, an ambition that reflected his maritime hopes. In 1593, Hideyoshi was to demand equal status with the Wan Li emperor of China, which was a major challenge to Chinese views of the world. He wished to be invested with the King of the Ming as a way to legitimate his seizure of power in Japan, as well as to receive the privileges of tribute trade.[3]

Hideyoshi's reach had exceeded his grasp. The invasion, with about 150,000 men, was initially successful in 1592 and Hideyoshi won victory at Ch'ungju, capturing the city of Seoul, and advanced north to the Yalu River, but Korean naval resistance eventually altered the situation. The Japanese fleet was defeated at the battle of the Yellow Sea by a fleet commanded by Yi Sun-Shin that included some of the more impressive warships of the age: Korean 'turtle ships', oar-driven boats, equipped with cannon and possibly covered by hexagonal metal plates in order to prevent grappling and boarding. They may also have been equipped with rams. In addition, Korean guerrilla tactics on land undermined Japanese control and the Japanese were also affected by logistical problems.

China, concerned about the situation on its frontier in a way that prefigured its position in 1950 when American forces advanced north towards the Yalu River during the Korean War, committed large forces to Korea in September 1592. Without this Ming aid, Korea would have fallen to Japan, at least for the short term. Instead, co-ordination by the Chinese–Korean allies proved effective: the Japanese were driven back and the city of P'yongyang was captured in February 1593. Japanese sources emphasised the size of the Chinese army in explaining their defeat, although its technology was also important, notably the use of cannon in the field, which was significant because the effectiveness of the Chinese was affected by the extent to which their northern forces, configured to fight steppe threats, were confronted in Korea by the Japanese – who had themselves transitioned to spear- and firearm-equipped infantry – who had driven cavalry from the field. Although the use of firearms in their army had spread, the Chinese also deployed large numbers armed with traditional weapons: bows, lances and swords. As with the South Koreans in 1950, the Japanese were pushed back to a bridgehead on the southern coast around Pusan, but the Chinese, who committed more than 200,000 troops to Korea in 1592–3, were unable to destroy the bridgehead. The numbers put into the field on both sides overshadow those employed in Western Europe.

In 1596, Hideyoshi rejected the Chinese attempt to get him to accept a more subordinate status, for example equivalent to that of the Altan Khan, the Mongol ruler,[4] and in 1597 a fresh invasion was mounted by 140,000 troops. However, the Chinese and Koreans were now prepared for attack and the Japanese were unable to repeat their success of 1592, although the Chinese were affected by grave logistical problems. In 1598, the Koreans were supported by a Chinese fleet under an artillery expert, Ch'en Lin. The Japanese had rapidly deployed cannon on their warships but their tactics remained focused on boarding, and their fleet was defeated in 1598 by Yi Sun-Shin at the battle of the Noryang Straits, the Korean and Chinese navies making more extensive use of cannon and firearms, although Yi was killed in the battle.[5]

Hideyoshi died in 1598 and his plans against China were not pursued, which was an important moment in East Asian and, thus, world history. Far from being invulnerable, China was to fall to Manchu attack in the 1640s, which raises the question whether the Japanese could have succeeded earlier. Despite problems the Japanese faced in securing their sea lines of communications, and the resource and logistical strains of invasions of East Asia (a strain also seen during the Russo-Japanese War of 1904–5 and then again when the Japanese invaded, first, Manchuria and, then, all of China between 1931 and 1945), the Japanese had the manpower and agricultural resource base necessary for operations in the 1600s. This capability was especially the case if they were not diverted into internal conflict, an aspect of international power in this period that was more generally important than administrative development. However, the Japanese did not have the comparative advantage over the Chinese provided by the mobility, flexibility and firepower of the Manchu mounted archers, a force the Chinese could not match as they lacked a supply of horses.

Hideyoshi's position in Japan was taken by Tokugawa Ieyasu, a *daimyō* whom Hideyoshi had never trusted. His rise to power was resisted by a rival league of *daimyō*, but Ieyasu had undermined his opponents by secretly winning several of them over, and this led to victory at the battle of Sekigahara on 21 October 1600. As with many battles, betrayal proved a key element, with Ieyasu benefiting from bringing over about 15,000 troops from the 82,000-strong opposing army.[6] Ieyasu then established the Tokugawa shōgunate, which lasted until 1868. Hideyoshi's son, Hideyori, and his supporters were defeated when Osaka castle was successfully besieged in 1614–15 by Ieyasu's 200,000-strong army. Thus, civil warfare in Japan, which briefly revived in 1638 when a rising by Christian converts was suppressed at Shimábava,[7] came to a close in a similar period (though before) as it did in France, where it stopped with the end of the *Frondes* in 1652.

War between Austria and the Ottomans

While decisive victory was eluding the combatants in Korea in the 1590s, the same was true in the Danube valley. A major war between the Austrians and Ottomans from 1593 until 1606 suggested for a while that the latter could be driven back from much of Hungary which, under Suleiman the Magnificent, they had conquered following their victory at Mohacs in 1526. Indeed, Buda, the major city in Hungary, was besieged (unsuccessfully) by the Austrians in 1598. The war, however, ended with scant territorial change. The campaigns focused on control over fortresses, the capture of which served as a demonstration of success. Attempts to relieve sieges also provided an opportunity for battle or for deciding not to launch an attack. In 1600, for example, the Ottomans captured the fortress of Kanissa and then successfully resisted an Austrian siege of it the following year, whereas, in 1601, the Austrians captured Székesfehérvár, blocking a relief attempt, only for the Ottomans to capture the fortress in 1602. Also in 1602, the Austrians captured Pest and besieged Buda, and in 1603 an Ottoman attempt to regain Pest was defeated. The Ottomans were more successful in 1604, advancing in strength and gaining Pest and Vac, followed by Esztergom (Gran) in 1605.

The Thirteen Years' War is interesting for the light it throws on the problems of assessing and using capability advantages. The Ottomans were able to capture many of the fortresses recently modified by the Austrians using the cutting-edge Italian expertise of the period, including Györ (Raab) in 1594, Eger in 1596, Kanissa in 1600 and Esztergom (Gran) in 1605. Thus, rather than providing a paradigm leap (or revolution) forward in the defensiveness of Christendom, it is necessary to consider the advances in fortification, like other developments, in terms of particular circumstances,[8] and not least to remember that defences were only as good as their defenders and logistical support. Moreover, although the Ottomans had no equivalent to the *trace italienne*, nor to the extensive fortifications built in the Austrian-ruled section of Hungary, as well as along the coasts of Naples and Sicily against Barbary raids, they did not require any such development as they had not been under equivalent attack. Thus, yet again, capability should be related to tasking, and means to goals, and this in a context in which Europeans and Ottomans had a realistic perception of the potential and might of the adversary.[9]

Nevertheless, it would be mistaken to suggest that there was not a change in the balance of advantage in some respects. Although accounts of the battle, as of so many battles, are unclear, Austrian firepower played a major role at Mezö-Kerésztés in 1596, although a break in formation to plunder the Ottoman camp permitted a successful counter-attack. Furthermore, Ottoman reports admiring Austrian cannon captured in the Thirteen Years' War suggest that a technological gap in cannon-casting had begun to open by then, but recent work has corrected the earlier view that the Ottomans concentrated on large cannon, rather than larger numbers of more manoeuvrable smaller cannon, and has instead emphasised that their ordnance was dominated by small and medium-sized cannon. It has also been shown that they were able to manufacture an adequate supply of gunpowder.[10]

The Thirteen Years' War also repeatedly indicated the significance of a form of coalition warfare, in the shape of the importance, yet unpredictability, of subordinate parts of imperial systems, notably Wallachia, Transylvania and Moldavia (each a part of modern Romania), the rulers of which followed an independent path creating important operational and strategic issues. The Austrians benefited from rebellions against Ottoman overlordship by the *voyvodas* (rulers) of Wallachia and Moldavia, until Prince Michael of Wallachia turned against the Austrians and was murdered at their behest in 1600. The Ottomans, in turn, profited in 1602 and 1603 from anti-Austrian rebellions in Transylvania.

Poland, Sweden and Russia

If the Ottomans and Habsburgs were unable to prevail in the Thirteen Years' War, that offered a parallel to the failures, in very different contexts in the conflicts in the 1590s and 1600s, of Sigismund III of Poland (r. 1587–1632) and of both Spain and its opponents. It would be normal to put Spain first and to consider its inability to suppress the Dutch Revolt, to prevent the accession of Henry of Navarre as Henry IV in France and to defeat the English as the key issues, but Sigismund III provides as instructive an instance of a failure to achieve goals that was of long-term significance for European history. In a reminder of the porosity of political arrangements and international alignments under the pressures of individual ambition and dynastic drive, Sigismund was also King of Sweden from 1592 until deposed in 1599, and he sought to put his son, Wladyslaw, on the throne of Russia.

The possibility of very different political circumstances across Eastern Europe were therefore present, and it is unclear why the ability of Spanish troops to reach Paris in 1590, relieving its siege by the future Henry IV, was less significant than that of Polish forces to reach Moscow. Both sets of conflicts are instructive in that they demonstrated the extent to which clashes between armies in battle and siege, the usual subjects of the Military Revolution, took on much of their meaning in terms of a politics in which violence was often more effective in the form of conspiracies, coups, urban and rural rebellions, and related conflict. Thus, the movements of troops in the Swedish civil war of 1597–8 were in many senses less consequential in explaining Sigismund's failure to maintain his position in Sweden than dynastic division and aristocratic factionalism. In particular, Sigismund's keen support for Catholicism, a support vital to his position in Poland, helped his uncle, Duke Charles of Södermanland, to organise the successful opposition to him in Protestant Sweden.

In turn, Sigismund's overthrow led to a serious rivalry between the two branches of the Vasa dynasty, those in Poland and Sweden, a rivalry that affected power politics around the Baltic. In Russia, competing Polish and Swedish intervention from 1609 reflected the chaotic situation in the country.[11] Boris Godunov, Tsar from 1598, had faced growing problems as a result of poor weather and the resulting crop failures from 1601, and in 1604 he was challenged by a man claiming to be Dmitrii, a son of Ivan the Terrible who had probably died in 1591. The False Dmitrii's claims provided the cover for opposition to Godonuv to reject him as a usurper, and in 1604, supported by some Polish nobles, the False Dmitrii invaded Russia and raised support among the Cossacks, essentially autonomous people living in the southern regions of Russia and Poland. The success of the False Dmitrii's cavalry thwarted the initial attempt to defeat him in December 1604, but, as a reminder of the need to advance hierarchies of relative military success with care, the second battle, at Dobrynichi in January 1605, produced a different verdict, with the success of the False Dmitrii's cavalry on the right flank followed, this time, by an unsuccessful attack on the centre which was repelled by Russian infantry protected by mobile fortifications. Designed to lessen vulnerability to steppe cavalry, such fortifications were a characteristic of Russian campaigning.

Although a serious defeat followed by mass executions of prisoners, Dobrynichi, like many battles in civil wars, did not mean the end of the conflict, because it did not lead the False Dmitrii and his supporters to surrender, which was the only way to end the war. Instead, the rebellion continued, Godunov died in April 1605, and his weak young son, deserted by many of the nobles, was overthrown and murdered in Moscow, the capital, in June 1605 in a riot. The False Dmitrii was then proclaimed Tsar, but his Polish connections helped make him unpopular and he, in turn, was overthrown and killed in May 1606 by a mob as part of a conspiracy organised by Prince Vasilii Shuiskii, who was proclaimed Tsar. However, like Li Zicheng in China in 1644 (see p. 51), he lacked support and legitimacy, while the serious social crisis continued.

Rebellion persisted in southern Muscovy, without any particular battles of note, until, in December 1606, rebel forces under Ivan Bolotnikov, who claimed to be acting for Dmitrii (although he could no longer produce him), were defeated at Kolomenskoe as a result of the defection of their second-in-command and his men. Defection was important anew, in May 1607, when Shuiskii's forces were defeated on the Pchelnia River by those of the False Peter, another claimant to the throne, and in June, at the Vosma River, when many of the rebels defected from the now joint forces of Bolotnikov and the False Peter. Betrayal as the battle winner reflected the porous nature of allegiance in a complex civil conflict, and was also frequent elsewhere, including in India and China, although it was not to be in the English Civil War of 1642–6. Later in 1607, the rebellion was brought to an end when the rebels in Tula surrendered. Attempts to storm the city had failed, but the damming of the Upa River flooded it, which is a reminder of the range of methods employed to take positions. Thus, in July 1611, the city of Novgorod fell to the Swedes when a gate in the walls was opened by a traitor.

A second False Dmitrii invaded, with Polish support, in September 1607, but he could not capture Moscow, although Shuiskii could not defeat him. The war became a matter of trying to win noble support, of raids designed to hit opponents' supplies and thus force them to retreat, and of a quest for foreign intervention. Swedish support for Shuiskii outweighed Polish backing for the False Dmitrii in 1609, although the weaknesses of the latter's support base were as significant, as was the skill of Mikhail Skopin-Shuiskii, the Tsar's nephew and general; in civil wars, such personal links are crucial in the choice of commanders.

Full-scale Polish intervention in 1610 combined with a collapse of support for the Tsar, who was suspected of murdering his nephew, and his abandonment by his Swedish mercenaries, culminating in the overthrow of Shuiskii in July 1610, again in a conspiracy involving noble leadership and mob action. Polish troops entered Moscow in September 1610 and its *boyars* (nobles) swore allegiance to Wladyslaw. The major fortress of Smolensk was stormed by the Poles the following year after its wall had been breached. Hostility in Russia to the prospect of Polish control and Catholicism, however, resulted in rising opposition and the besieged Polish garrison in Moscow surrendered in October 1612. The hostile reaction to Wladyslaw led, in 1613, to the election of a new tsar, Mikhail Romanov, whose family was to reign until 1917, and Mikhail restored order. The Cossacks were brought under restraint, the second False Dmitrii had already been murdered in December 1610, and the return of stability within Russia was followed and secured by a stabilisation of the international system. Wladyslaw and a Polish army was able to advance as far as Moscow in September 1618, but he failed to take the city, and, that year, Poland and Russia agreed a truce at Deulino which left Smolensk in Polish hands. Inconclusive fighting between Sweden and Russia from 1613 resulted in the Treaty of Solbovo in 1617, a compromise peace. As with the Dutch Revolt, the fate of fortified positions proved important, with the Swedish siege of Pskov ending in failure, and Russia only able to regain Novgorod as part of the peace settlement.

Rebellions in the Ottoman empire

Rebellions played a greater role in the warfare in Russia than in the Ottoman empire in the opening years of the century, as Mehmed III (r. 1595–1603), Ahmed I (r. 1603–17) and their Grand Viziers were able to put war with Austria and Persia first. Nevertheless, there was a large-scale rebellion in the important region of Anatolia from 1596, in part due to dissatisfied cavalrymen who lacked employment and favour, allegedly because they had not fought well against the Austrians at Mezö-Kerésztés. The initial rebellion was not defeated until 1601, and it revived under a new leader in 1602 who was victorious until removed by being appointed Governor-General of Bosnia. Rebellion, however, continued, and in 1605 the leading rebel, Tall Halil, won a major battle at Bolvadin, which provoked the Sultan to take the field, only for Tall Halil to avoid battle and be bought off with the Governor-Generalship of Baghdad. This rebellion was not the best basis for the successful pursuit of the war with Austria, but buying off rebels in this fashion was another instance of the porosity of allegiance and the role of betrayal.

Kalenderoghlu Mehmed then became the new rebel leader. An expedition against him in 1606 failed when the unpaid troops mutinied, and in 1607 Kalenderoghlu defeated Ottoman forces near Nif and at

Ladik, although the customary weakness of rebel forces, their lack of a capability, without artillery and assured supplies, to mount sieges, was shown with the failure to take the town of Ankara or the citadel, as opposed to the town, of Bursa. Another rebellion against Ottoman rule broke out in Syria when the execution of the Governor-General of Aleppo in 1605, for refusing to serve against Shah Abbas of Persia, led his son, Ali Janbulad, to rebel.

Kuyuju Murad, who became Grand Vizier in 1606, showed himself a resourceful commander able to match the military means of mounting campaigns and defeating rebels with the political skill necessary to divide his opponents. In 1607, he won Kalenderoghlu over by appointing him Governor of Ankara, before mounting a rapid-tempo campaign that led to the crushing of Ali Janbulad's forces that October, followed by the capture of the major city of Aleppo, and the execution or submission of most of the rebels. In 1608, Kuyuju Murad turned against Kalenderoghlu and defeated him near Malatya in a battle that was important to the stability of the empire. Victory and executions in 1609 further weakened the rebels in Anatolia. These successes indicated the intensely political character of a warfare in which opponents had to be divided and some bought off. The Ottomans were more successful against their rebels than the Spaniards proved to be in suppressing the Dutch Revolt, but the context was very different.

The crises of Spain

The failure of Spain appears even more important than the chaos in Russia and the checking of Sigismund, not least because, on the world scale, it ensured that the Hispanic system did not dominate the European presence. Instead, the Dutch, England and France all became major imperial powers in part because of the opportunities created by conflict with Spain. Philip II of Spain (r. 1556–98) was the ruler of the first empire on which the sun literally never set, and the global range of his power was indicated by the Philippines being named after him: a Spanish base was established there in 1565. However, Philip's success in Europe was mixed. Although the Ottomans were held in the mid-Mediterranean in the 1560s and Philip's forces successfully invaded Portugal in 1580 to enforce his claim on the throne, he was unable, despite major efforts, to suppress a rebellion in the Low Countries, to invade England successfully with his Armada in 1588, or to ensure the outcome to the French Wars of Religion (1562–98) that he sought. As with the eventual failure of his father, the Holy Roman Emperor Charles V, in 1552, to suppress the German

Protestants and defeat France, the outcome to Philip's plans reflected the extent to which hegemonic power was thwarted in Europe.

Yet, it was not only the Ottomans and Portuguese among Philip's opponents who failed. Henry of Navarre, the leader of the Huguenots (French Protestants), who became Henry IV of France in 1594, had had to convert to Catholicism to do so and, thereafter, he had only limited success in defeating the battle-hardened Spanish Army of Flanders on his north-east frontier. The Treaty of Vervins of 1598 essentially confirmed the leading position Philip had already imposed with the Treaty of Cateau-Cambrésis in 1559 after an earlier bout of conflict between the French and Spanish crowns. The English, at war with Spain from 1585 to 1604, defeated the Armada, an attempted Spanish invasion mounted in 1588, and, in 1601–3, overcame Irish opponents supported by Spain, crushing in 1601 at Kinsale an expeditionary force dispatched by Philip III. However, the English failed, in attacks in Portugal and in the Caribbean, to inflict decisive blows on the Spanish imperial system.

A 12-year truce agreed in 1609 marked the Spanish acceptance, after major efforts in the early 1600s, that the Dutch Revolt could not be suppressed, but, equally, the Dutch acceptance that Spanish persistence and successes had ended their hopes that independence could be won for all of the Low Countries, more particularly for what is now Belgium as well as for the areas further north that became the United Provinces (the Dutch republic). The Dutch had won a major victory at Nieuwpoort on 2 July 1600, Dutch firepower proving particularly deadly, although their cavalry also contributed significantly to the Dutch success.[12] However, as a reminder that victory in battle did not necessarily have automatic consequences in terms of territory gained, the subsequent Dutch siege of Nieuwpoort failed in the face of a strong garrison and with the Dutch lacking the necessary supplies. Furthermore, in 1604, the Spaniards captured the important fortress of Ostend after a long siege.[13] The war ended with inconclusive fighting comparable to that between Sweden and Russia from 1613 until the peace in 1617.

Overreach and military ambitions

Respective failures raise the question of how best to judge goals. In particular, there is the question of the validity of the concept of strategic overreach, at once a product of expansion and a cause of decline, as a key feature of great-power status. While apparently plausible, the thesis faces the serious conceptual difficulty of assuming a clear-cut measure of strategic reach, a point that is also pertinent for the USA today.

Indeed, the extent to which overreach is, in practice, a matter of perception, both for contemporaries and subsequently, needs underlining and leads to a questioning of whether there is any ready application for the concept, not least by returning it to the sphere of contention and debate in which policy was formulated and discussed. The charge of unsuccessful strategic overreach is usually applied to Spain, especially under Philip II and his successors, Philip III (r. 1598–1621) and Philip IV (r. 1621–65).[14] As such, Spain apparently takes on significance as the first major modern exemplar of such overreach, prefiguring Britain's position in the early twentieth century, and that of the USA at present. The concept also appears to provide an analytical approach to the trajectory of the power of each of these empires/states, with overreach explaining moves from success to failure. More particularly, overreach can be seen as a damaging general characteristic, but it can also be presented as the explanation of particular failures, notably the decline of Spain in the seventeenth century.

This multiple usage reflects the flexibility of the concept of overreach, and therefore of the related idea of imperial limits. Looked at in one respect, the very flexibility, as with the idea of military revolution, makes the concept of only partial value because it means that the idea of overreach is imprecise; however, from another perspective, the very value of terms such as overreach, limits, revolution, command quality or decisiveness is a product of their varied applicability and conceptual flexibility. Making this point, however, does not mean that the issue of conceptual looseness is not serious.

The assessment of feasible reach is in fact problematic. Financial problems, which hit Spain hard, notably (but not only) in the 1590s and 1620s, or a lack of adequate military resources, are not necessarily helpful as measures of overreach, as both are true of most combatants in history. Secondly, it is unclear that restraint, the presumed opposite of overreach, means much, either in prudential terms or with reference to the dominant strand of the political culture of the age, not least because of the honour involved in being bold. This point underlines the tension between contemporary cultural values[15] and subsequent analytical perceptions.

In normative as well as prudential terms, war and expansion appeared necessary and successful throughout the seventeenth century. Rulers sought simultaneously to consolidate authority and to gain territory, each goals that involved normative and prudential valuations; and to opt out would not have seemed sensible. With its stress on honour and dynastic responsibility, and its concern with *gloire* (which means more than glory but can be translated thus) and the normative values of combat, the dominant political culture was scarcely cautious or pacific, and this was the case across the world. For Philip II of Spain and his two successors not to oppose the Dutch Revolt would have appeared bizarre, and Philip III was only brought to accept a truce with the Dutch in 1609, and Philip IV in effect to acknowledge Dutch independence in 1648, after very serious difficulties for Spain. Similarly, it would have been implausible for the Kangxi emperor of China not to act against Dzhungar expansion in the 1690s. Moreover, to move from defending positions to territorial growth, a necessary defence of interests was at issue, and not overreach.

For Spain, and other powers, to seek to pursue an alternative response to rivals by trying to avoid conflict and, instead, defining mutually accept-able spheres of influence was difficult, if not impracticable, and, again, in very different circumstances, parallels with the modern USA may be considered. Such a policy would have been politically and ideologically problematic to Spain and would also have been a serious signalling of weakness. Lastly, for Spain as far as the Ottomans, the Dutch or France were concerned between 1560 and 1648, there seems little reason to believe that compromise could have been reached and sustained short of large-scale conflict. Thus, strategic reach could only be defined as part of, and yet also in response to, what others might see as overreach. Indeed, far from being alternatives, reach and overreach were part of the same process.

Moreover, the very success of Spain, as later of Britain, makes it clear that overreach is a difficult, although still useful, concept. The conquest, by rela-tively small forces, of large areas – for example by Spain of what, as a result of a bold initiative, could be designated as New Mexico in the 1590s – and the successful laying of claim to other areas, did not demonstrate the value of limits, and this point is also abundantly true, at another scale, for the Manchu invasion of China. A desire to avoid risk would have prevented William III of Orange from fighting on against the French invasion of the United Provinces (Netherlands) in 1672 or from invading England in 1688, or would have kept the Spaniards in the Caribbean offshore the American mainland in the early sixteenth century.

Furthermore, the element of perception in modern judgements that is in practice central to the apparently objective notion of strategic overreach also reflects the ideological and cultural assumptions of the perceiver, assumptions that are frequently subliminal, but nonetheless very signifi-cant. For the Ottomans, in a version of what has been termed Orientalism, there is a sense that they had an anachronistic social and political system, were bound to become the 'Sick Man of Europe', and therefore did not present a real threat to their neighbours, which leads to a downplaying of the need for, and significance of, their defeat, and thus of the value of the military system devised for conflict with them. For Spain, there is a longstanding perception, which can be described as Whiggish or liberal, that reflects critical views on Catholicism and, correspondingly, the customary association of progress with Protestantism. Aside from being anachronistic, the Spanish empire emerges in this account as something that had to be defeated in order to usher in the future, but also as an empire that was likely to fail. Given this perception, it is not surprising that the idea of overreach and inevitable defeat is frequently applied to Spain.

Aside from their misleading specific application, such issues also underline the problematic nature of the thesis that interests (in the sense of the interests of a state) and capabilities are clear and readily apparent, a point that needs stressing when there is discussion of imperial limits and military capability. In practice, just as interests can be variously defined and understood, so possible limits can be seen as much, if not more, in terms of policy and related debate, as of the geography of military strategy understood in terms of the constraints of environment and distance on successful operations. Indeed, a focus on the latter may seem to represent an emphasis on a militarisation of the limits of empire that is disproportionately important in the literature, for example as far as Philip II's policies towards the Dutch Revolt and the French Wars of Religion were concerned. In contrast to this militarisation of issues of policy and strategy, other policies would probably have led to very different situations, affecting the possibility of opposition to incorporation or conquest or of rebellion, the likelihood of support within the areas that rebelled, and the prospect for a reconciliation short of revolution. Thus, a different politics could have led to a different geography. This issue cuts to the quick of the question about limits because it removes this question from the realm of mechanistic theories of the state/empire – of the form 'thus far is appropriate, but more causes a reaction', rather like a machine cutting out, or a rubber band losing its stretch.

Instead, it is the very drive of the system that is at question when policies, and the pressures for obedience and order, are considered, and, partly for this reason, there is a need to include domestic policy as a key aspect of strategy, as with the moves against religious heterodoxy by Philip III of Spain and Louis XIV of France: respectively, the expulsion of the Moriscos, converted Moors, in 1609 as a potential fifth column who might help the Ottomans and the Barbary States of North Africa, and the Revocation of the Edict of Nantes in 1685, ending the rights of French Protestants. Similarly, religious considerations were important in the definition of Ottoman interests.[16] Indeed, as earlier with limits, the value of a flexible definition for strategy emerges. It is conventional to restrict the term to the military, but this practice is not terribly helpful from the perspective of limits, as strategy emerges as primarily political in background, goal and indeed means, with the use of force simply an aspect of these means, and frequently an aspect that is only to be employed as a substitute for other means. Thus, strategy should be understood in terms of a process of policy formation, execution and evaluation to which military purposes are frequently secondary.

In part, the definition and discussion, in recent decades, of an operational dimension to war, between the tactical and strategic levels, provides a valuable opportunity for reconceptualising strategy, away from its usual military location and, instead, towards an understanding of the concept that is more centrally political. In any event, even at the operational and tactical levels, political considerations played a crucial role in the seventeenth, as in other centuries. Indeed, they can be seen as aspects of the political character of warfare, notably again the sense of limits in means as well as goals. This is not a semantic play on the notion of limited war, instructive as that is in this context, but, instead, an emphasis on the extent to which war making involved limits or their absence, for example in the treatment of prisoners and civilians, or the extent of scorched earth policies, while, as a product of political factors, there were important differences between conflict designed to retain and/or incorporate territory and warfare more focused on battle with opposing forces, notably if intended to ensure their destruction.

Variations and limits in the tone of military policy bring up key cultural elements in war making which act as a qualification to any ahistorical transference of examples for analytical purpose from one state to another. For example, although the extent to which religion was important to various aspects of the character of Spanish imperialism can be qualified and debated, that very process underlines the degree to which the cultural or ideological dimension, and everything it entailed for an understanding and telling of interests and limits, has to be considered in terms of a specific historical context and cannot be readily reduced to, or by, any form of structuralism and determinism. Thus, for Spain, as for other seventeenth-century empires, for example Mughal India, the issue of limits serves as the basis for scrutinising the drive of a state and the character of an international system, but does so within a particular context framed by multiple political factors rather than solely military ones.

Ethiopia and Persia

This emphasis on politics is instructive since there is a tendency to downgrade this factor in military analysis and particularly when writing about non-Western cultures, as the latter are generally discussed solely in terms of their war making and, specifically, their technology and tactics. Moreover, if the politics of non-Western cultures are considered, there is a primitivisation, usually by means of reducing them to a simple account of causation and means of operation, as with a discussion in terms of nomadic peoples and raiding, the sophistication of which tends to be underrated. The implications of the choice of words can play a major role in such an analysis, but there is a need for more discussion. For example, to take the Horn of Africa and the Oromo peoples, nomadic pastoral-ists who moved into Ethiopia in part as a result of their effective use of cavalry, in practice more was at stake both in their challenge and in the response. This response was instructive, as Serse-Dingil, who became King of Abyssinia (Ethiopia) at the end of 1562, ruling until 1597, changed its military system so that the traditional reliance on the private forces of provincial governors and other regional potentates was complemented by an extension of the troops directly under royal control, both the royal bodyguard and the militia. This change can be seen in terms of centralisa-tion, but that analysis overlooks the extent to which such a royal policy was a traditional means of extending patronage and increasing control that had been seen for centuries across the world.

Possibly more significantly, Serse-Dingil's decision to lead the army in person, again a traditional response, also helped give a new direction to Ethiopian energies. The Sultanate of Adal, a nearby source of Islamic pressure, was defeated in 1576, as was an alliance of Ottoman forces with the Governor of Tigre two years later, which ended Ottoman attempts to overrun Ethiopia from the Red Sea. Serse-Dingil then expanded Ethiopia to the west. Susenyos (r. 1607–32) continued this expansion, but also followed the traditional policy of those confronted by 'barbarians', one that bridged politics and the military in a joint policy: he incorporated many of the Oromo into his army and settled many in his dominions. However, in a parallel to the factors limiting Sigismund III of Poland's appeal in Sweden and Russia, Susenyos's conversion to Catholicism led to serious rebellions and he abdicated.

Thus, in Ethiopia, as more generally, new (muskets) and existing weap-onry was impacted into a warfare shaped by the interaction of domestic and international politics. At the same time, the means of war were not simply a passive product of political forces. Yet, around the world, there was scant sign in the 1590s and 1600s of radical change in these means, or certainly of a military revolution in progress. For example, Idris Aloma, *mai* (ruler) of Bornu (r. 1569–c. 1600), a Muslim state based in the region of Lake Chad, probably obtained his musketeers from the Ottoman stronghold of Tripoli, across the Sahara on the Mediterranean, but Ibn Fartuwa's contemporary account of Aloma's wars with neighbouring Kanem makes no mention of guns playing a crucial role. Instead, Fartuwa concentrated on other units of Aloma's army, which included archers, shield-bearers, cavalry and camel-borne troops. Camel columns were sent into the Sahara. There was no mention of cannon. In his campaigns, Aloma made careful use of economic measures, attacking crops or keeping nomads from their grazing areas in order to make them submit, both longstanding practices in such campaigns.

At a greater scale, Abbas I of Persia (r. 1587–1629) also focused more on organisation than technology, although the latter played a role. Abbas sought to develop a strong, centrally controlled force based on Caucasian military slaves (*ghulams*). This force included a 12,000-strong corps of artillerymen with about 500 cannon, but most of the *ghulams* fought with traditional weapons, and in 1598, when Abbas defeated the Uzbeks at Rabát-i Pariyán, the battle was decided by an old-fashioned charge by Abbas's mounted bodyguard, led by the Shah himself. This victory gave Abbas control of the important city of Herat in what is now western Afghanistan.[17]

Earlier Uzbek successes, including, in 1589, the capture of Herat and an advance on the city of Mashhad further west, had weakened Abbas in the war with the Ottomans the latter had launched in 1578; and, in 1590, Abbas had had to accept peace terms leaving the Ottomans with major gains in the Caucasus and western Persia. In 1603, however, Abbas resumed the Safavids' struggle with the Ottomans, capturing the major city of Tabriz and, in 1604, after a long siege, Erivan. In 1605, the Ottomans attempted to regain Tabriz, only for their army to be routed by Abbas at Sufian. As was frequent in many battles of the century, defection played a role in the victory, with Abbas benefiting from the defection of some of the Kurdish leaders, although Abbas's superior tactics were also important in that he misled the Ottomans as to the direction of his attack. Abbas then captured the cities of Gänjä, Tblisi and, in 1606, after a long siege, Shirvan. After intermittent hostilities and periods of peace, Abbas captured Baghdad from the Ottomans in 1623, a crucial gain.

This Persian pressure throws light on the Ottoman ability, neverthe-less, to fight the Habsburgs to a standstill in the Thirteen Years' War of 1593–1606. Indeed, all three powers understood the interrelationships of the struggle. In 1592, Pope Clement VIII sent a mission to Abbas urging him to oppose the Ottomans, and in 1602 he sent another mission seeking to convert Abbas with the promise of Western military assistance against the Ottomans. Relations between Abbas and the Christians, however, collapsed in 1606 when Austria negotiated peace with the Ottomans. In turn, Abbas both offered Jerusalem (if he conquered it from the Ottomans) to the Christians in 1609 and pressed Spain (and thus Portugal also) to declare war on the Ottomans in order to avoid his making peace with them.[18] As further instances of the strength of his military system, Abbas, a talented expansionist, captured the city of Kandahar (in modern southern Afghanistan) from the Mughals and Hormuz on the Persian Gulf from Portugal, both in 1622. On the Persian Gulf, he had already taken Bahrain in 1602 and Bandar 'Abbas in 1614. In turn, the Portuguese helped the Ottomans hold Basra against Persian attack in 1624.

By increasing the land under his control, Abbas was able to fund his existing and new military systems, which contributed to his string of successes. Administrative changes allowed troops to be paid directly from the royal treasury, rather than from the revenues of provinces assigned to tribal governors. Moreover, *ghulams* became provincial governors, which strengthened Abbas's position, and the destruction of many fortifications may have arisen, as in seventeenth-century France and Cromwellian England, from a desire to concentrate power.[19] Such a programme of change, however, was not required in order to obtain success. Thus, in 1614, Louis XIII of France marched south with his army in order to impose his authority on Béarn, an independent territory in southern France that was a royal fief but where Catholic worship was not permitted. The Estates (Parliament) had protested against an order to restore Catholic worship and all church property, whereupon Louis resorted to the military option, which led to submission, not resistance.[20] Louis formally annexed Béarn to France. The use of force short of war had fully succeeded and the existing army had overawed resistance. The multiplicity of factors involved in military activity therefore serves as a reminder of the need to avoid any single explanation of success and capability, and thus provides a key context for considering the major upsurge of warfare in Europe from 1618.

4 Conflict, 1616–1650

The centrality of East and South Asia

It is worth rethinking the world in 1600 and 1700 in terms of equal-population cartograms. These provide demographically weighted maps (with territory mapped in proportion to its population) that have much to offer that is not provided by conventional, equal-area, maps. Notably, these cartograms, with their emphasis on East and South Asia where most of the world's population lived, would suggest that Western power was less central than the use of equal-area maps would imply. This contrast offers an important perspective because the subliminal quality of cartographic images conveys impressions of relative importance that, in turn, help dictate conclusions about political and military success. In many respects, the impressions created by equal-area maps are misleading and rethinking the world spatially in terms of equal-population cartograms very much revises the impression of Western success. For example, the Russian conquest of much of Siberia, with its low density of population, becomes of limited immediate importance, as indeed does that of eastern North America, whatever their eventual consequences. This approach also offers a different account of European history since more attention, for example, should be devoted to Italy, especially the populous north, than is usually the case in the discussion of seventeenth-century warfare. Furthermore, an emphasis on gaining control of people helps underline the importance of sieges, as major towns were fortified.

While the demographic approach encourages a reconceptualisation of European expansion, it is also important to the consideration of conflict between non-Western powers. Inevitably such an approach ensures that more attention is devoted to China, and indeed conflict within the country is, at this level, more significant than that between many European states, although it can be argued that the long-term consequences of the Thirty Years' War in Europe were more important for world history than those stemming from the Manchu conquest of China.

The Manchu conquest of China

Nevertheless, China found its fortunes transformed by war in this period and must take pride of place in any military history of the century. Nothing in the European world and nothing else in Eurasia compared to the scale and drama of the overthrow of Ming China, which brought down an empire established in the late 1360s. The Ming were to be replaced by the Manchu, descendants of the Jurchen Jin who, until overthrown by the Mongols, had controlled all of China north of the Huai river from 1126 to 1234, and this replacement by the Manchu lent new energy to the Chinese military and to Chinese expansionism, and, indeed, contributed to the longstanding bellicosity of Chinese history.[1] Originally based in the mountains of south-eastern Manchuria, the Jurchens expanded under Nurhaci (1559–1626) to dominate the lands to the north of the Great Wall in the early seventeenth century. He united the Jurchen tribes, by means of war, marriage alliances and exploiting the Chinese tributary system, and also developed a strong cavalry army based on horse archers. This army was organised into 'banners': units that incorporated tribal groups. Like Chinggis Khan and the Mongols in the late twelfth century, Nurhaci employed organisational methods in order to overcome the fissiparous tendencies of tribalism and also to bring cohesion to cavalry warfare.

Nurhaci used his army to gain control of most of northern Manchuria by 1616. Having renounced fealty to the Ming that year, a marked challenge to the usual pattern of Ming control over steppe areas, Nurhaci consolidated the Manchu state before attacking the Chinese in 1618, capturing the city of Fushun and defeating a far larger army at Sarhu. In an instructive instance of the relationship between events in different centuries and areas, the efforts required to defeat the Japanese invasions of Korea in the 1590s had exhausted the Chinese treasury, and led to a failure to maintain adequate defences against invasion from the steppe. Thus, imperial overstretch could be measured not in success, or failure, on a particular front, but on the eventual consequences elsewhere. Looked at differently, defences only appeared inadequate because of the unexpected effectiveness of the attack.

The Chinese defence system proved inadequate to the challenge. Korean-supported Chinese counter-attacks failed disastrously in 1619, with defeats at Siyanggiayan and Niu-mao chai: Chinese and Korean firearms and numbers could not counteract the tactical mobility of the determined, well-led and numerous Manchu cavalry.[2] Not only could the Chinese not match the Manchu cavalry, but they were also unable to formulate an effective infantry response to the Manchu. Moreover, Manchu adaptability was to lead them to benefit from the military technology of their rivals. By the end of the sixteenth century, a metallurgical industry had developed in Manchuria, an area rich in iron and coal, and cannon production followed. Actively seeking to capture the men able to manufacture and use cannon, and helped by a mutiny among them, the Manchu were able to adopt Portuguese cannon and cannon-founding technology, making effective use of the former, while the Chinese also sought advice.

More significantly, the Manchu also emulated the political techniques and administrative structures of imperial China, creating an effective system that was recognisably different from that of tribalism. This left the Manchu better able to benefit from the political chaos in China in 1644, and contrasted with the total failure of the Afghans, who overthrew Safavid Persia in 1721–2, to create a new political order there. The Manchu captured the major position of Liaoyang in 1621, blocking the overland route between China and Korea, as well as Shenyang, which became the Manchu capital from 1625. Nurhaci, instead of making over the conquered territory for looting and division among the banners, left it outside the tribal system to be administered by Chinese bureaucrats. Thus, a dual state, separately administering Chinese and Jurchens, was created, and this structure greatly increased the Manchu appeal to dissident and defeated Chinese. Authority was focused on the ruler and not on the ethnic group of invaders.

After invasions in 1627 and 1636–7, Korea, China's leading ally, was reduced to vassal status. The Koreans surrendered within two months in the face of the Manchu winter invasion of 1636–7. This surrender represented a frightening portent for China, as well as ensuring resources for the Manchu and giving them greater room for manoeuvre. Just as serious, the Chinese failed in their long-established policy of manipulating their steppe neighbours. Inner Mongolia became a Manchu dependency in 1633–4, as a result of disunity among the Mongols and a breakdown in relations between the Ming and the Čaqar Mongols, whose leader, Ligdan Khan, lost control of the steppe and was defeated by the Manchu. The latter also benefited from marriage alliances with the Mongol élite, from winning support by matching Ming payments in return for fealty, and from purchasing Mongol horses. Direct support was important and Mongol banners were organised by the Manchu. Moreover, Mongol co-operation made it easier to attack China, not least by circumventing Chinese defences. The Chinese attempt to move troops on the northern frontier eastward, from facing the Mongols in order to confront the Manchu, was no longer appropriate. The wide-ranging energy and expansion of the Manchu, and their concern with the steppe, was also shown by their conquest of the Amur region and the area further north to the Argun River, which were brought under Manchu control from 1643. This move north into an area of low population density very different to much of China prepared the way for the clash with the Russians in the Amur valley in the 1680s.

The Manchu still encountered many setbacks which reflected the challenge posed by the defence of the Chinese fortified border zone. Attacks on China in 1626 and 1630 were unsuccessful. Nurhaci failed to storm the fortress of Ningyuan in 1626, in part due to Ming cannon, but the fortress of Dalinghe fell in 1631 after Ming relief attempts were defeated. Co-operation with Chinese elements strengthened the Manchu militarily, again illustrating the importance of the political context and the value of combined arms operations. Chinese 'fifth columnists' helped the Manchu capture the fortified cities of Shenyang in 1619 and Liaoyang in 1621. In a battle near Dalinghe in 1631, the Chinese held off frontal assaults by Manchu cavalry, but were then disrupted by the artillery and fire arrows of the Manchu's Chinese allies, so that the Manchu cavalry ultimately triumphed. Nurhaci's successors, Abahai (r. 1626–43) and Dorgon (r. 1643–50), maintained his dynamism. Manchu plundering expeditions into northern China in 1632 and 1634 were followed by a major invasion in 1638–40 which captured many cities in the provinces of Shandong and Zhili.

Rather than simply thinking in terms of a victory for cavalry over the static military system and warfare of China, it is necessary to note a lack of unity on the Chinese side that weakened resistance and, in some key cases, directly abetted the Manchu advance. From 1582 there had been weak emperors, increasingly arbitrary central government, oppressive taxation and growing independence by ambitious figures, the first and last matching the situation in France during the Wars of Religion and in the Ottoman empire in the early 1620s. Large-scale rebellions included one in Fuchow (1607), the White Lotus uprising in Shandong (1625), and, from 1628, a major series in central China which, from 1636, spread to include much of the north.[3] These rebellions were far more extensive than anywhere else in Asia at the time, most prominently Japan, where the unsuccessful Shimábava Rebellion led to the siege of Hara Castle in 1638, which proved the last large-scale use of Japanese troops in action until the nineteenth century.

Out of this chaos in China, two regional warlords emerged without any matching improvement in the quality of the Emperor. In the early 1640s, Zhang Xianzhong dominated the Yangtze valley and the eastern plain, and, from 1644, established himself in the province of Sichuan. Li Zicheng, a former bandit, was more powerful in the north. From 1641, when he captured the walled city of Luoyang, he controlled the provinces of Shanxi, Hubei and Henen, and he benefited from the degree to which Ming forces and fortifications were concentrated further north and designed to resist Manchu attacks from the north. The city of Kaifeng fell the following year.

From 1596 to 1609 there were serious rebellions against Ottoman rule in Anatolia and Syria that were finally overcome by defeats, the buying off of some rebel leaders and the difficulties of sustaining rebellion in the impoverished countryside. In contrast, rebellion in China led to the overthrow of the dynasty, but the Ming were also engaged by Manchu attack, whereas, in his operations in 1607–9, the Ottoman Grand Vizier Kuyuju Murad Pasha benefited from the end of war with Austria in 1606.[4] The rebellions in China grew in scale at the same time that the treasury was exhausted by war and there was little money to pay the troops. In 1644, the garrison in Beijing marched out to confront Li's advancing army, but it proved unequal to the task. Allegedly, the garrison fled when they heard cannon fire, leaving Beijing to rely on only 3000 eunuch troops who proved unable to hold off the attackers, not least as Li was helped by supporters within the walls. As the capital fell, the incompetent Chongzhen emperor committed suicide.

Li proclaimed the Shun dynasty, but his army was poorly disciplined and he lacked the support of legitimacy, powerful allies and an administrative apparatus. Here there is a powerful parallel with some elements of European politics, where such support was also important, as was indicated by some aspects of the resilience of the Bourbon position in France in the face of the rebellions of the mid-century, the *Frondes*. The collapse of the Ming dynasty, and thus of the Chinese frontier defence system, thanks to Li, gave the Manchu their opportunity. Wu Sangui, who commanded the largest Chinese army on the northern frontier, initially decided to accept Li's offer of terms but, en route to negotiate, discovered that the rebels had killed his family. Fighting then broke out between Wu and the rebels who advanced on his position at Shanhaiguan at the eastern end of the Great Wall. Wu refused to submit to Li and, instead, turned to the Manchu who felt that the death of the Ming emperor provided them with greater opportunity and legitimacy for their attempt to take over China. Both opportunity and legitimacy were crucial; realist and idealist considerations each played a role, as they had long done in relations between China and the steppe people, and as they were to continue to do.[5]

The battle of Shanhaiguan (the Battle of the Mountain-Sea Pass) on 27 May 1644 was a key clash which rarely features in lists of decisive battles in world history, since these lists tend to be Eurocentric. In this battle, the joint Manchu–Ming army defeated Li, who commanded his 60,000 force in person. Li deployed his force in a broad and deep line, repulsing repeated attacks by Wu's army, about 50,000 strong and with another 50,000 local militia in support. Wu's forces took heavy casualties without defeating Li, but the ability of the Manchu cavalry under Dorgon to turn Li's left flank in a sandstorm proved decisive. The arrival of the Manchu cavalry behind Li's flank wrecked the cohesion of the latter army, but so also did the realisation that it was also up against the Manchu, who had only just arrived. Li's army was routed with heavy casualties. After being defeated, Li returned to Beijing, hastily crowning himself Emperor on 3 June (29 April in the traditional Chinese calendar). No longer able, however, as a result of his defeat, to protect or dominate Beijing, Li abandoned the city and the Manchu army occupied it without resistance on 5 June 1644. Wu pursued Li into Shanxi and Hubei, being responsible for his death in October 1645.

In turn, Chinese units were reorganised by the Manchu, who recruited some of the leading Ming generals and used them to help in the conquest of central and southern China. Hong Chengchou became a Manchu general, capturing Hankou in 1645 and Nanjing in 1646, and pacifying Fujian in 1646, a major extension of Manchu power into southern China. Geng Jingzhong also became a Manchu general. In an instructive comparison, central and southern China fell more speedily than when the Mongols had invaded China in the thirteenth century, although the Mongols had faced the need to overcome two Chinese states, one in north and one in south China. The provinces of Shandong, Jiangsu, Anhui and Hubei were conquered in 1645, Sichuan in 1646, and Gansu in 1649. Zhang Xianzhong was defeated and executed in 1647. The contrast between the campaigns of these years and the difficulty, in the latter stages of the Thirty Years' War in Europe, in ensuring a comparable relationship between advances and outcomes is notable.

The south was quickly conquered because of the Chinese troops that fell into Manchu hands due to opposition to Li, but, despite Ming awareness of their problems and the scale of the area of operations, the Manchu would probably have succeeded in destroying the Ming even without Li. They were already well advanced in the process of shifting to conquest from raiding, and the Manchu benefited from having a stronger and more coherent military and political system than any Chinese contenders to the Ming. Moreover, the success of Li was really a sign of Ming political paralysis as the court veered between devoting resources to suppressing the rebels and then backing off before someone could obtain political capital by succeeding.[6] Poor leadership by the Chongzhen emperor (r. 1628–44) was critical, as he executed several of his most prominent commanders and, unlike his predecessors, most notably the Wan Li emperor, did not shield his generals from unfair criticism by civil officials. The Ming defence was plagued by factional squabbles.

Again, the key clash was scarcely with the West, while, moreover, Western forces did not play any role in the struggles within China, a marked contrast with the situation during the Taiping Revolution of the mid-nineteenth century. An instructive comparison with the willingness of the Manchu to recruit former enemies was provided by England and France in the 1660s, each of which also used one-time rebels: former Cromwellians and *Frondeurs* respectively.

China and military capability

These Manchu campaigns indicate the need for care in reading from models of military capability and progress based on Western Europe. More particularly, the literature on state development and military revolution presumes a synergy in which governmental sophistication and needs play a key role for each and also provide definitions for progress and success. Instead, the overthrow of the Ming underlines the extent to which administrative continuity and sophistication (which, alongside legitimacy, the Ming certainly possessed) did not suffice for victory, a point that can be paralleled with the complete Mongol conquest of China in the thirteenth century. Yet, the Manchu had to develop, adopt and adapt administrative mechanisms and strategies of legitimation in order to help anchor their military success and to obtain political benefit from it. It is unclear how much emphasis should be placed on the mechanisms rather than the strategies.

Manchu success also suggests that it is mistaken to read back from the modern perception of the effectiveness of infantry and artillery fire-power, and of the attendant relationship between disciplined, well-drilled and well-armed permanent firepower forces, and, on the other hand, those that were not so armed. In practice, the balance of advantage was much closer, with factors such as experience, terrain, leadership and tactics all affecting the use and value of particular arms, albeit in varying circumstances and to differing degrees. At the level of force structure and tactics, the Manchu conquest of China demonstrated that cavalry remained the key to much conflict. As in Europe, cavalry provided a mobility towards and on the battlefield, and an ability to develop and sustain an attack across a changing battlefield that infantry lacked. In Europe, cavalry continued to be important, for example in battles such as Rocroi (1643), Naseby (1645) and Vienna (1683) and, more generally, in the latter stages of the Thirty

Years' War (1618–48),[7] as well as in Eastern Europe. Social and cultural as well as functional factors focused on mobility played a role, and the prestige of cavalry was indicated by the greater social prominence of cavalry service and command compared to those of the infantry. Moreover, works on military horsemanship were popular, for example Lodovico Melzo's *Regole Militari sopra il govierno e servito particolare della cavaleria* (Antwerp, 1611), which was translated into French, Spanish, German and English. Born in Milan, the centre of Spanish power in northern Italy, and a member of the Order of the Knights of St John of Jerusalem, Melzo might appear a marginal figure if military progress is understood in terms of the rise of infantry, but that was not a view that made much sense in the 1610s or the 1640s.

On the world scale, the principal limit on cavalry was not infantry firepower, as might be implied if the stress is on the Military Revolution, a thesis that does not engage satisfactorily with the continued role of cavalry, but, rather, disease and climate, which, for example, greatly restricted the use of horses in sub-Saharan Africa, most of which was affected by the tsetse fly. Heavily forested regions, such as much of South-East Asia, also proved inappropriate for cavalry. Cavalry tactics and weaponry varied across the world, but most cavalry did not make a transition to the use of firearms and this was particularly the case in Asia where the Manchu, the most effective cavalry force of the century, employed archery.

Military 'progress' is difficult to define, whether assessed in terms of capability, effectiveness or sophistication, and what was entailed for forces to be fit for purpose varied very greatly around the world. The same was true for political 'progress', and this is significant because implicit assumptions about the latter tend to play a major role in the definition and discussion of military developments. In the case of China, progress is a problematic concept. As with the 'decline and fall' of imperial Rome, notably the role of 'barbarians', both in defeating Rome and in fighting for it in the fourth and fifth centuries, there were not clear-cut sides in seventeenth-century China, and the 'overthrow' that is to be explained is not as readily apparent as it might appear. Instead, the Manchu conquest involved redefinitions of cultural loyalty in which distinctions between Chinese and 'barbarian' became less apparent and definitions less rigid. Advancing and contesting this process of redefinition was an important aspect of the conquest. Indeed, the Manchu state owed its lasting success in large part to its syncretic character (drawing on and adapting to different traditions), which highlighted the extent to which such a means, while crucial for European success and consolidation in the aptly named Latin America and, later and in a different fashion, nineteenth-century India, did not operate solely for the Europeans, nor indeed similarly for them in the seventeenth century in North America, Africa or the Balkans.[8]

Mughal India

The contrasting nature of military tasking was amply demonstrated by the different challenges facing Mughal India. There was no recurrence in the seventeenth century of the invasion from Central Asia seen in the sixteenth with the Mughal conquest of northern India, and no repetition of the overthrow of Persia by foreign invasion. Indeed, in an important reminder of significant contrasts within the early-modern period, and despite environmental continuities and similarities, Mughal India, Safavid Persia and Ottoman Turkey did not have to cope with problems comparable to those posed to Ming China by the Manchu invasion, although they all faced external pressures as well as related challenges in frontier zones. Indeed, the Mughals, the leading land military power in the world after China, encountered serious setbacks, both within India and in neighbouring regions.

Such setbacks for the Mughals were particularly the case where the terrain was not suited to their forces. For example, in the forested valley of the River Brahmaputra in what is now north-east India, the Ahom, a Shan people originally from upper Burma, proved a serious challenge from 1612, not least because they mobilised all their resources for war. Although the Ahom were outnumbered, their fighting techniques were well adapted to the terrain. They relied on infantry armed with muskets or bows and arrows, used flexible tactics, including surprise night attacks, and rapidly created fortified positions based on bamboo stockades which made attacking them a costly and difficult task. The riverine and jungle terrain were very different from the plains and low hills of Rajasthan, a more strategically significant region, where the Mughals had campaigned extensively and for which their weaponry and tactics were far more appropriate.[9] There is a parallel with the problems that faced the British Indian Army, a force used largely for conflict on the dry upland terrain of India's North-West Frontier, when it was sent in 1941–2 to resist Japanese advances in Malaya and Burma.[10]

As a result of the terrain and vegetation, the Mughals made little use of horses against the Ahom. Instead, in a clear sign of a resilient military system, both force structure and tactics were adapted. Elephants were employed to provide shock power, both in battle and against stockades; they were also used in conflict in southern China, as in the Rebellion of the Three Feudatories (see pp. 81–2). The Mughals also made extensive use of boats equipped with cannon, including floating platforms carrying heavy cannon, while they matched Ahom stockades by constructing entrenchments. The Mughals manned them with musketeers and cannon. A fierce war with the Ahom in 1636–8 saw the Mughals win a major battle at Burpetah (1637) and, having advanced, lose one further east at Kajali (1638). The war led to a compromise peace which preserved Ahom independence but advanced Mughal authority to Kamrup.

In a conflict of greater scale and significance, Afghanistan also proved difficult terrain for the Mughals, who sought to recover their ancient Central Asian homeland of the region of Ferghana from their ancestral enemies, the Uzbeks, who ruled Bukhara and Samarqand north of the Oxus River and Balkh and Badakhshan to its south. Benefiting from an Uzbek civil war, a Mughal army was instructed to restore the exiled ruler, Nazar Muhammad Khan, as a tributary, or to annex the state. Some 50,000 cavalry and 10,000 infantry were sent to Kabul in early 1646. After the road had been improved, the army moved through the mountains of the Hindu Kush, occupying Badakhshan, and the cities of Kunduz and Balkh, now in northern Afghanistan. This was a formidable achievement which can be favourably judged after the difficulties faced by Britain, the Soviet Union and the USA when operating in Afghanistan from the 1830s and at the present time.

Little fighting was involved in the initial advance but, again like campaigns there from the 1830s, it proved impossible to prevent the situation from deteriorating. Uzbek guerrilla raids inflicted a heavy burden on Mughal logistics and, although Mughal firearms proved effective against attacks by mounted archers, the range of Uzbek war making included the fouling of the Balkh River, which helped cause an epidemic. Such techniques were used frequently, as disease was seen as a weapon. Thus, the besieging Omani Arabs fired corpses within the walls of Fort Jesus in Mombasa, contributing to an epidemic among the garrison that, after many deaths, led the Portuguese to surrender the position in 1698.

In 1647, the Mughals sent reinforcements to Afghanistan under Prince Aurangzeb, second son of the Emperor, Shan Jahan. Unlike in 1646, they had to fight their way across the Hindu Kush, although they did so successfully, helped by a shock force of war elephants, as well as by firearms, including rockets which were in effect fireworks. Once near Balkh, however, the Uzbeks employed the customary harrying tactics of horse archers in undermining the Mughal position. Mughal field artillery and musketeers were unable to defeat their more mobile opponents, even when the Mughals sought mobility by leaving their equipment behind. They also found it impossible to obtain adequate supplies from the harsh region where local knowledge, supplies and military adaptability were essential to success. In late 1647, Aurangzeb evacuated Balkh and retreated through the snowbound Hindu Kush, his force suffering heavy losses as a result of attacks from local tribesmen.

In a clear reminder of the interdependence of operations on different fronts, Mughal weakness in the aftermath of this campaign affected the competition with the Safavids over the city of Kandahar, a key commercial point and the gateway for the Persians to advance into southern Afghanistan and towards the Indus Valley. Lost by the Mughals in 1622 to Shah Abbas I of Persia, Kandahar had been regained in 1638 when the Persian commander surrendered, fearing execution by his sovereign. Helped by Mughal weakness in the aftermath of their campaign in Afghanistan, Shah Abbas II recaptured the city in 1648. Nevertheless, the Safavids were no longer an expansionist power and, instead, had become more defensive, which reflected the evolution of the Safavid state from a tribal formation to a sedentary policy.[11] Whereas, in 1739, Nadir Shah of Persia was to push on from Afghanistan to invade northern India, capturing Delhi after victory at Karnal, there was no such advance in the 1640s.

The Mughals also had a number of important successes. To the south in India, they sought expansion in order to gain new sources of men and money. The Nizam Shahis of Ahmadnagar, the ruling dynasty, were attacked by the Mughal ruler, Akbar, in 1596, and the territory of Barar, which they had annexed in 1574, was ceded to the Mughals that year, in a clear acknowledgement of Mughal superiority. The Mughals pressed on to take the capital of Ahmadnagar in 1600, but conflict continued, with independence asserted in a vigorous resistance, especially from 1609. The Mughals were driven back, and the Nizam Shahis invaded both Barar, which they occupied from 1616 to 1626, and the territory of Khandesh. A coalition, established in 1615 with the major Deccan Sultanates to the south, the Qutb Shahis of Golconda and the Adil Shahis of Bijapur, provided the Nizam Shahis with major advantages, but the coalition collapsed in 1621, enabling the Mughals to gain much territory in 1622, and in 1633 the final conquest and annexation of Ahmadnagar occurred. In this expansion, the Mughals, generally adept at recruiting local allies, followed their usual pattern, obtaining, for example, support from the Marathas.

After periods of civil war in 1622–4 and 1627–9, Mughal expansion resumed during the reign of Shah Jahan (1627–58); aside from conquering Ahmadnagar, he reduced Bijapur and Golconda to vassalage in 1635–6. Golconda swiftly complied, but Bijapur did so only after three Mughal armies invaded and ravaged the countryside. Such devastation serves as a reminder of the potential operational and strategic value of attacks on civil society, which, in turn, provides a perspective in which to look at the notorious anti-societal violence of troops in Europe during the Thirty Years' War. Such devastation was not only employed by the Mughals. Bijapur and Golconda responded in the mid-1640s to opposition to their claims to overlordship by Hindu rulers to the south by successful campaigns, including Golconda's conquest of the state of Vijayangara in 1646. Allegedly, over 150,000 people were seized for slaves.

To the north of India, the Mughals pushed into the territories of Baltistan and Ladakh in the Himalayas in 1637–9 after a difficult expedition over hazardous mountain passes by 12,000 men, who had to carry all their supplies with them because the route was largely barren. Mughal success there contrasted with the difficulties encountered by the French when operating in the Alps in the mid-1630s, especially in the valley of the Valtelline. The Himalayan state of Garhwal, however, fought off the Mughals in 1635.

Mughal control of their frontiers was maintained by clientage, local alliances which, in turn, helped sustain the size of the army, and by force. Thus, to the west in the dry province of Sind, a network of small forts manned by cavalry and musketeers extended Mughal power. More generally, the Mughals were also able to preserve their dominance of northern India. Force was a key element, not least in providing a focus for clientage, and, although the Mughals paid insufficient attention to the quality of their firearms or to artillery, they maintained a formidable mixed-arms army. In 1647, Abdul Hamid Lahori listed Mughal military strength as 200,000 stipendiary cavalry, 185,000 other cavalry, and a central force of 40,000 garrisoned musketeers and gunners, 10,000 of whom were posted with the Emperor.[12]

The cavalry were dominant, not only numerically but also in terms of the ethos of the army, and this dominance affected the use of combined arms. Thus, the Mughals had only a limited interest in field artillery, and this interest was largely in a light artillery that could be integrated with the cavalry, rather than a heavier field artillery more appropriate for the less mobile infantry. Siege artillery was a different matter, as the Mughals favoured large guns that could make a major impact at sieges, not least as a display of power and, in particular, greater power over rivals. These guns were designed, like the very large European warships of the early sixteenth century, to proclaim status as well as to intimidate.[13] The nature of their army provided the Mughals with a multi-layered response to crisis. The *zamindari* militia generally took care of most peasant unrest, while the main-force *mansabdari* armies took on larger challenges.

Mughal activity on a number of fronts was matched by that of the Safavids and Ottomans. The former fought both Mughals and Ottomans, the latter Safavids and Christian powers. Compared to these powers, much of the military history of Christian Europe seems rather small-scale. Yet, there were similarities at the general level. If Mughal India, Safavid Persia and the Ottoman empire all operated in an obvious context of pressure and rivalry, the same was also true of the European states, and, in each case, this context encouraged a process of competitive emulation. Other key similarities were found in force structure and political context. Although a long-term perspective would note an increasing emphasis on firepower in European armies, with a declining percentage of pikemen among the infantry, the overwhelming stress in the first half of the century, both in Europe and elsewhere, was on combined forces. Thus, Iskandar Muda (r. 1607–36), the dynamic Sultan of Aceh in Sumatra and an opponent of the Portuguese, had not only a fleet with large galleys capable of carrying over 600 men, but also an army including many cannon, as well as infantry, cavalry and elephants. Although his land and sea attack on the Portuguese base of Malacca in 1629 was totally unsuccessful, the army was well up to the task of dominating northern Sumatra.[14]

Organisational differences may well have been more significant to capability than those in weaponry, although there is again the issue of fitness for purpose. A key contrast was that between the use of conscript troops, as in Arakan, Burma and Nepal, and of mercenaries, as in northern India. Environmental factors were also significant to differences in tactical, operational and strategic goals and possibilities. Thus, at the tactical level, the skilful use of stockades in Arakan, Burma, Kerala and Nepal reflected the availability of timber. Indeed, the major differences between warfare in Kerala and northern India are a reminder of the dangers of assuming that there was a common pattern or trajectory to warfare in India, let alone further afield. Northern India was a less varied military environment than the south, but the former also posed a range of challenges.

The Thirty Years' War

This methodological point provides an appropriate way with which to approach the situation in Europe because there is a tendency to assume that there was a clear best practice there. With a lack of precision, this best practice is seen as both being defined by, and indeed defining, the Military Revolution. Moreover, the Thirty Years' War (1618–48) apparently serves to provide a demonstration of the process as it provides the opportunity to describe and demonstrate this Revolution, notably with the warfare of, first, the Dutch and, then, the Swedes under Gustavus Adolphus (r. 1611–32), who defeated, respectively, Spain and Austria.

The war was, from the outset, effectively a Europe-wide civil war, although the participation of England, Russia and the Ottoman empire was only indirect and limited. Nevertheless, the Thirty Years' War brought together several different conflicts, notably, but not only, the Austrian Habsburg attempt to assert control of the Habsburg hereditary lands and authority in the Holy Roman Empire, as well as hostilities in the long war between Spain and the Dutch, rivalries between France and Spain, and Sweden and Russia, and a dynastic struggle within the Vasa family between the rulers of Poland and Sweden. Rivalry between Protestants and Catholics was also such that the conflict can be seen as one of the European wars of religion stemming from the Reformation. Although there were significant alliances across confessional boundaries, notably between France and Sweden, religious antagonism and paranoia contributed to the violence of the struggle.[15]

The war initially began as a rising in 1618 against Habsburg (Austrian) authority in Bohemia (in the modern Czech Republic), a rising in which Protestant opposition played a major role. This was crushed by superior forces at the Battle of the White Mountain outside Prague on 8 November 1620.[16] Prague then fell, Habsburg authority was reimposed in the person of the Holy Roman Emperor Ferdinand II, and Bohemia was re-Catholicised. Ferdinand was supported by his relative, Philip IV of Spain, but also by the Lutheran Elector of Saxony, John George. The Bohemians had offered the throne to the Protestant Frederick, Elector Palatine, the ruler of an important principality in Germany, and, in 1620, Spanish troops from the Army of Flanders under Ambrogio Spinola overran much of the Lower Palatinate, helped by units from Bavaria.[17] Duke Maximilian of Bavaria, a Catholic and a relative of Frederick, saw the war as an opportunity to supersede the Protestant branch of the Wittelsbach dynasty. Such competition within dynasties was common and serves as a reminder of the complexity of dynasticism as a motivating force and means of operation in international relations.

The overrunning of the Lower Palatinate, a wealthy area in the middle Rhine, provided a clear example of the potential decisiveness of conflict in this period. On 6 May 1622, at Wimpfen, the army of the Bavarian-led Catholic League under Jean, Count of Tilly and a Spanish force under Don Gonzalo Fernández de Córdoba heavily defeated an army under George of Baden-Durlach that was seeking to prevent the conquest of the Lower Palatinate. By the end of the year, the principality's leading cities, Heidelberg and Mannheim, had fallen. Bavaria also annexed the Upper Palatinate to its north, and began a process of re-Catholicisation there. To reward his supporter and further entrench the Catholic position in the Holy Roman Empire, Ferdinand II transferred the position of Elector (one of the seven princes of the Holy Roman Empire able to vote for the Emperor) from the Palatine to the Bavarian branch of the Wittelsbachs.

War began anew between the Dutch and Spain in 1621, with Spain determined to resume the drive to end the Dutch War of Independence, and hoping to benefit from the new weakness of the United Provinces' German allies. The context seemed favourable as James I of England preferred the illusion that he might serve as the mediator of Christendom's divisions to the task of helping the Dutch pursued (eventually) by his predecessor Elizabeth I, while, in 1621, the anti-Spanish faction was not yet dominant in France. Searching for aid, the Dutch encouraged opposition to the Habsburgs in Germany and, in turn, Ferdinand II entrusted his troops to a Bohemian military entrepreneur, Albrecht von Wallenstein,[18] who defeated the Dutch-financed German army under Ernst, Count of Mansfeld at Dessau on 25 April 1626. At Lutter, on 27 August 1626, Tilly defeated Christian IV of Denmark who had intervened to support the Protestant cause and to pursue his territorial interests in northern Germany by seizing Catholic prince-bishoprics, territories ruled by clerics, such as the bishoprics of Hildesheim, Paderborn and Verden.[19]

As a reminder, of the number of participants in the Thirty Years' War and the range of operations, Wallenstein marched east after Lutter to prevent Bethlen Gabor, Prince of Transylvania, an Ottoman-backed Protestant, from advancing on Vienna from the east. Wallenstein and Tilly then drove the Danes from northern Germany, defeating a counter-attack at Wolgast in 1628, before, in 1629, invading Jutland and forcing Christian IV out of the war. Wallenstein's freedom of action as an individual commander contrasted markedly with the greater control of military affairs by rulers 50 years later.

As a parallel to the challenges confronting the Austrian Habsburgs, the Ottomans faced not only foreign war with Poland (1620–1) and Persia (intermittently from 1603 to 1640), but also dynastic division leading to the overthrow and murder of one Sultan, Osman, in 1622, and the dethroning of another, Mustafa, in 1623, and provincial opposition, notably rebellions in eastern Anatolia and Lebanon. Precipitated by a rebellion by Caspar Gratiani, the *Voyvoda* (subordinate ruler) of Moldavia who had been deposed by the Sultan for hostile behaviour, the war with Poland had led to victory over the Poles and Moldavians at Iasi in September 1620 but then to a failed siege of the fortress of Chotin in 1621, which led to a rebellion in the army. The contrast between the outcome of the battles of the White Mountain and Iasi was instructive. As also for Ferdinand II, the recovery of authority by Murad IV (r. 1623–40) was difficult, with rebellions, notably by the Governor of Erzurum, Abkhaz Mehmed Pasha, limiting Murad's ability to operate successfully against the foreign challenge of Abbas I of Persia who could not be dislodged from his capture of Baghdad, despite attempts in 1626 and 1630, although the city of Kirkuk was regained by the Ottomans in 1624. This long conflict with Persia was important to Habsburg survival in the Thirty Years' War as the 1606 Peace of Zsitvatorok with the Ottomans continued, indeed being renewed, notably in 1629.

After Lutter, and, even more, the end of the Danish war, Ferdinand dominated the (Holy Roman) Empire until the Swedish intervention, but, although he was able to send help to the Spaniards in Italy and the Low Countries, he failed to use this period to win support and exploit his position, preferring the latter to the former, and this preference provided an opportunity for opponents. In September 1629, French mediation rescued Gustavus Adolphus from an indecisive war with Poland, a conflict that had shown that an ability to win battles, in this case by the Swedes, did not necessarily yield outcomes, as the Poles, with their largely cavalry army, were able to refuse battle if they chose. With Denmark defeated, the French wished to use Sweden to weaken the Habsburg position in the Empire. This ploy was important to the anti-Habsburg strategy of Cardinal Richelieu, the leading French minister, who pursued a policy of suppressing Protestant independence at home while seeking the alliance of Protestant powers abroad, a policy that was criticised within France by those who sought a more coherent Catholic policy.

In July 1630, in order to advance Swedish interests including the cause of international Protestantism,[20] Gustavus landed at Peenemünde on Germany's Baltic coast. One of his major concerns was to prevent the Habsburgs establishing their power on the southern shores of the Baltic, a prospect which was seen as a threat not only to Sweden but also to the Dutch ability to derive key supplies of food and naval stores from the Baltic, and thus to continue to resist Spain. Having overrun the regions of Pomerania and Mecklenburg, Gustavus advanced south into Brandenburg in April 1631 and then followed Tilly into Saxony, crushing his force at Breitenfeld on 17 September, a victory that established Gustavus as the leading general of the war.

The Imperialists were outnumbered at Breitenfeld, and also outgunned by the mobile and numerous Swedish artillery. The allied Saxon infantry on the Swedish left quickly broke when attacked by the Imperialists, but the flexible and well-disciplined Swedish infantry formations in the centre of Gustavus's line were able to halt Tilly's attack with musketry and artillery fire. The Swedish cavalry on the flank overcame their Imperialist opponents and drove them from the field before turning on the Imperialist centre. Tilly's infantry, exposed to artillery, infantry and cavalry, took a heavy battering before retreating. Imperialist casualties were 7600 killed compared to 1500 Swedes and 3000 Saxons. The killing of experienced troops was a clear means and measure of success, as such troops were difficult to replace, but victory owed much to the ability to win the battlefield. As a result, all of Tilly's artillery was lost, while over 7000 Imperialists were taken prisoner. Tilly retreated west over the River Weser, leaving Bohemia and the Main Valley to the south exposed to Saxon and Swedish advances respectively.

Victory had political consequences, with many German Protestant princes rallying to Gustavus as he advanced into central Germany, taking the cities of Würzburg and Frankfurt, while his Saxon allies captured Prague. A general of great ability and flexibility in command of an experienced and well-honed war machine, Gustavus had won far greater success than his rival Christian IV of Denmark. In 1632, Gustavus planned to overrun Bavaria and then conquer Austria, which would truly have been a knock-out blow. Tilly was killed at the river Lech in an unsuccessful attempt to prevent the invasion of Bavaria, the Swedes crossing under powerful artillery cover. Munich, the Bavarian capital, fell on 17 May. However, Ferdinand II then reappointed Wallenstein as overall commander, and his threat to Gustavus's lines of communications and to Saxony led the Swedes to return northwards. The campaign, indeed, demonstrated the difficulty of maintaining a consistent pattern of victory, as the Swedes were unable to drive Wallenstein's forces from a heavily fortified position at the Alte Veste, where Gustavus could not make effective use of his cavalry or artillery. With the impetus of success gone, and the accompanying logistical benefit of the advance lost, the Swedish army suffered seriously from desertion, which owed much to the supply problems posed by the devastated countryside.

Convinced that the campaign was over, Wallenstein began to disperse his troops, only for Gustavus to attack at Lützen on 16 November 1632. In a fog-shrouded and bitterly fought battle in which each side had about 19,000 men, Wallenstein remained on the defensive, deepening a ditch to the front of his position. Such ditches were important features in many battles as they limited or constrained advances by opposing forces. Thus, at the battle of the Paitan River in India in 1616, a ditch in front of the Mughal army broke the cavalry attack by the forces of Malik Ambar of Ahmadnagar. At Lützen, the Swedes eventually won a cavalry battle on their right after the Austrian cavalry commander, Pappenheim, who had initially turned the tide there with the arrival of his men, and who had had seven horses shot from under him, was mortally injured by a cannonball. In the centre, the Swedish infantry, led by Gustavus (who was shot in the arm but pressed on), pushed back the opposing musketeers holding the ditch at the front of Wallenstein's position, but were unable to drive back the main Austrian line. Advancing boldly but too far, Gustavus died in the mêlée, shot three times. Wallenstein stabilised the situation on his left by sending Piccolomini and his cavalry reinforcements there, but, at the close of the battle, the Swedes on their left captured the village of Lützen and the nearby Austrian artillery that had commanded the battlefield from a rise, and Wallenstein retreated under cover of darkness. Both sides lost about one-third of their strength and Wallenstein retreated to Bohemia, leaving the Swedes in control of Saxony, a key battleground not least because of its political weight as the leading Protestant Electorate in the Holy Roman Empire.

More successful in battle than Tilly, Wallenstein, however, proved a politically problematic force whose increasing determination to devise, rather than implement, policy led to his being killed by some of his own officers on 25 February 1634 on the orders of Ferdinand II. As a result, Wallenstein was not to become a Hideyōshi-type figure, although, even during the most serious moments of the Thirty Years' War, Austrian power and German support for the Imperial ideal did not collapse sufficiently for such a parallel to be plausible. The challenge posed by armies was indicated in the Ottoman empire by the *janissary* revolt that led to the murder of Sultan Osman in 1622 and that of the *janissaries* and cavalrymen in 1632 that Murad IV only assuaged by executing, as demanded, his principal advisers.

On 6 September 1634, the serious defeat at Nördlingen of the main Swedish army in Germany by an Austro-Spanish force indicated that the capability gap between the two sides was far from insurmountable and that Habsburg co-operation was still a potent force. That the Swedish army was so far south in Germany revealed the extent to which, in what was a true crisis of German power in the sense of the integrity of the Holy Roman Empire, the Baltic powers could not be kept to the periphery. Yet, Nördlingen was followed by the retreat of Swedish power and, in 1635, by an apparent consolidation of the Imperial position in Germany as a result of the Peace of Prague.

The Thirty Years' War and the Military Revolution

The battles of the Thirty Years' War permit a re-examination of some of the claims made on behalf of Michael Roberts's argument that the Swedish army was the key force of the Military Revolution.[21] While tactical deployment was certainly important to success in the battles of the Thirty Years' War, experienced troops were more useful not least if employed by commanders able to direct the flow of the battle by seizing and using the initiative and responding to the moves of opponents in a fashion that denied them control of the tempo. Moreover, it is necessary to be sceptical about the automatic superiority of novel formations. The more innovative linear formations, only five or six ranks deep, notably were far more vulnerable to flank and rear attack than the long-established blocs of troops, for example those formed by the Spanish *tercios*. Duke Bernard of Saxe-Weimar, a young German prince who served Sweden in 1630–5, before transferring with the army he had raised to French service, won a number of battles, such as Rheinfelden on 2 March 1638, by manoeuvre, battles described in pamphlets as far away as neutral England. Significantly, Bernard did not adopt Dutch-style tactics or formations.[22]

Indeed, the Dutch focused not on battle with Spanish forces in the Low Countries, but on sieges such as those of 's-Hertogenbosch in 1629, Maastricht and Venlo in 1632, Breda in 1637 and Hulst in 1645, all of which were successful. It was scarcely surprising that these years also saw the development of a distinctive Dutch style of fortification which owed much to Simon Stevin and the Prussian-born Christian Otter (1598–1660) whose *Specimen problematum hercotectonico-geometricorum quo ut fortificationis modi universalis ita sectionis rationalis linearum vestigium exhibetur* was published in Amsterdam in 1646. The work of Adam Freitag was also influential, with his *Architectura militaries nova et aucta*, published in Amsterdam in 1631 and having its third and final reprint in 1665. Freitag's work also had an impact in Paris where editions of a French translation appeared in 1635, 1640 and 1668. *La Nouvelle fortification de Nicolas Goldman*, published in Leiden in 1645, served as a reminder of the international character of publications: the Leiden mathematician had been born in Breslau (now Wroclaw), and the book was published in French by the major Dutch publisher Elzevir.

The sieges in the Low Countries were also followed with great attention by foreign audiences, and thus, although lacking the drama of Gustavus Adolphus's campaigns, played an important role in maintaining an impression of campaigning in which sieges were highly significant. Hermannus Hugo, the chaplain to Ambrogio Spinola, the commander of the Spanish Army of Flanders, was present at the latter's successful siege of Breda in 1625, and published an account of it in 1626. This account appeared in Latin, with a second edition in 1629, and was translated into English (twice), French, Italian and Spanish. The standard emphasis on Dutch thought and Dutch and Swedish practice can lead to an underplaying of the degree elsewhere of military thought and receptiveness to opportunities. For example, one of the more influential works on artillery was the *Tratado Dela Artilleria y uso della platicado ... en las guerras de Flandes* (Brussels, 1613), by Diego Ufano, a Spanish captain who had served in the Low Countries and northern France.

This treatise was rapidly translated into French and German and was used by other writers, such as Robert Norton in *The Gunner* (London, 1635) and William Eldred in *The Gunners Glasse* (London, 1646). Spanish interest in artillery was also shown in two works by Julio Firrufino, *Platica manual y breve compendio de artilleria* (Madrid, 1626) and *El perfeto artillero theorica y pratica* (Madrid, 1648). Spanish work on fortifications included *Arquitectura Militar Mallorca* (1664) by Vincente Mut, who was a military engineer on the island of Majorca, and the *Epitome de la Fortificaciion Moderna* (Brussels, 1669) by Alonzo Zepeda y Adradas, who was governor of a fortress in the Spanish Netherlands. Continued Italian interest in fortifications was shown with the expanded second edition in 1609 of Buonaiuto Lorini's *Le Fortificationi*, Pietro Ruggiero's *La Militare Aichittura overo Moderna Fortificatione* (Milan, 1661), and with Francesco Eschinardi's *Architettura Militare, Ridotto e Metodo Facile* (Rome, 1684).

Whatever the formations employed – and the square was not much used in Russia – the general deployment on the European battlefield was linear, with infantry in the centre and cavalry on the flanks. Because, in the absence of the tactics of horse archers, such as feint retreats, Western cavalry was effective largely on the attack, there was a major premium to launching an attack at the most opportune moment, with cavalry victory on the wings helping support the infantry assault in the centre; and the detailed topography of the battlefield provided local opportunities of height, slope and surface drainage. The advantage of launching an attack at the most opportune moment, like that of seizing and using the initiative, were aspects of the value of surprise which was so important to success both tactically and operationally.

Manoeuvre was also important to success, as at the battle of Jankov on 6 March 1645, the major clash in the campaign of 1645 when the Swedes under Lennart Torstensson invaded Bohemia. Supported by Hessian forces, they were initially unable in the battle to defeat roughly equal Austrian forces, but succeeded by outmanoeuvring and attacking them from the rear. The Austrian army under Melchior von Hatzfeld was destroyed, and the Swedes thus benefited from the tactical flexibility of their more experienced force. Emperor Ferdinand III fled Prague for more distant Graz the day after the battle. However, although Torstensson advanced to the Danube at Krems, he lacked sufficient strength to move on to Vienna.

The course of the Thirty Years' War indicated the problems of judging capability in terms of tactical innovations. In practice, victory tended to go to larger and more experienced armies, like the Spaniards, Swedes, and some of the Austrian and Bavarian units, rather than simply to those which adopted new Dutch-style tactics. At the White Mountain, there were

28,000 men in the army of the Catholic League against 21,000 Bohemians and German Protestants; at Breitenfeld, Gustavus Adolphus outnumbered this opponents by 42,000 to 35,000; at Nördlingen, there were 33,000 Catholics to 25,000 Protestants; and at Rocroi, 24,000 French to 17,000 Spaniards. In contrast, at Lützen the armies were evenly balanced and, partly for that reason, the engagement was essentially inconclusive. At Breitenfeld, it was not tactical formations that were crucial but numerical superiority, the resilience of the Swedes despite the collapse of the Saxons, and the defensive position from which Gustavus's superior artillery could attack Tilly's army. The weakness of Dutch tactics was also seen in Brazil in the 1630s as the Neapolitan troops in Spanish/Portuguese service proved better able than their Dutch opponents to adapt to the possibilities of the terrain, adopting far more open formations as well as using frequent ambushes.[23]

Around the world, numbers of troops was an important factor, but also posed serious issues of use. They could be unwieldy on the battlefield, there were problems in ensuring sufficient numbers of troops, let alone experienced troops, and logistical difficulties gravely affected their operational capability by encouraging campaigning focused on a search for supplies. This campaigning pressed in Germany during the Thirty Years' War, on an exhausted economy and a ravaged society, hit by a climate downturn that affected crop yields, as well as by the length, severity and disruptive consequences of the war.[24] Thus, it was difficult to support the numbers of troops that might be judged appropriate, while a combination of heavy earlier losses and, especially from the 1620s, the population downturn of the century (or, at best, demographic stagnation) made it hard to recruit sufficient soldiers. This was a European-wide problem and one that could not be addressed by recruiting soldiers from outside Europe. Indeed, it is an interesting insight into cultural norms and preferences, and their significance, that (Christian) European societies shipped slaves to plantation economies in the Americas but were unwilling to raise slave forces comparable to those seen in the Islamic world.

The result of the problems posed by recruiting and sustaining troop numbers was a marked tendency in the latter stages of the Thirty Years' War to resort to smaller forces. The war, moreover, contributed greatly to the population crisis because armies spread diseases, as when Austrian forces were moved into northern Italy during the War of the Mantuan Succession between 1628 and 1631. Recruiting sufficient troops was generally less serious an issue in Asia, but logistical problems were also a problem for the large Mughal armies that operated in the Deccan in the 1620s and 1630s. Thus, in 1624, when the logistical system collapsed, the soldiers, denied pay and food, joined Diwan Malik Ambar, the Ahmadnagar warlord against whom they were campaigning, because he promised them both.

For Western Europe, the numbers at Breitenfeld were exceptional as field armies during the Thirty Years' War rarely had more than 30,000 men. Alongside the shift, subsequently, to smaller numbers in the second half of the Thirty Years' War, there was a change to a greater reliance on cavalry. Cavalrymen cost more to hire and pay than infantry, while the logistical burden of feeding the horses was heavy and also posed operational problems regarding the availability of fodder. Yet, far from this shift to smaller armies and cavalry leading to limited outcomes, it helped provide important opportunities for campaigning, which poses an important qualification to the usual assumption that larger armies offered greater success. The latter stages of the war saw wide-ranging campaigns in which control over much of Germany, especially Saxony, was bitterly contested. The Swedes played a key role, with Johan Baner, for example, advancing to the Danube in 1640, Torstensson into Moravia, capturing Olomouc, in 1642, and to the Danube in 1645, and Karl Gustav von Wrangel invading Bavaria in 1646 and Bohemia in 1647. Despite her commitment against Spain, France also sent a number of armies under Turenne and Condé across the Rhine, notably in the period 1644–8. Although these expeditions were not always successful, Turenne being defeated at Mergentheim in 1645, they contributed to the heavy military pressure on the Austrians.

It is possible to emphasise failures. Swedish sieges of Brno (1645) and Prague (1648) were unsuccessful, and advances into Bohemia and Moravia, for example by Torstensson in 1645 and by Wrangel in 1647, did not knock the Austrian Habsburgs out of the war. More generally, the uncertain outcomes of the campaigns reflected in large part serious difficulties in the supply of men, money and provisions. There were also the operational problems posed by the strength of fortifications, as well as the strategic issues arising from the size of the disputed areas, and the security of the key political centres of Vienna, Paris, The Hague, Stockholm and Madrid. Yet, it is a mistake to assume that military capability should only be judged by a decisiveness measured by the total surrender of one of the parties, an approach to war based in part on the end of the Second World War in 1945. Instead, war can deliver results by showing the parties that they have to negotiate and by indicating the likely bases for a successful negotiation, as in France in 1622. Following an earlier royal victory in the field in April, the failure of the Huguenots in October to relieve their besieged stronghold at Montpellier in the face of the king's army induced them to sign the Peace of Montpellier, which provided for the destruction of most Huguenot fortifications.[25]

The Thirty Years' War produced such verdicts on a number of occasions, notably with the Peace of Prague of 1635, which left Ferdinand II dominant in Germany and, crucially, allied to (Protestant) Saxony so that few Protestant principalities remained leagued with Sweden, only to have the situation affected by the intervention of another outside power, most prominently Sweden in 1630 and France in 1635. Indeed, Richelieu's decision to act directly from 1635, rather than through surrogates, in part reflected the sense that, otherwise, an Austrian-dominated Empire would provide support to Spain and its ally, Charles IV, Duke of Lorraine, thus weakening France's position in its crucial eastern borderlands, the vulnerability of which were fully displayed when eastern and north-eastern France was invaded in 1636. In the latter stages of the war, peace negotiations continued during the conflict, often in tandem with operations and being affected by them or by reports and rumours about them. This situation put a premium on Intelligence.[26]

The war ended in 1648, with treaties signed at Münster and Osnabrück that are collectively known as the Peace of Westphalia. This peace is seen as a marker in the development of international relations, notably the beginning of the modern state system, and this assumption affects the discussion of military history. Spain in effect acknowledged Dutch independence, bringing the Dutch Revolt that had begun in 1566 to an end, while Austrian Habsburg control over their dominions, notably Bohemia, was accepted, ending the ability of these dominions to pursue autonomous courses, with the exception of Hungary.[27] The view of Westphalia as a key departure in the establishment of the modern state system also owes much to the acceptance in the treaty that German princes were free to pursue their own foreign policy. This acceptance marked an effective end to the pretensions of Christian unity provided since the ninth century by the Holy Roman Empire. Indeed, the decline of the Imperial ideal has been seen as a transition from medievalism to modernity.

This analysis, however, places too much weight on the changes brought by Westphalia. As frequently also in the case of military history, which similarly often shows a Whiggish teleological progression (see p. 1), the stress on Westphalia is an instance of the pronounced historical preference for crucial turning points (usually the subject of the author's research) and the repeated belief that major developments must be marked by a crucial occasion of transition. In practice, the impact of the changes in Germany was limited, while their wider consequences are unclear. Effective autonomy had long existed for the princes within the Empire, and they had negotiated accordingly, while the process of Imperial disunity and the effective sovereignty of individual princes had been greatly advanced as a result of the Protestant Reformation. Thus, the changes brought by Westphalia represented the adaptation of a weak federal system, in which what in effect was inter-state diplomacy had already occurred, rather than a turning point. The latter idea bears little reference to the more circumspect shift in the relationships between Emperor, Empire and Princes actually seen in and after the Peace.[28] Analogy is always a difficult, not to say risky, process, and it is all too often that simple parallels are sought, parallels that somehow support the thesis of the author. Yet, a revisionist approach to Westphalia can certainly sit alongside one towards the Military Revolution.

It is also instructive to consider long-term parallels in military history. The extent to which, in the Thirty Years' War, experienced and well-deployed infantry were usually safe against frontal attack threatened a tactical impasse in infantry conflict, one that prefigured the trench warfare of the First World War (1914–18), rather than suggesting a revolutionary turning point. In the case of the Thirty Years' War, this impasse led to a particular need for skills in generalship and for flexible and effective cavalry.

The close of the Thirty Years' War did not mean the end of conflict in Western Europe, notably because wars to which it had given rise continued, especially that between France and Spain declared in 1635 and the Portuguese and Catalan wars of independence that began in 1640. The Franco-Spanish conflict ended in 1659 and the Portuguese war in 1668, while Catalan resistance was suppressed in 1652. These conflicts registered both the continued importance of Spain as a military power and yet also a decline in skill and quality that are associated in particular with the mishandling of Spanish imperial governance, specifically its Portuguese and Catalan politics,[29] and also with the military flaws for which the defeat of the Army of Flanders by a French force under Louis, Prince of Condé at Rocroi on 19 May 1643 provides both summary and symbol.

These failures contribute to an understanding of military history in progressive terms, with the baton of quality passing from Spain to the forces of the classic Military Revolution, the Dutch and Sweden, and then to France. There were, indeed, serious flaws with the Spanish system and it is easy to see why a sense of decline existed and exists, notably in contrast to the effectiveness of the Army of Flanders in the 1560s under the Duke of Alba. He was a general who also swiftly overran Portugal in 1580, in marked contrast with the frequent Spanish failures there between 1640 and 1668. Particular attention has focused on the failure to ensure quality among Spanish officers and commanders, a failure traced to a preference for patronage over competence, the patronage being designed to further the incorporation of the aristocracy into the state.[30]

Yet, the problem of patronage was apparent already in the 1580s, years, in fact, of great success for the Army of Flanders. Moreover, command and officership in the French army were also characterised by patronage, and this certainly played the key role in command at Rocroi. In addition, rather than seeing Rocroi as an indicator of the end of Spanish military prowess, the resilience of the Spanish army thereafter is notable,[31] and this resilience was demonstrated before the *Frondes* brought serious problems of instability for France from 1648.[32] There is also the issue posed by the readiness of scholars to cite comments by the *arbistras* and others, contemporary Spanish commentators who offered critical remarks about their own country, state and governance, comments that generally lacked comparative insight. Such comments indicate an awareness of serious problems, but all states had such problems in this period. In conclusion, the Spanish army remained more effective than talk of decline might suggest.

Eastern Europe and the value of cavalry

As a further reminder of the possibility of a variety of narratives and the need not to assume an automatic typicality for the Thirty Years' War, the value of cavalry was demonstrated more clearly in Eastern Europe where, as in the First World War, the force–space ratio was less dense than in Western Europe. Polish victories over the Swedes at Kircholm (1605), and over a far larger Swedish and Russian army at Klushino (1610), suggest the limits of effectiveness of musket and pike against cavalry, in this case hussar lancers.[33] Knowledge of Eastern European developments will hopefully reflect the greater political prominence of the region since the 1980s. Generally seen as a completed political development, the fall of the Iron Curtain is in fact an incomplete cultural project, as the longstanding tendency to regard Eastern Europe as primitive[34] remains all too potent. The impact of the problems that other scholars often face with Eastern European languages may well be lessened as research flourishes in Eastern Europe and is presented to the outside world in English. Research on developments in Eastern Europe needs to abandon conceptions framed on a Western European teleology, not least by addressing the extent of 'sub-state' violence. The imperial character of states in Eastern Europe was matched by an often only limited control over frontier regions, such as Transylvania and Ukraine, and it is necessary, first, to devote appropriate attention to their military history and its particular characteristics,[35] and, secondly, to integrate the resulting conclusions into studies at the continent level.

The role of cavalry was prominent not only in Eastern Europe, the latter stages of the Thirty Years' War and the English Civil War, but also in the war between Portugal and Spain from 1640 to 1668, as the forme successfully struggled to assert and defend its independence. The nature o the campaigning zone in this conflict encouraged a resort to cavalry, no least because of the difficulty of mounting operations with large infantr forces in what, due in part to the climate, were short campaigning seasons in which such forces moved slowly. The use of cavalry was also favoure by a tactical emphasis on irregular warfare with, in particular, the ambus of crucial supply convoys. Raids, moreover, led to scorched-earth tactic in order to make defensive positions untenable, as well as providing display of power which was particularly important in seeking to maintai support and sow fear.[36]

The British civil wars

Alongside an emphasis on the dynamic relationships between militar environments, force structures and tactics, the purposes of military activit acted as a key variable. This was particularly seen in civil warfare. Th desired and/or eventual outcome might be a compromise arising fron the war, with conflict thus serving as a negotiation of power, which wa the case with the *Frondes* in France. However, civil warfare could also pos issues that were not subject to such a compromise, and this could lea to a drive for total victory. The British civil wars of 1638–52 provided key instance of this process. They began with a rising in Scotland in 163 that reflected opposition to Charles I's commitment to religious change His uncompromising response led to the Bishops' Wars of 1639–40, bu Charles lacked the means to sustain the struggle. He made a poor choice commanders, while inadequate finance wrecked the logistics necessary fo operations against the Scots.[37] Poorly prepared and deployed, the Englis army collapsed in 1640 when attacked by the large and professionall officered Scottish army, much of which had gained experience in Dutc and Swedish service.[38]

The Scots, indeed, successfully invaded northern England. That 1640 an 1641 were, across the world, years of extreme weather – a point of particula crisis in a decade of persistent climatic catastrophes – was pertinent, a the results not only encouraged misery but also more specifically hit th crops important to royal and seigneurial revenues and borrowing.[39] As s often, war affected authority by sapping power, just as a crisis of Ottoma authority in 1648 was to stem from serious problems in the war wit Venice. Charles I was weakened in England first by the undermining of hi finances and then by failure. Threatened with bankruptcy as a result of th Scottish invasion, the king was forced to turn to Parliament, a recourse h had avoided since 1629. In turn, Parliament chipped away at royal powers until, in an atmosphere of mounting crisis, the need to raise an army to deal with a major Catholic uprising in Ireland in November 1641 polarised the situation. The question of who was to control this army proved highly divisive in a situation where paranoia fed differences. As the century was repeatedly to show, the control of armies was indeed a key issue in domestic politics, because rulers, for example William II of Orange against Amsterdam in 1650, Frederick William I of Brandenburg-Prussia, 'the Great Elector' (r. 1640–88), and Louis XIV of France, sought to use forces under their control to overawe domestic opposition.

Charles responded to the crisis by trying, in a display of force, to seize hostile Parliamentarians on 4 January 1642, but he mishandled the attempt and opposition increased. The Common Council of the City of London elected a Committee of Safety to defend London and, on 5 January, rumours of a Royalist attack led to the mobilisation of the Trained Bands (in effect the militia), and much of the population, in defence of London. The balance of force proved crucial, as it also did at Paris with the outbreak of the first *Fronde* in 1648. Lacking the strength to overawe London, the centre of opposition, Charles, on 10 January, left the capital to raise support elsewhere in England. This proved a serious mistake, as London-based institutions represented fundamental sources of legitimation.

Fighting in England between Royalists and Parliamentarians started in the summer of 1642, creating a revolutionary situation as the bold claims to authority made on behalf of Parliamentary views led to violence. In the resulting First English Civil War (1642–6), control over London was a key strategic issue, but there was also a series of local struggles across the British Isles as conflict in England interacted with that in Ireland, Scotland and Wales.[40] This pattern was more generally indicative of the nature of conflict in the period, and indeed most others, and it was one that raises important questions for the judgement of best practice, and, notably, for understanding the extent to which this was not solely defined by battle-winning. It has been calculated that 47 per cent of the soldiers who died in conflict in England died in skirmishes in which fewer than 250 fought, while only 15 per cent died in major battles. Military units had a strong sense of locality, many were reluctant to travel far from home, and the role of local garrisons and their search for supplies were crucial to the struggle in the regions.

As with other civil wars, this conflict saw growing demands on the localities from both sides, as the cost of the war rose, while resources available in the early stages were used up. In order to try to achieve central control, reliable and experienced commanders replaced local gentlemen in positions of local power. Localism was eroded, just as neutralism had been ended when people were forced to commit to one side or the other. This led to a violent response in the shape of the Clubmen movement in which, in 1644–5, local people sought to keep troops out, and, in particular, to limit the demands of garrisons, only for the Clubmen to be dispersed by Parliamentary forces.[41]

The fate of local struggles was influenced, and at times determined, by the campaigns of the main field armies, and, ultimately, all the local struggles were ended by the fate of the latter. In the first major battle, Edgehill on 23 October 1642, Charles narrowly defeated the Earl of Essex, the uninspired general who commanded the main Parliamentary army, but Charles failed to follow up by driving decisively on to London, and was checked at Turnham Green to the west of the city on 13 November. He failed to press home an advantage in what were difficult circumstances, and retreated to establish his headquarters at Oxford. His best chance of winning the war had passed. The outbreak of war also encouraged the publication of relevant works on the military art, including John Cruso's *Castrametation, or the measuring out of the quarters for the encamping of an army* (London, 1642).

In 1643, the Royalists overran most of western England, crushing the Parliamentarians at Stratton and Roundway Down, while Bristol, the major port on the west coast, fell to Royalist assault after a brief siege. However, the Royalist sieges of Gloucester and Hull were both unsuccessful, and the principal battle in the vital Thames Valley and surrounding area, the First Battle of Newbury (20 September), was inconclusive: the Royalist cavalry outfought their opponents, but their infantry was less successful. The Royalists had many successes in 1643, but their plan of concentrating their forces on Oxford and then advancing on London[42] failed. More generally, they could not challenge the Parliamentary heartland, a situation that, albeit on a very different scale, matched that both for the combatants in the Thirty Years' War and for the Manchu in their attacks on China prior to the mid-1640s. The 11-mile-long defence system rapidly constructed for London – an earthen bank and ditch with a series of forts and batteries – was never tested in action, but was a testimony to the resources available for the Parliamentary cause. London did not suffer the fate of Beijing at rebel hands in 1644.

The British dimension played the key role in 1644. The Scots entered northern England on the side of Parliament that January. Both were united by opposition to Charles and suspicious of his religious leanings. Scots and Parliamentarians jointly besieged York, the major city in northern England, control over cities yet again serving as the major focus of campaigns. The Royalist attempt to relieve York led, on nearby Marston Moor on 2 July 1644, to one of the two decisive battles of the war, an instance of the frequency with which sieges provoked battles. The application of cavalry power again proved important to the fate of battle: the victory of Parliamentarian/Scots cavalry on their left was followed by their joining the assault on the Royalist infantry in the centre, and the latter succumbed. The nature of conflict in these densely packed formations was grim, with troops crushed, hot, thirsty and standing on, or by, the dead or wounded. The noise and smell (of the black powder used for firearms and of the excrement and urine of the troops) were terrible.

Without hope of relief after the Royalist defeat, York surrendered, and the north of England had been lost to Charles. As with the general tendency elsewhere, experience and discipline were important in the development of what finally became the war-winning Parliamentarian force in England, the New Model Army, which was eventually commanded by Oliver Cromwell, whose wartime background was that of a cavalry commander. This army's equipment and tactics were essentially similar to those of their British opponents. The major difference was that the New Model was better disciplined and supported by a more effective infrastructure and supply system. Promotion was by merit, and Cromwell favoured officers and men imbued with equal religious fervour to his own, although the Royalist military regulations also stressed religious obligations, including the need to take Holy Communion, veneration of the sacraments, and the importance of catechising and decency.[43]

The social practice of war varied between the two sides in England. The Royalists essentially relied on traditional notions of honour, obligation and loyalty to raise troops: Charles I headed the social hierarchy and his armies reflected this. Leadership for the Royalists was, in large part, a function of social position, and prominent landowners, such as Henry, 5th Earl of Worcester, provided much support, although an increasing number of Royalist officers came from outside the social élite. Aristocrats, notably the Earls of Essex and Manchester and Lord Fairfax, played a major role in the Parliamentary leadership in the early stages, but far less subsequently as a result of the Self-Denying Ordinance of 1644, and the contrast between Cromwell, who was from the poor gentry, and the Royalist cavalry commander Prince Rupert was one of different attitudes towards responsibility, position, quality and merit. In this respect, the New Model prefigured the Continental Army of the American War of Independence, the Republican Army of the French Revolution and the Red Army in the Russian Civil War, each serving as the expression of the political thrust of the revolution as well as providing its force.[44] In contrast, other seventeenth-century rebellions were unable to generate a comparable force.

Aside from the role of conviction, the New Model is seen, by the composition of its officer corps, as providing an exception to the process by which, in the seventeenth century, the remilitarisation of the English aristocracy, it has been suggested, obstructed the emergence of a professional officer corps based upon merit. This remilitarisation is linked to a chivalric revival which is presented as focused on anachronistic values, specifically a preference for edged weapons over firearms, an emphasis on honour, and a disinclination to accept 'the technological innovations associated with the military revolution and the pursuit of military and political objectives dictated by the needs of state'.[45] This thesis is an important one, as the New Model serves in this account to support a linked analysis of military progress and social politics. In particular, there is an assumption that the principles of good military leadership were incompatible with aristocratic culture, notably by including a disdain of the quest for honour and glory. Such an account, however, risks anachronism in a number of respects, notably by assuming the presence of an effective bureaucratic state that could readily serve as a model for more desirable alternative practices. In addition, the notion that honour and glory were outdated values clashes with understandings of military prowess that note their significance not least for unit cohesion and morale. Moreover, the emphasis on aristocratic officers was important not just for political reasons but also for recruitment in the localities.

Alongside the stress on the New Model and a meritocratic command culture, it is also necessary to note other factors in Parliament's success. The New Model benefited from a strong infrastructure, in part because Parliament was backed by the wealthiest parts of the country, London, the major ports and the navy, and, although this support did not make the result of the war inevitable, it helped finance and sustain the war effort. For example, when they invaded Ireland in 1649, Cromwell's forces were well supplied, enabling them to operate most of the year round. Well equipped with carts, wagons and draft horses, they retained the initiative.[46]

Alongside fervour and resources, the combat experience of the New Model was also important, as was the role in battle of chance, which was significant, alongside much else, at Naseby on 14 June 1645, the second decisive battle of the war. Due to detaching substantial forces from the field army to operate in other areas, the Royalists were outnumbered by about 14,000 men to 7600, which crucially limited their reserves, but the battle was decided by the superior discipline of the Parliamentary cavalry. Prince Rupert, the Royalist cavalry commander, swept the cavalry on the Parliamentary left from the field, but was unable to prevent his troops from dispersing to attack and loot the Parliamentary baggage train, a frequent problem with cavalry attacks. In contrast, Cromwell, on the right, defeated the Royalist cavalry opposite, and then retained sufficient control to turn on the veteran, but heavily outnumbered, Royalist infantry in the centre. This infantry had advanced and driven back the front line of the New Model's infantry, but the most experienced troops were deployed in the second line, and they held fast, stopping the Royalist infantry. It was this struggle that Cromwell swayed by attacking the flank and rear of the Royalist infantry, which succumbed with about 5000 men taken prisoner. The leading Royalist field army, poorly commanded by Charles I, had been destroyed.

Naseby, like Marston Moor and Cromwell's sweeping victory over a far larger Scottish force at Dunbar in 1650, demonstrated the importance of cavalry for success. This importance underlined the issue of command skills, since some commanders, such as Cromwell, were far better at retaining control over their cavalry than others, most obviously Prince Rupert. Another aspect of command skills was provided by creating and making effective use of a substantial reserve line.[47] The nature of attack victories such as Marston Moor, Naseby and Dunbar, in which shock played the key role, ensures that battles should not be seen primarily in terms of firefights, with the accompanying temptation to view military progress in terms of technological and tactical innovations designed to increase firepower. A general who stressed the attack, Cromwell was a vigorous leader who led from the front, which was a characteristic of much – particularly, but not only, cavalry – generalship in this period, for example that of Gustavus Adolphus, Condé, Turenne and John Sobieski.

Yet, alongside the emphasis on shock cavalry, it would be bizarre to neglect the role of firearms, whether in battle, skirmish and siege, different categories of combat that picked out contrasting emphases in firearms. An instrument of terror as well as a weapon designed to be used with precision in the implementation of calculated tactics, cannon were most important in sieges both for opening breaches and for inviting civilian unrest at the prospect of a damaging defence.[48] In contrast, cannon were least effective in skirmishes, which tended to be fast-developing as well as fast-moving. In battle, cannon could play a role in causing casualties in the dense-packed ranks of opponents, both infantry and cavalry, hitting their morale and precipitating an attack. The latter factor could play to the advantage of receiving an attack, especially on favourable terrain, but, if an army remained on the defence, cannon could pound it heavily. As a result of these advantages, cannon were often deployed on the battlefield in front of the main formation or between the squares. Indirect fire over the heads of formations was uncommon, although mortars were used in sieges.

This battlefield disposition was also used in India, where, for example, at the battle of Samuargarh in 1658, Aurangzeb's cannon were deployed to the front of his army, as were those of his opponent, Dara Shikoh.

In Europe, the cannon used on the battlefield were generally light pieces – three-pounders in the English Civil War – as these could be moved most readily. Heavier pieces, however, were necessary at sieges, indeed a key requirement. Armies that lacked the necessary cannon, shot and gunpowder tended to be unable to capture fortified positions unless they could mount a surprise storming, climbing over the walls, a tactic which was unlikely to succeed if a position was well fortified, supported by an adequate and alert garrison, and under a commander able to respond rapidly to circumstances. At the same time, these cannon were very difficult to move, and they and their supplies required plentiful draught horses and carts. Furthermore, the manufacture and use of all cannon faced many difficulties, not least the difficulty of casting true cylinders, as well as limited knowledge of ballistics, and problems with the availability of sufficient powder and shot. However, there were also significant developments in artillery during the century, not least those leading to the use, in the Thirty Years' and English Civil Wars, of lightweight 'leather guns', which, in fact, were tubes of copper bound with wire and then covered in leather. Moreover, there was a use of demountable brass cannon which looked towards later screw-guns. Thus, a stress on cavalry must not detract from developments in firepower.[49] Furthermore, published information about war increased in this period. The year 1639 saw the publication of Richard Norwood's *Fortification or Architecture Military*, the earliest full-scale work in English on the topic, while Nathaniel Nye, Master Gunner of Worcester during the Civil War, wrote *The Art of Gunnery* (London, 1647).

Conclusion

The contrasts between the fall of the Ming, the end of the Thirty Years' War, and the English Civil War, all of which occurred within six years, indicated the variety of contexts within which conflict occurred, even in only the 1640s. There was a diffusion of experience, technique and weaponry, as in the case of Sir Henry Gage (1597–1645). A Catholic, he was a cavalry captain in the Spanish army that successfully besieged Breda in 1625 and he translated Hermannus Hugo's account of the siege into English. Gage later fought for Charles I in the English Civil War, being mortally wounded in 1645. Yet, the combatants in the English Civil War had different goals to those of the major participants in the Thirty Years' War, and such a variety of contexts should take precedence in analysis and helps explain why general attempts to provide accounts of relative capability are problematic. This uncertainty was also felt by contemporaries and indeed helped explain why it was worth engaging in war. The results of conflict were scarcely seen as predictable, and this situation appeared amply justified by the varied flow of campaigning, notably with the Ming–Manchu conflict and the Thirty Years' War.

Aside from uncertainties in the field, there were the marked variations in international and domestic politics. The former could lead to the deployment or loss of allied forces, so that, for example, France's entry into war with the Habsburgs in 1635 significantly reduced the pressure on Sweden. Moreover, domestic politics was important, as opposition, indeed rebellions, greatly qualified the ability to raise resources for warfare, and also forced the diversion of troops. Austria, in the 1620s, and France, in the 1630s, had to overcome serious peasant uprisings, while many states, including Spain, France, China and the Ottoman empire, faced grave domestic political crises in the 1640s. In addition to these uncertainties, there was scant sign at the time that the course of military progress and, thus, such a basis for a judgement of capability and proficiency, were widely agreed.

5 Conflict, 1650–1683

China

A key theme in this period was that of the consolidation of authority. In part, this consolidation can be seen as the sequel to the series of problems and number of crises grouped together as the mid-seventeenth century crisis, but there was also a longer-term process of seeking to establish control over states. This was particularly true of the Manchu in China but was also the case, for example, in Abyssinia (Ethiopia) and the lands of the Austrian Habsburgs. In contrast, in India and much of Europe the political and military situation was more clearly a response to the immediate crises of mid-century.

In terms of scale, the most important campaigns were those in China. The rapid conquest of northern and central China by the Manchu and their Chinese allies was followed by the conquest of much of the south by 1652, the city of Guangzhou (Canton) and the province of Guangxi being conquered in 1650, as the Ming cause succumbed to the military strength and political opportunities presented by its opponents. However, strong resistance was subsequently encountered in the south,[1] notably as the Manchu were challenged by the Japanese-born Zheng Chenggong, known to Europeans as Coxinga, who, with the profits of piracy and trade, developed a large fleet based in the south-east province of Fujian and amassed a substantial army of over 50,000 troops. In 1656–8, he regained some of the coastline of southern China for the Ming, reflecting the precarious nature of the Manchu system at this point. The weaponry of Zheng's forces reflected the general Chinese tendency to field a variety of arms, rather than the greater uniformity seen in the West. Some of his troops were equipped with European-style weapons, although, like other Chinese armies, they did not use flintlocks. However, the large force Zheng led to the siege of Nanjing in 1659 was mostly armed with swords: two-handed, long, heavy swords, or short swords carried with shields. The soldiers wore mail coats to provide protection against bullets. Alongside cannon and musketeers, Zheng's army included an archery corps that was more effective than his musketeers.[2]

This army, however, was defeated outside Nanjing by Manchu cavalry and infantry attacks. The Manchu then advanced into Fujian, while they also conquered south-west China, overrunning the province of Guizhou in 1658 and Yunnan in 1659. The last Ming pretender was killed in Burma by Wu Sangui in 1662. These impressive operations are worthy of attention for they were on a far greater scale than the New Model's consolidation on the British scale of its earlier successes in England, and also brought a closure to the war on the Chinese mainland that contrasted with the inability to do the same in the (admittedly) far more complex environment of the Thirty Years' War. Chinese unity over recent centuries was important as it encouraged a sense that provinces could not retain their independence from the consolidation of Manchu control elsewhere.

Deprived of his mainland bases, Zheng turned his attention to Taiwan, which had not previously been Chinese and which was partly under Dutch control from the bases of Fort Zeelandia and Keelung. Zheng invaded in 1661, with a force of 25,000 men and 300 junks, and, after a nine-month siege, in which he employed 28 European-style cannon, he took the Dutch base of Fort Zeelandia. Attempts were made from distant Batavia in June to relieve the outnumbered garrison, but they failed, and Fort Zeelandia surrendered in February 1662 after the walls of its Utrecht redoubt collapsed under heavy fire. The fate of this position indicates the need to be cautious in ascribing too great a battle-winning character to the artillery fortress.[3] Such fortifications provided a very valuable force multiplier, but so did effective siegecraft. Keelung also fell in 1662. Dutch attempts to re-establish their position in 1662, 1663 and 1664 were all unsuccessful and contrasted greatly with the situation two centuries later when, by the Treaty of Nanjing of 1842, the British were able to force the Chinese to accept their capture of Hong Kong. European powers never again established a presence on Taiwan; when it fell, it was to the Japanese as a result of the Sino-Japanese War of 1894–5. In 1662, Zheng was succeeded by his eldest son, Zheng Jing, who consolidated his father's position. After his death, however, the family was divided and, in 1681, their forces were badly defeated by a newly constructed Manchu navy. Taiwan itself surrendered in 1683 after the Manchu fleet defeated the nearby Pescadores' pirates.

This conquest was the last stage in the suppression of the Rebellion of the Three Feudatories, a rebellion begun in December 1673 by powerful generals who were the governors of the southern and western provinces, especially Wu Sangui, who, as Governor of Yunnan and Guizhou, controlled most of south-western China. He had been rewarded by the Manchu with considerable power and autonomy for his role in the conquest of southern China, and his eventually treasonable response reflected both the difficulty of managing patronage politics when the legitimacy of the regime was poorly grounded and, more immediately, the determination of the Kangxi Emperor to end the power of the Feudatories, specifically their military strength. Wu's rebellion was followed in 1674 by that of Geng Jingzhong, and in 1676 by Shang Kexi. The Rebellion of the Three Feudatories was particularly serious because it arose from within the structure of the Chinese state as altered by Manchu conquest, whereas eighteenth-century rebellions were not from within the political structure. In a conflict that spanned more territory than that contested in the contemporaneous Dutch War in Europe, the Feudatories overran most of southern China and came close to overthrowing the Manchu, leading the Emperor to campaign in person. However, as a result of their earlier policies, Wu and his allies could not readily win Ming support and were unable to translate their success in south China into the conquest of the north. Key figures refused to join the rebellion, notably Fan Chengmo, Governor of Fujian, and Zhang Yong, Wu's godson, the Governor of Gansu. The Feudatories were driven back to the south-west by 1677 thanks to the use of Green Standard troops: loyal Chinese forces.

Earlier, Manchu units had failed to defeat the rebels, and this failure helped in the consolidation of a new political system in which Manchu tribesmen could no longer[4] challenge the adoption of Chinese administrative techniques, personnel and priorities. Indeed, the army increasingly saw the effective integration of Manchu, Mongol and Chinese units, which permitted the successful co-ordination of cavalry with infantry. Wu died in 1678, but order was not restored in his former provinces until 1681, after a full-scale campaign that year that included the siege of Yunnanfu,[5] while Taiwan, which had supported the rebellion, was not conquered until 1683.[6] After the 1680s, there was no major internal disorder in China, and revenues rose, reflecting both stability and an improvement in the climate. This situation permitted the determined and effective Kangxi Emperor (r. 1662–1723) to turn against the Dzunghars, the latest (and last) of the major steppe challenges to China. Thus, internal stability was significant to external power projection, not only in ensuring sufficient resources, but also in enabling the dispatch of troops.

Mughal India

The crisis in Mughal India had a different genesis. Fratricidal conflict in the Mughal ruling dynasty in the 1620s had led to the reign of Shah Jahan (1624–58), and his final illness, in turn, resulted in a war over the succession between his four sons. Their armies were similar, the crucial elements being cavalry and artillery, and victory was the reward for superior tactics or superior fighting qualities, especially better-disciplined cavalry. The early-morning surprise attack that led to the defeat of the Bengali forces of Muhammad Shuja near Benares in February 1658 demonstrated the former, while Aurangzeb's victories at Dharmat (February) and Samuagarh (29 May) displayed the latter. At Samuagarh, the crucial battle of the war over the Mughal succession, Aurangzeb's generalship and his well-disciplined cavalry and cannon defeated the repeated attacks of Rajput cavalry launched by his elder brother, the designated heir, Dara Shikoh. As a reminder, however, of the complexity of accounting for results, that of Samuagarh has also been explained in terms of the betrayal of Dara by Khalilullah Khan, one of his nobles.

The cannon of each brother was manned by Europeans, that of Aurangzeb, which was regarded as better, being manned by French gunners. This was an important aspect of the diffusion of technique but also of the extent to which armies (and navies) were composite forces drawing on different military skills and traditions. Therefore, to see the need to use Western gunners as a sign of weakness is unhelpful as it underplays the extent to which military labour markets were designed to foster and profit from comparative advantage in particular skills, but as part of creating a powerful combined force. This situation can only be regarded as flawed and anachronistic if a teleological approach towards military development is adopted, but imperial systems were a norm in this period across much of the world, and such systems inherently relied on composite forces.

As a consequence of victory at Samuagarh, Aurangzeb gained possession of Shahjahanabad (Delhi), where he crowned himself Alamgir or 'world-seizer'. After his coronation, he routed, in the battle of Khajwa (5 January 1659), the heavily outnumbered and outgunned forces of his second brother, Muhammad Shuja, the Subadar of Bengal, who used Portuguese refugees from Sri Lanka (by then Dutch-run on the coast) for manning his cannon. The use of artillery was important at Khajwa, but so also was betrayal, with both Mukarram Khan and Abdur Rahman betraying Shuja and not only transferring their contingents to Aurangzeb but also providing information on his dispositions.

Aurangzeb then defeated Dara again, in a bitter three-day battle at Deora near Ajmer in March 1659. Dara fled, but was betrayed by Malik Jiwan, an Afghan chief with whom he had taken refuge. In August 1659, Aurangzeb had Dara killed and heavily defeated Shuja at Tanda after a fierce campaign involving flotillas on the river Ganges; Suja was killed when he sought refuge with the King of Arakan. The third brother, Murad, who had joined with Aurangzeb to defeat their father's forces at Dharmat, was imprisoned in June 1658, and executed in 1661.

This warfare is ignored in most accounts of seventeenth-century conflict, but it is unclear why it should be regarded as without significance. Instead, the high-tempo warfare in India in the late 1650s showed the importance of competition within the royal family for control of both territory and forces, and also underlined the extent to which success in battle was important to the position of rulers and would-be rulers. Moreover, it is clear that symmetrical warfare in India between similar forces nevertheless entailed important differences in quality, notably in the cavalry. These campaigns coincided with the last stages of the Manchu conquest of southern China and of the Franco-Spanish War of 1635–59, and indicated, yet again, the varied nature of warfare. At the same time, in each case, there was a shared role for determination, specifically an ability to persist in making an effort, as well as a success in exploiting weaknesses and creating alliances, however short term, for example, in the late 1650s, that between republican Protestant England and Catholic monarchical France against Catholic monarchical Spain.

The year 1659 marked a turning point in seventeenth-century Indian warfare as Aurangzeb, who ruled until 1707, was thereafter able to focus on external threats. As such, it parallels the end of the Rebellion of the Three Feudatories in China in 1681, and of the *Frondes* for the French government in 1652, although there was a continuum, rather than a sharp divide, between external and internal (foreign and domestic) challenges in the case of India, as there had also been in France in the 1640s. From 1670, Aurangzeb came to focus on challenges and opportunities to the south, notably the Marathas and the sultanates of the Deccan, but, until then, Aurangzeb's activities reflected the wide-ranging commitments of Mughal power. At the same time, despite their military strength and determination, the Mughals were unable to prevail in adverse circumstances in frontier zones. In particular, there was no resumption of the conflict with Persia over Kandahar, which serves as a reminder of the extent to which the campaigns and battles that did *not* occur were part of military history. Mughal attempts to regain the city in 1649, 1652 and 1653 had all failed. As with the attempts to operate north of the Hindu Kush in 1646–7 (see pp. 56–7), it was difficult to campaign effectively so far from the centres of Mughal power, and success had to be achieved before the harsh winter set in. Mughal siege artillery was also of poorer quality and less accurate than the Persian cannon, which inflicted heavy casualties on the besiegers. In 1653, three specially-cast Mughal heavy guns made breaches in the walls, but the onset of winter and logistical problems made it impossible to exploit them.

Moreover, any Mughal interest in expansion into Central Asia diminished with a series of Pathan tribal revolts in what is now the Pakistani–Afghan borderlands. The revolt of the Yusufzai in 1667 was suppressed, but the Afridi, who rebelled in 1672, successfully ambushed Mughal armies in 1672, 1673 and 1674. This tactical and operational challenge to Mughal power was matched by a strategic one, as Mughal forces were diverted from their campaigns in the Deccan. Aurangzeb was able to restore order only by lavish payments and the construction of new fortresses. The situation prefigured later and more recent problems for state control in the North-West Frontier Province of British India and, subsequently, Pakistan. Politics and force in combination served at best to offer partial stabilisation.

In contrast, Aurangzeb, like Louis XIV, had a number of successes in limited external conflicts at the start of his reign. Thus, he annexed the forested chiefdom of Palamu (1661), sent an army that pushed back the Ahom from 1661 and forced them to sue for peace in 1663, and seized Sandwip Island and the port of Chittagong on the Bay of Bengal in an amphibious operation in 1665–6, a deployment supported by the making of an all-weather road from Shangramgarh to Dacca, a measure which was significant for the integration of territories under imperial sway. Similarly, Louis XIV supported road-building in France, in part in order to be able to speed his troops and also supplies to his system of magazines.

None of Aurangzeb's campaigns in the early 1660s involved operations on the scale of the problems posed by the Deccan. In the western Deccan, around Poona, Shivaji Bhonsla (1627–80), leader of the Marathas, a Hindu warrior caste, was creating a powerful state; by the 1660s he commanded 60,000 troops, substantial revenues and important fortresses, and he raided to Ahmadnagar in 1657. In 1665, a major advance by Aurangzeb's forces under the Hindu Rajput Raja, Jai Singh I, forced Shivaji to accept an agreement which conceded most of the fortresses. This advance was typical of many operations in India, as sieges were accompanied by negotiations intended to win Shivaji's support, which was seen as particularly important to the forthcoming Mughal attack on Bijapur further east. These negotiations were an aspect of the dependence of operations on the politics created by the preference for sequential war making: engaging with opponents one after the other and in a way that took advantage of the support of those last coerced into co-operation. This preference was characteristic of Indian warfare, but was complicated by the unstable basis of alliances and, as a result, the conditional nature of co-operation against opponents who might soon be allies.

Relations between Shivaji and Aurangzeb rapidly deteriorated and, in 1669, Shivaji asserted his independence by recapturing the fort of Sinhagad. In 1670, moreover, Shivaji sacked the major port of Surat, challenging the revenue stream yielded by overseas trade, and pressed the Mughals onto the defensive in west-central India. In the following year, he drove them from their surviving regional bases around Poona and advanced into, first, Bijapur and, then, Golconda. Thus, the Marathas acted to benefit from the weakness of the Deccan sultanates, challenging the Mughal aspiration to dominate them, but, at the same time, lessened the possibility of co-operation with the sultanates against Aurangzeb.

The Marathas were able to hold their own against Mughal heavy cavalry and field artillery thanks to their own cavalry's superior mobility. Maratha cavalry used small horses from the region, rather than the large, heavier horses imported from Central Asia that were the Mughal goal, not least because Mughal cavalry were armoured and carried more weaponry. Moreover, the Maratha cavalry did not ride stirrup to stirrup in order to provide the shock and impact of their Mughal opponents. Instead, they relied on harassing the Mughals, staying out of the range of charges while weakening them by raiding tactics and the use of missiles. These tactics were matched by an operational preference for gaining logistical mastery by cutting the supply lines of opponents, and a related strategy of exhausting them by devastating territory rather than risking battle. In 1677, Shivaji successfully invaded the Carnatic in south-eastern India, occupying Veluru, Arni, Jinji and Tanjore, an impressive force projection, and, when he died in 1680, he left a powerful position in the Maratha homeland and a strong presence elsewhere. Aurangzeb was unable to defeat the Marathas in the early 1680s, although, in 1683, when Portuguese positions at Goa and Chaul were attacked by the Marathas, they were saved by their fortifications and because the Mughals attacked the Marathas the same year.

All comparisons risk problems. The Mughals were unable to overcome the Marathas at a time when the Manchu were defeating the Rebellion of the Three Feudatories. Nevertheless, albeit facing a different threat environment, the Mughals were far more successful in the seventeenth century than the Ming, even if their eventual collapse in the nineteenth century had some echoes of the fall of the Ming in the seventeenth. The Mughals in the seventeenth century also proved more effective than both the states of southern India and the Mughals in the eighteenth.[7] Moreover, the Mughals displayed an ability to adapt to a bewildering variety of environments, from the equatorial heat and humidity of the forested Brahmaputra valley, where they fought the Ahom, to the arid plains and snowy mountains of Central Asia. Their troops, military system, generalship and (on the whole) logistics, proved equal to the challenge, even if success could not always be won. This range is an important measure of military capability, but range tends to be underrated, not least because many famous Western forces, such as those of Frederick the Great, Napoleon and Moltke the Elder, largely operated only in one type of military environment.

Europe

The range confronted by Aurangzeb's forces was not faced by the Western Europeans, with the exception of the minority of troops sent outside Europe. As in China and India, however, there was a need to consolidate power in the 1650s in the face of internal challenges. In the case of France, Spain and Poland, these challenges interacted with external threats, while the republican regime in England was spared such a problem, which helped explain its success until it collapsed as a result of internal divisions and its lack of broad-based support.

Beginning a full-scale war in 1635, neither France nor Spain was able to impose a crippling defeat on the other, but the fiscal burdens of war had posed growing political problems for both. Although France was the most populous state in Western Europe, and had a well-developed agricultural base, the French lacked a system of effective military administration and sound finances, and the strains of the war revealed the inadequacies of their reliance on expedients. After the mid-1640s, it had been less a question of French victories or defeats in the war with Spain than of a failure by France to make much progress, and certainly progress commensurate with the need to defeat Spain before debt overwhelmed France's finances and made it difficult to continue anchoring the personal credit of royal officials and allies.

Spain had the largest empire in Western Europe, but its financial, political and military system also proved unequal to the strains of the war. The character of the two crises, however, was different, as Spain faced rebellions in parts of the empire, notably Catalonia in 1640 and Naples and Sicily in 1647, while France faced the *Frondes*, rebellions in the centre of power that broke out in 1648 and lasted until 1652. The Parliamentary and aristocratic *Frondes* indicated a serious breakdown in the political and aristocratic process, one that was precipitated by the crisis of war finance, in a similar fashion to the Catalan rising against Spain in 1640.

Each side sought to exploit the rebellions in the other, France sending forces into Catalonia and using the opportunity of the rebellion there to conquer the in-between province of Roussillon, the fortress-city of Perpignan falling in 1642. However, French attempts to exploit rebellions in Palermo and Naples in the Spanish empire met with scant success, which was an aspect of the more general resilience of Spanish power, a resilience that stands as a contrast to standard views on Spanish decline.[8] The failure was also a reflection of the difficulties of amphibious force projection. Similarly, Spain's attempt to intervene directly in the *Frondes* by invading Gascony to help rebels in the city of Bordeaux failed. The *Frondes* proved more useful to Spain in permitting the reconquest of Catalonia, the capital of which, Barcelona, fell in 1652 after a 14-month Spanish blockade had reduced the population to starvation. The war between France and Spain continued until the Peace of the Pyrenees in 1659, but, although leading to major pressures, the conflict did not help cause any comparable political breakdown to those in the 1640s. Instead, the defeat of the rebellions provided a wider margin of opportunity for the two powers while, at the same time, there was a more cautious attempt in each to co-operate with the politically influential.

In Britain, there was also a consolidation of power, although, in this case initially on behalf of the revolutionary Parliamentarian regime. Having won the First Civil War in 1646, the victors fell out. Parliament, the army leadership and the Scots clashed over church government, negotiations with the captured Charles I, and army pay arrears. Delegates appointed by regiments of the New Model Army pressed Parliament for arrears, and, in August 1647, the army occupied London. The Scots were appalled by the rising influence of radical Protestantism in England and, in 1648, in the Second Civil War, invaded on behalf of Charles. There was also a series of Royalist risings, particularly in Kent and South Wales. All, however, were speedily crushed, especially with Cromwell's victory over the overstretched and poorly co-ordinated Scottish forces at Preston on 17 August. In contrast, when earlier allied with the Parliamentarians, the Scots had been able to campaign as far south as Hereford in 1645. The rapid end to the campaign reflected the strength, flexibility and determination of the New Model Army and the qualities of its leaders. The army's determination to punish Charles I and crush Royalism was central to his execution in 1649 and to the declaration of a republic.

The Parliamentary forces pressed on to overcome opposition in Ireland and Scotland, an impressive success that had eluded English monarchs throughout history, as well as to capture the remaining Royalist bases in the Channel Isles, the Isles of Scilly, the Isle of Man and the colonies. The war in Ireland had involved a number of parties, as the civil wars in England and Scotland came to interact with the Catholic rising against English rule in 1641, and the conflict lacked a central focus, since control over towns did not ensure dominance in their hinterlands. In 1649, the Royalists were in control of most of Ireland when Cromwell landed with 12,000 New Model veterans. His campaign, especially the storming of the fortified towns of Drogheda (10 September) and Wexford (11 October), has since become proverbial in Irish consciousness for its cruelty. In fact, the conflict of the 1640s was as much an Irish civil war as an English invasion, and the struggle had begun with a Catholic uprising in 1641 in which Protestant were massacred. At neither Drogheda nor Wexford were there attacks on women and children, although at Drogheda, where Cromwell's siege artillery achieved a firing rate of 200 cannonballs per day, the garrison of about 2500 men was slaughtered, the few who received quarter being sent to work on the sugar plantations in Barbados. Both then and later, Cromwell's well-supplied forces demonstrated the value of good logistics in permitting a high tempo of operations that took and kept the initiative, enabling a relatively small number of troops to conquer a large area.[9]

Before Cromwell left in May 1650, his forces had overrun the south-east of Ireland, and his successor, his son-in-law Henry Ireton, showed the value of combining victory in battle with the capture of positions. Victory at Scarrifhollis (21 June 1650) was followed by the capture of the cities of Waterford (1650), Limerick (1651) and Galway (1652), and, as significantly, a sense of inexorable power was created. Ireton himself had become more radical as a consequence of war, and the combination of his radicalism and his conviction that he did God's will helped further to accentuate the disruptive consequences of the conquest for Gaelic society, although Ireton died in November 1651 as a result of a fever contracted while campaigning.[10] Largely as a result of subsequent famine, plague and emigration, the conquest led to the loss of about 40 per cent of the Irish population, and was followed by widespread expropriation of Catholic land as the Anglo-Irish Catholics lost power and status.

In a parallel to the role of sequential campaigning in facilitating success in India and elsewhere, Scottish quiescence was crucial to the early stages of the Parliamentary conquest of Ireland, but in 1650 Charles I's eldest son, Charles II, came to terms with the Scots. In response, Cromwell invaded Scotland on 22 July. Unable, however, to breach the Scottish fortified positions around Edinburgh and outmanoeuvred by the Scottish commander, David Leslie, Cromwell fell back to Dunbar to the east where he was cut off from retreat to England by a force twice the size of his own. On 3 September, Cromwell launched a surprise attack which defeated the Scottish cavalry, while much of the infantry surrendered. Edinburgh was then captured, in a classic instance of battle ensuring the surrender of a defended position. In the following summer, Cromwell used his command of the sea to outflank the Scots blocking his way north at Stirling and occupied the town of Perth, a demonstration of the value of naval power and maritime capability.

Rather than fighting Cromwell in Scotland, Charles, however, then marched south into England, hoping to ignite a Royalist rebellion. He reached Wigan on 15 August, but, short of recruits, decided to head for the Welsh Borders, rather than march directly on London. The town of Shrewsbury, however, resisted the Royalist advance, and when Charles reached the town of Worcester on 22 August, he had recruited few additional men. The Parliamentarians under Cromwell, who numbered about 30,000 men, drove at Worcester on 3 September from several directions. The Royalists, with about 12,000 troops, launched an initially successful frontal attack on Cromwell's position, but numbers told and the Royalist army was overwhelmed. Hiding in an oak tree and supporters' houses en route, Charles fled to France, leaving the Royalist cause crushed, although his survival was strategically important. By the summer of 1652, all Scotland had fallen to Cromwell's forces. No subsequent conspiracies or rebellions came close to success.

Very different attempts at consolidation were seen in Ukraine and Poland in the 1640s and 1650s, as the protagonists, in a complex and overlapping series of conflicts that involved Russia, Poland, Sweden and the Cossacks, undertook and resisted attempts to create a new order. Ukraine provided a key instance, with Russia trying to use Poland's difficulties stemming from the Cossack rebellion there in 1648 in order to advance its power southwards, a major Russian goal in order to provide security against the Crimean Tatars who had been a considerable problem earlier in the century. As a reminder of the challenge posed by multiple commitments, their invasions of central Muscovy helped force Tsar Mikhail's government to negotiate peace with the Poles in 1634 and to turn attention to the securing of Muscovy's southern steppe frontier, which was done by developing the earlier programme of constructing new fortress towns and defensive lines. The repair and extension in 1638 of the Abatis Line involved over 20,000 labourers, while from 1635 a new line, the Belgorod Line, was built further south. Largely completed by 1653, it was an earthen wall, strengthened by fortifications, that ran for about 1000 kilometres from Akhtyrka to Tambov. Built between 1647 and 1654, a Simbirsk Line extended this system to Simbirsk on the Volga, and subsequently the line was to be extended further east to the Urals, when the Trans-Kama Line linked Simbirsk to Mensenlinsk on the Ik River.

Defensive and offensive were, as ever, related, with the extension of Russian interests and power into Ukraine, notably by taking the Dnieper Cossacks under the protection of the Tsar at Perejaslaw in 1654,[11] linked to major efforts to project strength south across the steppe in order to crush the Tatars and to establish bases on and near the Black Sea. Fortress towns and defensive lines represented one way to try to consolidate power, with a comparable attempt made by the Habsburgs to establish military colonies in Croatia in order to provide protection against Ottoman attack. This method, however, required much effort, and was best pursued in regions with low population density, notably with the attempt to stabilise frontiers of control in the face of semi-nomadic peoples who classically used light cavalry, such as the Cossacks and the Crimean Tatars.

The consolidation of control was resisted by means of harassment, which repeatedly affected Swedish attempts to dominate Poland. In 1626–9, Polish cavalry attacks on supply lines and small units impeded Swedish operations there. Later, in response to invasion by Charles X of Sweden, the Poles, after their defeats at Zarnów and Wojinicz in 1655, avoided battle with large Swedish formations, relying instead upon surprise attacks and raids. In 1656, Stefan Czarniecki successfully used tactics of harassment, obliging the Swedes, who were not able to maintain their supplies, to withdraw. A Swedish force under Margrave Frederick of Baden was then destroyed by Polish cavalry at Warka, and Charles X, who had captured Warsaw in 1655, was forced to abandon the city, a key instance of failure, and to fall back on Polish Prussia towards his lines of communication across the Baltic. The Swedes had to admit failure.[12] They were to face fewer problems when they next invaded Poland, in the 1700s, but only because they then backed a Pole as their client for king.

As Poland clearly demonstrated, consolidation was another's conquest. Nevertheless, the theme of consolidation was important to the politics and conflicts of the 1650s, notably in terms of strategic goals and operational means. The military consequences included those of command and control, for civil conflict, followed by political consolidation, put a premium on the loyalty of commanders. Talent alone might be unreliable, as shown when Louis, Prince of Condé, the French victor over the Spaniards at Rocroi in 1643, joined the *Frondes* and, in 1652, became a general fighting the French on behalf of Philip IV of Spain, victoriously so at Valenciennes in 1656. Condé's career provides an instance of the degree to which states in this period should be seen not as nations but as regimes manifest in institutions but with the fundamental cohesion generally provided by personal loyalty to the ruler. These institutions could go beyond the bounds of personal loyalty, and this was especially true of republics, notably the United Provinces (Dutch Republic), which was based on the Union of Utrecht that had rejected Philip II of Spain, and on the ideologies of the Dutch Revolt. Nevertheless, in general, thanks to the potent role of personal loyalties and relationships in government, commanders chose themselves, as much as were chosen, and armies were in part raised through the links of these commanders. These links were of varied character, in a pattern that went back centuries and did not begin with the early-modern period. The two key elements were the local sway facilitated by positions of local prominence, notably those of landlords, and the opportunities to hire provided by individual wealth, credit-worthiness and speculation. These functional reasons that led rulers to rely on the resources of their commanders were accentuated by the limitations of bureaucratic mechanisms and the resulting co-operative character of governance, government, and thus the state. The latter interacted with political factors linked to the search for stability by means of co-operation with the élite.

These elements provided a similarity to military activity around the world, and also a continuity across the century – one that took precedence over changes, whether or not described in terms of a military revolution. Conflict was intended to facilitate consolidation, while the latter helped provide resources for war. The political consolidation of the 1650s was closely linked to continuing conflict between states, notably, in Europe, the Franco-Spanish War and the struggle in the eastern Baltic. Indeed, resource issues provided a linkage between stability and war, as did the prestige to be gained or lost through campaigning, for success was a vital lubricant of obedience, a functional explanation that matches the fact that such *gloire* was also enjoyable to most rulers and many members of the social élite. The political stability stemming from obedience, in turn, produced resources for war. Moreover, the political consolidation of the decade was an important background to the growth of standing armies in Europe both then and later in the century, with these armies, in turn, facilitating consolidation. The establishment of Manchu power in southern China proved a variant on this process, as it increased the tax base for the army, although the successful end of the Manchu conquest reduced the actual need for an expansion in the size of the army. The same was true of Aurangzeb's success in the civil war in Mughal India, which also consolidated the tax base.

Yet, a period that in hindsight could be described in terms of consolidation and success did not always appear so positive at the time. This point was demonstrated in China by Zheng Chenggong's operations and subsequently by the Rebellion of the Three Feudatories. Furthermore, in Europe, in contrast to the teleological practice of discussing the period 1640–60 in terms of France's rise, the end of the *Frondes* in 1652 brought little improvement in French prospects, and while in 1654 a Spanish attempt to regain the town of Arras was defeated by Turenne, the Spaniards captured Rocroi, a step that is scarcely ever mentioned, in contrast to the French victory there over a Spanish army in 1643. In addition, resource issues helped explain the pressure of war on France in the 1650s, as earlier in the 1640s. Serious French defeats at Pavia (1655) and Valenciennes (1656) led France to offer reasonable peace terms, only for Philip IV to reject them. Pavia was followed by Spain overrunning the Duchy of Modena, whose Duke, Francesco I, had abandoned Spain, and the victory also encouraged Cardinal Mazarin, the leading French minister, to revive France's longstanding and repeatedly unsuccessful attempt to dominate Italy. This attempt underlined the strategic importance of Italy, notably of the routes through northern Italy along which the Spanish Habsburgs could deploy and support their power. The conquest of Modena underlined another significant strategic point, that France was unable to protect its clients. In 1657, Spain won two more victories in Lombardy, showing how fruitless were Mazarin's Italian hopes, not least as these battles affected the possibility of staging successful sieges. Many battles arose from attempts to relieve sieges, as with Valenciennes and in 1659 when the Portuguese relieved the fortress of Elvas which had been besieged by Spain from late 1658.

Eventual victory over Spain for France reflected the military consequences of the political strategy of alliance-building, as the intervention of fresh English forces on the side of France tipped the balance in Flanders. On 14 June 1658, English troops helped Turenne to defeat the Army of Flanders under Archduke John of Austria at the Battle of the Dunes, as the Spaniards tried to relieve besieged Dunkirk. The Spanish army was outnumbered, its artillery had not arrived, the sandy terrain prevented it from taking advantage of its superiority in cavalry, and its flank was bombarded by English warships in a classic demonstration of the value of naval power for operations on land.[13] After the battle, Turenne captured the fortified positions of Dunkirk, Gravelines, Menin and Ypres, and threatened an advance on Brussels, the capital of the Spanish Netherlands. The Peace of the Pyrenees followed in November 1659, with France gaining the provinces of Roussillon and Artois from Spain, as well as the marriage of Philip IV's daughter with the young Louis XIV, a step that gave him a stake in the Spanish succession. The following year, peace between England and Spain left the former with Dunkirk, although it was subsequently sold to France.

Similarly, a series of treaties in 1660–7 brought the wars in Eastern Europe and the Baltic to an end. The Swedes acknowledged their failure to dominate Poland, the Danes that of their attempt to challenge Sweden's hegemony in the Baltic, and the Russians that of their drive to conquer Livonia from Sweden and win a major presence on the Baltic. These treaties of 1660–1 enabled Poland to concentrate its efforts against Russia, which it did successfully in the early 1660s with a number of victories, for example at Cudnów in 1660. Although the infantry techniques of countermarching and volley fire were not without relevance in Eastern Europe, the small number of engagements fought between linear formations and settled by firepower is a reminder that these innovations were not all-powerful. Infantry firepower was emphasised more by Tsar Alexei (r. 1645–76) than his predecessors, but cavalry operations remained especially important, not least as raiding could be employed to undermine an opponent's logistics.

Sieges also played only a relatively minor role, although control of bases such as Smolensk (captured by Alexei in 1654) and Kiev was of great importance.

Alongside the emphasis on the strength and weakness of military factors, Poland was affected by fiscal exhaustion and political discontent, culminating in a civil war in 1665–6. The Russians, in turn, had been exhausted by the length of the conflict, and frequent advances had failed to deliver the necessary closure. Alexei introduced regular conscription from the peasantry, but this did not produce well-trained or -motivated troops, while civilian morale was hit by the debasement of the coinage. The war became a stalemate in which both sides could launch attacks but not hold the ground covered. This situation led in 1667 to a 13-year truce with Russia agreed at Andrusovo, a truce that settled both the Ukraine and the struggle over Belarus: Alexei kept Smolensk and took the eastern Ukraine as well as Kiev, while the Poles were to retain the western Ukraine.[14] The gain of the eastern Ukraine took Russian interests closer to the Black Sea and, in 1679–80, the Russians began work on the Iziuma Line, a 530 kilometre-long defensive position that was further south than the Belgorod Line. However, the increase in governmental pressure on the southern borderlands resulted in a major rebellion, under the leadership of Stenka Razin. It was mounted by disaffected Cossacks and peasants, many of whom had run away from conscription, in the Volga valley in 1670.

The early wars of Louis XIV

Having taken personal charge of French policy in 1661 following the death of Mazarin, Louis XIV added a marked tone of bellicosity. His first war, that of Devolution (1667–8), was a relatively modest affair motivated by an opportunistic claim to part of the succession of Philip IV of Spain, his late father-in-law, who died in 1665. Military operations and political strategy were in line, for Louis was helped by the diplomatic isolation of Spain. Already at war with Portugal, whose 1640 rebellion it had failed to suppress despite major efforts, the Spanish government found England and the Dutch engaged in the Second Anglo-Dutch War (1665–7), while Leopold I of Austria was unable and unwilling to provide support.

The French were helped by the international situation and by the weak state of the defences of the Spanish Netherlands (Belgium), which lacked both soldiers and *matériel*, with the militia unpaid and the fortifications requiring repair.[15] In 1665, the French under Turenne rapidly seized a large number of fortresses in the Spanish Netherlands, including the important positions of Lille and Tournai. Under Condé, who had received Louis's forgiveness after the Peace of the Pyrenees, the French also invaded Franche-Comté, a Spanish territory to the east of France (with its capital at Besançon) that had once been part of the Burgundian inheritance, much of which the Habsburgs had inherited.

The Spanish forces were not able to offer effective resistance, and on 31 August 1667 were defeated at Bruges by a larger French force under François de Créqui. Alarmed at French success, England, the Dutch and Sweden formed the Triple Alliance in January 1668. The ostensible purpose of the Alliance was to mediate between the combatants, but the Alliance secretly agreed to back Spain if Louis refused to compromise. Louis, in turn, negotiated, in March 1668, the Treaty of Aix-la-Chapelle with Spain whereby he returned Franche-Comté, but kept Lille and Tournai. These gains, however, were far less than those won by Russia, at the expense of Poland, in the Truce of Andrusovo of 1667. In part, that reflected the presence in Western Europe of a number of second-rank powers able and willing to combine against any potential hegemon, and thus to restrict its growth.

Thus, for Louis to attack again with success, he needed to prevent such a combination. In planning a war on the Dutch, Louis won over the support or neutrality of England, Leopold I and a number of German princes. This backing had operational as well as political value. Thanks, in part, to the support of the Elector of Cologne, French forces under Condé crossed the Rhine and invaded the United Provinces from the east in 1672, capturing the city of Utrecht and only being stopped from advancing further west when the dykes were breached on 20 June. The province of Holland was thus saved, but the French had made a far greater impact in one campaign than the Spaniards had done against the Dutch in 1621–48. Rather than this contrast arising from a decline in the Spanish army (which, in fact, did better across the century than is often appreciated), in large part, it reflected the French ability to concentrate all their resources on one front, which greatly differed from the situation facing Spain, but it was also important that France in 1672 was not exhausted in either military or economic terms.

Louis had won a quick triumph, but had little sense of how the war would develop diplomatically and militarily. The Dutch offered terms, but an overconfident Louis, hopeful that the war would widen to include Spain so that he could resume the conquest of the Spanish Netherlands, issued excessive demands, including for major territorial gains and the acceptance of Catholic worship. The last reflected the extent to which religion was an important goal for all of the powers, with Louis also determined to gain prestige by being seen as a champion of Catholicism, thus supplanting the Habsburgs in this role.

Louis's harsh stance towards the United Provinces was unwise, not least because an Orangeist coup in Holland in July 1672 brought the anti-French William III of Orange to power as stadtholder (governor), a figure of great prestige in its politics that had been in abeyance in Holland since 1650. William was to prove Louis's staunchest opponent and was unwilling to accept a settlement under which he became hereditary ruler of the United Provinces in return for yielding to English and French demands. Instead, William combined political determination with a measure of military energy, although not always military ability. Moreover, his position in the German princely system helped ensure a measure of German support, a pattern seen since the Dutch Revolt that was important to the raising of troops and provision of officers. However, there was also a tension between the Orangeists and the republican urban oligarchs, notably in Holland, who did not want a stadtholder, and this tension led to serious political differences that affected war goals, strategy, the operational use of the army and the provision of troops.

In 1673–4, the conflict changed shape, in part because of Louis's overconfidence and maladroit handling of others, but also because the coalition that Louis had created was unstable. He lost his ability to manipulate German politics in order to create a potent alliance. Leopold I's decision to oppose Louis proved particularly significant and helped transform the strategic parameters of the war. In August 1673, Leopold, the Dutch, Spain and Duke Charles IV of Lorraine agreed to force Louis back to the frontiers laid down at the Peace of the Pyrenees of 1659, undoing French gains in the War of Devolution and in 1672–3. In the face of the development of the largest coalition France had had to face that century, the geopolitical situation changed. In 1673, rather than resume his attack on Holland, Louis besieged and captured the Dutch-held fortress of Maastricht on the River Meuse in order to improve his strategic position to the east of the bulk of the Spanish Netherlands as well as further east in the Rhineland. However, 1673 also saw the fall of French-garrisoned Bonn, the capital of the Electorate of Cologne, as the Italian-born Austrian general Count Montecuccoli outmanoeuvred Turenne and forced him to retreat from east of the Rhine. Indeed, in 1673, Louis abandoned his position in the United Provinces in order to protect his frontier in Alsace.

In 1674, Turenne seized the Rhine crossing point at Strasbourg, a key step as there were few crossing points of that mighty river, while Franche-Comté was conquered in an impressive display of the French ability to deliver a decisive operational result. This success was, significantly, a result of sieges, of Dôle and Besançon, rather than of battles, although the latter proved important in a surprise winter campaign of 1674–5 when Turenne outmanoeuvred the Austrian forces out of Alsace, defeating them at Mulhouse (29 December 1674) and Turckheim (5 January 1675). However, after Turenne was killed by a cannonball during the battle of Sasbach (27 July 1675), Montecuccoli advanced deep into Alsace, before being driven back across the Rhine by Condé. In 1676–8, Créqui for the French and Duke Charles V of Lorraine for the Austrians campaigned in the Rhineland with mixed results, but with Créqui victorious at Kochersberg (17 October 1677), Rheinfelden (6 July 1678) and Gengenbach (23 July 1678). The battles of these years, for example Sinsheim and Enzheim in 1674 and Conzerbrücke in 1675, have not received much attention, but they reflect the extent to which the campaigns were not solely a matter of sieges, although they were important, as with Charles of Lorraine's capture of Philippsburg in 1676 and the French gains of Freiburg and Kehl in 1677 and 1678 respectively.

The battles, which in many respects were like those of the 1640s, demonstrated the continued importance of cavalry, the willingness to fight in the winter, as at Mulhouse and Turckheim, and the role, as in the Thirty Years' War, of experienced troops and of gaining experience through a high level of conflict. An ability to respond rapidly to opportunities was important, as at Turckheim where Turenne, faced by Austrians deployed behind a stream, successfully turned their right flank.

At the same time, as with the latter stages of that war, commanders had to face the problems posed by the growing exhaustion both of their own resources and of those in the campaign zone, which was more compact than those in Eastern Europe in the 1670s. In May 1677, William Skelton, the English envoy in Vienna, noted that Charles V of Lorraine 'wants ammunition and cannon … besides he will ruin his army if he goes from the Rhine but four days march'.[16] That September, he added, 'where money and bread is wanting no general can do wonders',[17] Charles was defeated by Créqui at Kochersberg on 17 October. The results of this situation pressed hard on the local economy, but were exacerbated by deliberate destructiveness, as after the battle of Rheinfelden when the French burned down the nearby town of Sackingen.

England left what, for it, was the Third Anglo-Dutch War in 1674, abandoning Louis XIV in favour of a peace with the Dutch that greatly reduced the fiscal, and thus political, burden on Charles II. However, in 1674, Charles XI of Sweden entered the conflict on the French side, only to be defeated on 28 June 1675 at Fehrbellin by a smaller force under Frederick William I, the Great Elector of Brandenburg-Prussia. Fehrbellin was a small-scale engagement that became very important in the Prussian public myth;[18] it also affected the perception of Swedish strength. The Swedes were also defeated in the Baltic by the Danish navy. However, a Danish invasion of southern

Sweden was defeated at Lund on 14 October 1676 by Charles XI, who went on to defeat the Danes the following July at Landskrona. Ultimately, Sweden prevailed repeatedly over Denmark because of superior war making.

In the Spanish Netherlands, the French took a large number of fortresses, including Dinant, Huy and Limburg in 1675, Condé, Bouchain and Aire in 1676, Valenciennes, Cambrai and St Omer in 1677, and Ghent and Ypres in 1678. These successes owed much to French competence in siegecraft, which was largely due to the work of Sébastien Le Prestre de Vauban, although his ideas and work built on the experience and publications of earlier experts, for example Antoine de Ville, who became Military Engineer to Louis XIII in 1627. His *Les fortifications ... contenans la maniere de fortifier toute sorte de places tant regulierement, qu'irregulierement* (Lyon, 1628) was reprinted in 1640 and 1666 and used by Vauban, which provides an instructive instance of the interrelationship of developments in the two halves of the century. De Ville also published *De la charge des gouverneurs des places ... un abrégé de la fortification* (Paris, 1639).

A master of positional warfare, of siegecraft as of fortification, Vauban showed in the siege of Maastricht in June 1673 how trenches could more safely be advanced close to fortifications under artillery cover by parallel and zigzag approaches. The garrison capitulated after a siege of less than a month, as also, for example, did those of Valenciennes and Ypres, while some positions fell very rapidly – Limbourg in June 1676, a week after the trenches were opened. Vauban's many successes in siegecraft and fortification had a more lasting reputation than did the campaign victories of Louis XIV's forces, in part because the Austrians, British and Russians, although all later gaining prestige through victorious battles between 1683 and 1718, were far less successful in siege and fortification. Vauban's reputation led to the publication of his works well into the eighteenth century even outside France. The fifth edition of his *New Method of Fortification* was published in London in 1748, while an edition of his collected work was published in Amsterdam and Leipzig in 1771.

The importance of fortifications and sieges was such that Vauban's writings scarcely exhausted the subject of relevant publications, while his work and that of others in the field encouraged further publications, as best practice was much discussed by writers. Moreover, translations spread knowledge. Thus, Tomaso Moretti's *Trattato dell' artigliera* appeared in English editions in 1673 and 1683, with the translator, Jonas Moore, also publishing his own *Modern Fortification* (London, 1689). Among the many works that followed, Sebastián Fernández de Medrano's *L'Ingenieur Pratique ou L'Architecture Militaire et Moderne* appeared in Brussels in 1696. Skill in siegecraft, however, still faced the serious problems of conflict in the period, notably logistics, but also, for example, the impact of a lack of water on river levels and, thus, on the ability to move cannon.[19]

Sieges required an ability to deploy and support forces that relied on preventing blocking moves by opposing armies, let alone the attempts at relief that resulted in many battles. Thus, French sieges in the Spanish Netherlands were ultimately dependent on battles, notably successive victories over William III at Seneffe (1674) and Mont Cassel (1677). The latter arose from a failed effort by William to relieve St Omer, while the battle of St Denis in 1678 was a result of his attempt to relieve Mons. In this battle, cavalry played only a minor role due to the terrain. The French siege of Rheinfelden in July 1676, begun after the battle nearby, ended when Charles V of Lorraine appeared at the head of an Austrian force.

Alongside the famous battles and sieges, the French were able to use 'small warfare' to serve operational goals. In particular, there was a more systematic approach to supplies and contributions in order to make it easier to support the burden of conflict than the situation earlier in the century, as well as improved reconnaissance: the systematic gathering of Intelligence by the French increased the possibilities for, and of, planning. Raids took on a meaning within the calculus of supplies, and also as a means of putting pressure on hostile garrisons, all points that could also be made about Maratha war making in India. There, as in Europe, West and East, there was no easy division between 'small warfare' and large-scale engagements, but rather a continuum. Thus, in July 1678, a force of about 1000 Dutch troops sent from the fortress of Mons to escort in a supply convoy beat a similar French force that tried to stop it.

There was an offensive–defensive character to French war making, with the French, in particular, trying to protect their own northern frontier, as well as to put pressure on the Spaniards. It was impossible to seal off the frontier, but the French authorities dispatched war parties, prepared defences, issued ordinances, cajoled local officials and organised militia, all with the intention of slowing and disrupting the Spanish imposition and collection of contributions. Moreover, French reprisal raids and escalating demands for contributions were intended to inflict harm on the inhabitants of the Spanish Netherlands, and to weaken their resolve. The French defences worked well, but driving the Spanish garrisons from their fortresses was the only sure means to prevent Spanish raids. To that end, blockades of fortresses were an important prelude to sieges and demonstrated the potency of French 'small war'. Blockades wore down the Spaniards, enervating their garrisons or ensuring that French sieges were more rapid. Blockades, crucially, continued during the period of winter quarters in what was a war of outposts. This was a particularly important part of French operations from 1676, and it has been argued that 'The operational emphasis on blockades led Louis XIV and Louvois [the Secretary of War] to perceive military actions in interrelated, and mutually supporting terms, rather than as discrete expeditions. It constituted a kind of "operational revolution"', and French war making has been presented as part of 'the birth of a more modern style of military operations',[20] which is seen to lie in French operations emphasising sieges and smaller actions of war that aimed at attrition as a way to avoid battle and the risks it contained.

This claim, however, requires a wider assessment of other operations, both in Europe and further afield. Indeed, the extent to which there was a doctrinal shift in France is unclear, while, as so often in military history, it is helpful to think of incremental changes rather than a revolution. Earlier commanders, such as the Duke of Parma in the 1580s, Maurice of Nassau in the 1590s and Spinola in the 1600s and 1620s, also had a very clear conception of how minor raids linked up with campaigning as aspects of a big picture, an understanding that contributed to the impressive operational and strategic grasp they displayed. The notion of modernity in this context may be challenged, since such warfare was in fact fairly constant in many military environments, and if it can be argued that the French under Louis XIV provided an impression of modernity by using regular forces for these operations and by conducting them with a co-ordination not always seen elsewhere,[21] such activity had long occurred and it is important not to assume that regular forces necessarily provided more sophisticated campaigning. Moreover, it is necessary to appreciate that co-ordination takes many forms: it is unclear why Louis XIV's forces should be seen as better co-ordinated than those of the thirteenth-century Mongols.

The details of conflict in the 'small war' of the 1670s do not suggest much change from earlier small warfare. There was an emphasis on surprise, march security, and cover. As a consequence, many actions took place around cemeteries, churchyards, villages and walled farms which one side had occupied for their defensive value. Most infantry actions were decided within minutes of the first volley, and, in 'small war', formations on foot fought using the same volley fire tactics employed by troops in large battles. Indeed, large battles can be thought of as a series of small engagements in which men fought in relative isolation from one another, which is correct up to a point, although it minimises the extent to which units did move on the battlefield; and there was a flow to many conflicts, one that was often very important to success. In small-scale conflict, there was little all-out pursuit as victorious detachments feared ambush. More generally, the nature of this warfare, alongside the more prominent operations, underlines the serious financial issues that affected military capability and policy, and were pursued and exacerbated by raiding.

In addition to an emphasis on campaigning, as seeking stages in the defeat of opposing forces, it is necessary to adopt a broader approach to victory and to underline the extent to which success had a symbolic value. From this perspective, decisiveness has to be reconceptualised, away from an emphasis on total victory, understood in modern terms as the destruction of opposing armies and the capture of their territory, and towards a notion that may have had more meaning in terms of the values of the period. In Western Europe, territory was understood in terms of legal/feudal jurisdictions, which ensured that the capture of centres of jurisdictions was important, irrespective of their abstract military value. Control of these centres had to be grasped symbolically as well as practically, not least to help secure the international and domestic responses that would register and legitimate a transfer of territory. The presence of the monarch at a successful siege best ensured this grasp.

Moreover, although European theorists such as Francisco de Vitoria and Justus Lipsius insisted that neither honour nor glory should play any role in decision making linked to warfare – and neither factor played the leading role in wars conducted by the Dutch with their republican culture – the values of the period involved a struggle of will and a struggle for prestige. The ends sought were, first, a retention of domestic and international backing that rested on the gaining of *gloire*, and, secondly, persuading other rulers to accept a new configuration of relative *gloire*. This focus led to a concentration of forces on campaigns and sieges made important largely by the presence of the king as commander. Like other rulers, Louis XIV enjoyed both commanding and reviewing troops. His triumphs, such as the crossing of the Rhine in 1672, and the successful sieges of Maastricht (1673), Ghent (1678), Luxembourg (1684) and Mons (1691), were celebrated with religious services and commemorative displays. In the *Salon de la Guerre* at the royal palace of Versailles, finished and opened to the public in 1686, Antoine Coysevox presented Louis as a stuccoed Mars, the God of War.[22] Louis also appeared as a warrior in works of art that had a different theme, for example Charles Le Brun's painting *The Resurrection of Christ* (1674), which was painted while France was at war. By the 1690s, over 20,000 French nobles were serving in the army and navy, a bond that testified to aristocratic confidence in Louis and that underlined the political value of his position as war leader.

Louis was scarcely alone. Similarly, Frederick William, the Great Elector of Brandenburg-Prussia, commissioned Andreas Schlüter to design an equestrian statue depicting him as a military commander: in armour and holding a field marshal's baton.[23] Rulers were conspicuous in martial activities, since a reputation for resolution was of great significance, both to them and to their subjects, as well as proving important in operations.

Thus, during the Dutch siege of Maastricht in 1676, William III spent much time in the trenches and was shot in the arm. Two years later, he was described at the battle of St Denis as armoured with breastplate and helmet 'with thousands of bullets about his ears'.[24]

The Dutch War closed with the Treaty of Nijmegen of 1678 under which Louis XIV gained Franche-Comté, the fortresses of Freiburg and Bouillon, and more of the Spanish Netherlands. These terms helped cement an impression that France was not only the dominant military power but also one that could deliver results, results that have impressed scholars who have seen Louis's victories as a key indicator of his domestic strength. Indeed, the conventional view has been to present French capability and success in terms of the achievements of a more capable state. In this account, Louis and his ministers successfully re-established a state-controlled, state-funded military. Helped by rising tax revenues and better-regulated administration, the government sought to avoid reliance on military entrepreneurs, and, instead, there was a theme of order and uniformity. The payment of troops was regulated; progress was made in the standardisation of drill, training and equipment; and, in 1670, distinctive uniforms chosen by Louis were introduced, asserting royal control and making desertion more difficult. The name of Martinet, commander of the *Régiment du Roi* and, from 1667, Inspector-General of the Infantry, entered the language as a term for a strict disciplinarian; and the conduct of French troops towards their compatriots became considerably better, not least because pillaging was punished. The command structure was also revised, and a table of ranks established in 1672.

Moreover, the French developed the most effective logistical system in Western Europe, with the supply networks of men, money, munitions and provisions greatly improved. Alongside a supporting system of *étapes* (supply depots along marching routes), there was a network of magazines near France's frontiers from which campaigns could be supplied. This network was used with considerable success in launching the War of Devolution and the Dutch War in 1667 and 1672, respectively. Thanks to these magazines, the French could seize the initiative by beginning campaigns early. These achievements owed much to two successive Secretaries of War, Michel Le Tellier and his son, Louvois, who between them held office from 1643 to 1691, and who presided over a well-organised War Office. Thus supported, the army was employed to great effect under the inspired leadership of Condé, Turenne and Luxembourg, and French innovations subsequently had a great influence on military developments in the rest of Western Europe. Physical evidence of France's military prowess was provided in the shape of the fortresses built under Louis, most notably the fortified naval bases, especially Brest and Toulon, but also the large number of positions constructed or improved to protect France's borders and, in doing so, to protect France and to entrench Louis's conquests. This process was also seen elsewhere in Europe, but the French received most attention for their fortification work, which was particularly associated with Vauban. This summary covers some of the major themes in the conventional account of France's increased peacetime and wartime strength under Louis XIV, and this account has considerable weight and draws on important scholarship.[25] Moreover, the French military appeared impressive to Western European observers after the Dutch War, and this encouraged the translation of French texts on military affairs, translations which were given further authority by an inclusion of their attribution, as with Archibald Lovell's *The Military Duties of the Officers of Cavalry … written originally in French, by the Sieur de la Fontain* (London, 1678).

Yet, an alternative perspective has also been offered in recent years, one that emphasises the often-limited nature of the state's control over the army, as well as particular deficiencies in French war making, notably the issues created by emphasising dynastic prestige as a fundamental strategic goal.[26] This revisionist approach draws on the critical perspective on the admittedly much more serious situation in France earlier in the century,[27] and, while accepting that there were certainly changes from the often parlous French military situation in the 1630s, argues that it is important not to emphasise the transformation. It is instructive to note an English memoir on French resources, written in 1678 after a tour of the country, that suggests that, although the army had 265,000 troops listed as in pay, at least a fifth 'may be deducted by false musters and other devices of officers, notwithstanding all the great rigour used against those that are found faulty'.[28]

In a parallel fashion, recent work on the development of the French navy suggests that, under Richelieu, it was less the case of major institutional innovations than of traditional methods of government through personal politics.[29] This situation only changed to a certain extent from the 1660s under Jean-Baptiste Colbert, who in 1669 became Secretary of State for the Navy, a new post; and the central agencies of the French navy still had scant control of the, in effect, autonomous naval bases: the agencies could move levers but, frequently, little happened at the naval bases.

A stress on the limitations of the French army has a number of implications both for France and more generally. These categories are linked because of the tendency to present the French army under Louis XIV as the paradigmatic army of the late seventeenth century, as a result of which this army becomes a sort of successor, in the Whiggish account of military history, to the classic Military Revolution. Putting aside the hyperbole of the description, it is obvious that changes were indeed made in the French army and navy, which provides an empirical basis for the conceptual argument rejecting the notion that conservative societies lack the capacity for reform and that they are necessarily weaker than revolutionary counterparts. Rather than seeing a fundamental military problem that required reform, it is clear that the challenges for France and other powers were far more specific and contingent, namely the tasks of the moment, and those seen as likely to arise in terms of what would subsequently be referred to as strategic culture. Thus, there was no dominant teleology forcing the pace of change, and this perspective provides another way to reject the notion of *ancien régime* redundancy.

Yet, whatever its many strengths and successes, France was unable even to secure the defeat of the isolated United Provinces (Dutch Republic) when it attacked in 1672, let alone to operate further afield with sustained success. French dominance of neighbouring areas in the Spanish Netherlands and (less consistently) the Rhineland was not an indicator of a wider capability. Thus, during the Dutch War, an attempt in 1675–6 to undermine the Spanish position in Sicily failed. Moreover, French success in the Nine Years' War (1688–97) was more limited than in the Dutch War, while France suffered heavily in the War of the Spanish Succession (1701–14). France's territorial gains in Louis's reign (1643–1715) did not lead to a major shift in Western European geopolitics, and the possibility of French hegemony, which Louis's opponents emphasised when they sought to encourage opposition to his policies, was unlikely.

The need to contextualise French achievements by considering a range of European armies will be indicated in Chapter 7, while, conversely, a critical consideration of the French army opens up an understanding of European armies as a whole in this period. In doing so it is important to consider the general constraints within which they operated. Within limits, absolutism, the dominant political system of the period, relied in Europe, as elsewhere, on the consent of the social élite,[30] and, as will be discussed in Chapter 9, this consent had key consequences for the command of the military and for recruitment. Indeed, the benign consequences of élite consent notably included ensuring recruiting as, for example, for the Austrian army.[31]

The hegemony that Louis's opponents decried was only practicable if, as with the Franks under Charlemagne in the early ninth century, other Christian powers were very weak and divided. In the early 1680s, such dominance seemed possible, with Austria threatened by the Ottomans' advance, England, in the Exclusion Crisis, affected by serious political contention, and Spain under Charles II, a weak ruler. These weaknesses encouraged a reversion to the intimidatory French tactics of the 1660s. In the winter of 1678–9, French forces occupied much of the Spanish Netherlands, in order to collect contributions owed to the army, and also seized fortresses in the lower Rhineland, in order to exert pressure on the local rulers. Moreover, using force, Louis advanced and enforced a series of territorial claims. The weakness of potential opponents encouraged Louis to press his aggressive schemes, notably through using the *Chambre des Réunions* to pursue often very flimsy territorial claims to the subordinate territories of his newly won possessions. Intimidation seemed an end as much as a means, the creation of a situation in which diplomacy was not necessary other than to cement military gains. Thus, in 1683, troops were sent into the Spanish Netherlands, while the dispatch of a fleet to the Baltic reflected France's ability to challenge the Dutch in an area of traditional interest.

Conclusion

In Japan, in marked contrast, Ieyasu had initiated what was to be a long period of external peace, and did not seek foreign conquests. The Japanese still cast cannon, but made no serious attempt to extend their control in the northern island of Yezo (Hokkaido), where there had been rigorous Ainu resistance to Japanese power in the sixteenth century.[32] Other powers adopted a very different strategic culture. Empires probed their limits in 1683, with French forces in the Spanish Netherlands, the unsuccessful Ottoman siege of Vienna and the Chinese occupation of Taiwan, while Aurangzeb prepared for expansion south into the Deccan. The role of force seemed normative, but, on both the world and European scales, there was no clear guide to relative capability and strength on land. This situation was to be even more the case in the remaining years of the century.

6 The Expansion of Europe

Sieges and fortresses

Vienna, Luxembourg, Tangier, Bijapur, Albazin, Golconda: six significant sieges, each from the mid-1680s, all, bar the first, successful, and each benefiting from being considered alongside the others. Indeed, it is the resulting comparisons that make it possible to discuss relative capability and effectiveness, just as, for example, when considering eighteenth-century India it is appropriate to look not only at the British victory at Plassey in 1757 but also at British defeats, such as Wadgaon in 1779, as well as at major battles between non-Western forces, such as Karnal in 1739 and Third Panipat in 1761.

Reading between the different sieges of the 1680s prevents glib conclusions. Thus, the success for (Christian) Europe indicated by the total defeat of the Ottoman besiegers outside Vienna in 1683 is qualified, albeit to a limited extent, by the English withdrawal from Tangier in 1684 in the face of longstanding Moroccan pressure,[1] and by the successful Chinese sieges of Russian-held Albazin in the Amur valley in 1685 and 1686. More pertinently, the European capacity for capturing major fortresses, displayed in the successful siege of Spanish-held Luxembourg in 1684 by the French with their state-of-the-art siegecraft, was matched by the Mughal capture of the mighty fortresses of Bijapur and Golconda in 1685 and 1687; although, as frequently happened in India (and not only there), betrayal played a decisive role in the fall of Golconda.

Moreover, the sieges of the 1680s indicate the key extent to which conflict was impacted by political contexts and considerations. This was true not simply of the general strategic drives and suppositions, but also of the conduct of wars at the operational and, indeed, tactical levels. Thus, the presence at the siege of Luxembourg of Louis XIV of France reflected not so much military need for his participation as a political drive for monarchs, and thus the dynasty, to be associated with success, one frequently seen with Louis XIII and Louis XIV, as with Louis XIII's presence at the siege of La Rochelle. Much of the drama of majesty and rulership around the world related to victory in war, and this was seen in the public celebration of conflict.

At the global level, this political emphasis requires attention, and indeed discussion at length, in part because it subverts the conventional stress on the role of technology but, more generally, because an understanding of the political dimension makes sense of the purpose and assessment of military operations, and thus of the cross-cultural meanings of capability. Once stated, this point appears obvious, but it is striking how far much operational military history underplays the political dimension once the obligatory passages on the causes of a conflict have been produced.

Technology, therefore, has to be understood as part of a dynamic context that includes the independent or autonomous variables of politics, social structures and pressures, ideology, doctrine and military organisation.[2] This context, however, is underplayed, so that, in the case of fortifications, the combination of an emphasis on technological dominance with Eurocentricity has led to a misleading focus, for the sixteenth and seventeenth centuries, in explaining Western success by means of reference to artillery fortresses[3] – those constructed on the European model of the *trace italienne* with artillery as a key force multiplier for the defence. This focus can indeed be pertinent in the more narrowly military dimension, and notably for the tactics of defence, which helps explain the extent of contemporary publication on fortifications, including finely illustrated works showing fire-lines that provided an explanation of favoured plans, as in Francesco Tensini's *La Fortificatione* ... (Venice, 1630), a book by a military engineer who had planned fortifications in northern Italy. Yet, the standard focus on the artillery fortress underplays the extent to which fortresses, like sieges, served political purposes and were fully understood in that light, both in Europe and more widely. The capability of these fortresses as defensive positions, and as bases for offensive operations, played a role in the matrix of power, but did not dictate it.[4] Moreover, such expensive and difficult-to-maintain structures were not invariably valuable everywhere, and, indeed, less costly systems proved more useful in many contexts, for example the defensive lines the Russians established in the steppes.

The disproportionate nature of the attention devoted to the individual sieges of the 1680s, as well as to other sieges then and in different decades, also indicates the clearly Eurocentric nature of much of the literature. An emphasis on Vienna and, to a far lesser extent, Luxembourg usually drives out discussion of Bijapur and Golconda. This point can be made across the full span of military history,[5] but is also one that is especially unfortunate for particular periods. It is particularly ironic that warfare in Europe dominates the attention of military historians during the seventeenth century, as, despite talk of the Military Revolution, this was not a period in which that warfare, and indeed developments in conflict there on land, transformed Europe's relative capability on the world scale. This point was particularly the case for Michael Roberts's century, 1560–1660, albeit less so subsequently, notably in the Balkans from 1683. French fortifications and siegecraft both improved notably during the reign of Louis XIV (1643–1715), who took a close interest in fortifications and sieges;[6] however, although fortifications, for example Québec and Pondicherry, anchored French colonial presence, neither they nor French siegecraft transformed France's position on the world scale. Indeed, however significant in Europe, French activity was less consequential on this scale than either that of Britain or of Russia. As a reminder of the problems associated with an emphasis on the supposed leading military power – usually France for European commentators from mid-century – Austria, Britain and Russia were each important to warfare against other Christian states and to expansion at the expense of non-Christian polities.[7]

Limited European expansion

More significantly, this was not an age in which the European powers greatly increased their overseas sway. Like all comments, this one can be qualified and refined, although alongside attempts to argue for more significant European developments, it is relevant to note the largely independent character of non-Western developments.[8] An awareness of the limited extent of European expansion can be dramatised by reference to failures and setbacks, which stand as an important qualification of the impression created by the major Ottoman defeat outside Vienna in 1683. Prominent among these European failures are those of the Dutch in Taiwan, the French in Siam (Thailand),[9] the English in Tangier,[10] the Russians in the Amur valley[11] and the Portuguese in Mombasa. The list of European failures culminates with two defeats at the hands of the Ottomans, those of Peter the Great of Russia on the River Pruth in 1711 and of the Venetians in the Morea (Peloponnese) in 1715. The former was more impressive, because Peter had already won considerable renown by his success in totally defeating Charles XII of Sweden at Poltava in 1709. That the Ottomans were more successful than Charles was due to a range of factors, and there is no comparison of like with like; but the comparison is an instructive one, not least because both Charles and Peter rashly advanced into areas where they were outnumbered and lacked logistical support: Ukraine and Bessarabia (modern Moldova) respectively. On the Pruth, Peter came close to suffering the same catastrophe as he had inflicted on Charles: the Ottomans had the Russians trapped against a river, always a vulnerable position (as the Ottomans had fatally experienced at the hands of the Austrians at Zenta in 1697), and could have destroyed them if the Grand Vizier had not preferred to negotiate peace.

The interpretative context for Western failures is usually given as that of European history, European power, and the upward trajectory of the rise of the West. Thus, defeats are smoothed out in terms of a longer-term success, a process also, subsequently and more reasonably, seen with American expansion in North America from 1783. Yet, a more pertinent context is provided, notably for the seventeenth century, by that of the dynamism and variety of military capability and warfare across the world, an approach that does not put the supposed Military Revolution centre stage. As a separate, but related, point, the Europeans were not greatly influenced by other powers, which was a contrast with the situation in Eastern Europe in the fifteenth and, to a lesser extent, sixteenth centuries, but, in turn, their own military systems did not lead to wholesale transformation elsewhere.

In order to understand this process of dynamism in variety and variety in dynamism, it is necessary to see these other powers not as lesser forces that were bound to fail – in, for example, some chronologically receding aspect of what came to be termed the Eastern Question (the fate of the Ottoman empire) – but, instead, as powers that did not operate, and were not considered, in terms of obvious and inevitable failure. A similar point can be made for the eighteenth century, but this point becomes less pertinent from the late 1830s, with the major defeats of China and Egypt at Western hands proving particularly indicative of a major change.

China

If this situation was true, in the seventeenth century, for powers that competed with Western states, it was even more the case for those for whom such competition was non-existent in this period, for example Japan and Burma. Moreover, even if the former category of powers is considered, it is mistaken to imagine that confrontation and conflict with the West necessarily came first in concern, or set the pattern for developments in military capability, a mistake more generally made with the assessment of episodes of warfare between Western and non-Western powers, for example the Crusades that began in the 1090s. China was certainly not as concerned by war with Russia in the 1680s, nor the control of Taiwan, as a Western-centric account, or a discussion of developments in terms of a military revolution defined on European terms, might suggest. Instead, the Chinese were primarily worried about challenges from the steppe: from the Manchu to the north-east in the early seventeenth century and from the Dzhungars in Xiankiang later in the century, and about rebellions, both against Ming rule and, subsequently, the Rebellion of the Three Feudatories. Far from responding to contact with Europeans, Manchu success was important to the subsequent strategic culture and military organisation of China. As a reminder of the significance of tasking for military systems, the size and diversity of Chinese forces and the variety of environments in which they had to fight helps explain why Chinese forces had less standardised equipment than their Western counterparts, and the same was true for Mughal India and the Ottomans. By the end of the seventeenth century, China, unlike the Ottomans (with the Christian Europeans) and, to a now limited extent, the Mughals (with the Marathas), was not threatened on her land and sea frontiers by any power with significant offensive capability. Partly as a result, Chinese fortifications were less concerned with repelling cannon fire than their European counterparts, although, in the mid-nineteenth century, Chinese earth forts were to be surprisingly effective against British warships.

Indians, Ottomans and Persians

For the Indians, the European presence was militarily tangential on land (although not at sea) until the 1740s, and it is unhelpful to consider seventeenth-century developments in terms of what came later. Conflict with the Portuguese and, even more, English was of only local importance. Moreover, the Ottomans remained as worried about Persia, with whom there was to be another serious struggle from the 1720s to the 1740s, repeating that of a century earlier, as about the Western powers. The Persians challenged Ottoman primacy in the world of Islam, not least by encouraging Shi'i heterodoxy within the Ottoman empire, which had a Sunni orthodoxy. Furthermore, the Persians could threaten such key Muslim cities as Baghdad and Mosul, although the Ottomans succeeded in repelling the challenge and did not experience a crisis comparable to that posed for the Mughals by the invasion by Nadir Shah of Persia that led, in 1739, to defeat at Karnal and to the capture of Delhi. Baghdad, a centre of government and economic activity, was more significant for the Ottomans than Buda, let alone Azov, which fell respectively to Austria in 1686 and Russia in 1696. Given the extent to which military relations with the Ottomans are seen as a key instance of the particular sophistication and effectiveness of (Christian) European developments, as in comparisons of successive conflicts between Austria and the Ottomans, it is important to offer a wider consideration of Ottoman military activity, notably with reference to Persia.

Siberia

Alongside the limitations of Western powers, a basis for assessing their capability was provided by their expansion, which was a key aspect of the global dimension of military power, although not the sole one. Until the unsuccessful Ottoman siege of Vienna in 1683, the seventeenth century lacks the drama of the sixteenth in terms of Western success, but there were, nevertheless, important developments. For example, Russian power spread across Siberia to the Pacific, ensuring that China acquired a land frontier with a European state, although the significance of this for China did not become apparent until the 1850s. Moreover, from the 1600s, the English and French took over much of the eastern seaboard of North America, while the Dutch, defeated there by the English, had already won control over some of the key spice-producing regions of the East Indies. The crucial feature in the first two cases was that of demography, in particular in Siberia where the population was small; but in Siberia, North America and the East Indies there was also an absence of any major power capable of mounting a large-scale organised resistance, or, indeed, of intervening to contest Western expansion.

The Russians were attracted into Siberia by its fur, a vital form of wealth and prestige. A vast area, inhabited by nomadic and semi-nomadic peoples, Siberia was subjugated by the Russian construction of forts, while resistance was weakened by local divisions, as well as the higher level of Russian military technology. With their gunpowder weaponry, the Russians had a clear technological edge, and they used firearms effectively to overcome Siberian aborigines and to fight against the remnants of the Tatar Golden Horde, which had earlier held Muscovy to ransom with repeated raiding. The inroads of smallpox also greatly weakened resistance to Russian expansion. Yakutsk was established as a Russian base in 1632, the Pacific was first reached in 1639, and Okhotsk was founded as a base on the coast in 1647.

The Russians were still opposed, however, both by the horsemen of the lands between the Caspian and China, and by the aboriginal peoples of north-eastern Siberia. Military success did not correspond to this hierarchy. Whereas the Russians had a measure of success against the horsemen, they found the conquest of the frozen fastnesses of Siberia an intractable task: distance, climate, terrain and the determination of their opponents more than made up for the superior Russian firepower. Aboriginal people, the Chukchi, the Itelmen and Koryaks, were armed with bone- or stone-tipped arrows and their only firearms were those captured from the Russians. The Russians could anchor their presence with fortresses, but the latter could only achieve so much: although they were difficult for the native peoples to overrun, the fortresses did not really dominate the surrounding countryside and they had to be supplied by vulnerable convoys in a war of ambushes, raids and destruction, not battles.[12]

North America

In North America, the European impact was less sweeping, in large part due to stronger local resistance from a more densely populated Native population benefiting from the extent to which most of North America has a more temperate climate than Siberia. In addition, the Europeans devoted much of their effort to fighting one another, with competition between the English and French providing the key element after the independent Dutch presence was ended in 1674 when the end of the Third Anglo-Dutch War brought an acceptance of England's conquest of Dutch North America. This competition led to conflict in the 1620s and from the late 1680s.

Local resistance to the Europeans in North America was helped by the acquisition of firearms and horses by the Natives, to which (as in West Africa) rivalry among the European powers directly contributed. Firearms were sold in exchange for furs and in an attempt to obtain influence, particularly from the 1640s,[13] and the latter process was encouraged by concern that Native protégés would succumb to local rivals. As experts with bows and arrows, the Native Americans were adept at missile warfare, and thus more readily able to make the transition to muskets, which were easier to aim, and the bullets of which, unlike arrows, were less likely to be deflected by brush, and also could not be dodged. The Natives' general lack of fixed battle positions made it difficult for the Europeans to devise clear military goals, and ensured that there was scant role for volley fire. Native use of weapons and tactics allowed for autonomy on the part of individual warriors,[14] although it is important not to underrate the role of organised tactics and discipline among Native Americans, nor of leadership by officers. Moreover, the ability of the Europeans to travel by sea became less valuable militarily once they moved away from coastal regions.[15]

As with the Portuguese in Angola in Africa, European success in frontier warfare in North America depended on Native assistance or adaptation to the Native way of war. Thus, in King Philip's War in New England in 1675–6, the English colonists moved in loose order, adapted to the available cover, fired at specific targets, and benefited from Native support against rival Natives, who were crushed with considerable savagery. More generally, the clash of military cultures proved a challenge to each side, which encouraged a high level of violence,[16] and the power balance in North America was shifted less by weaponry than by demography: the Europeans came to colonise rather than to trade and they came in increasing numbers, especially the English, who were willing to emigrate overseas in relatively large numbers; more so than the French. There was no comparable emigration from East or South Asia to overseas colonies, not least because there were no such colonies.

In contrast, hit by smallpox and other diseases brought by the Europeans to North America, Native numbers did not grow but, instead, fell greatly, a fall that was important to their economies and military strength. In North America and other parts of the world with limited state development, such as Amazonia, Patagonia, Australasia, the Pacific and parts of South-West Africa, there was no specialisation of the military, and all fit adult males were expected to act as warriors, which increased the significance of disease. As the economies of these regions were also limited, mostly dependent on pastoral or shifting cultivation, they supported only relatively small populations, primitive governmental systems, and a resource base that could carry neither a large army nor what would later be termed a military-industrial complex.

Instead, it was the rising colonial population of Europeans and their ability, thanks to advantages of mobility, logistical support and reinforcement, to concentrate forces at points of conflict, which proved crucial. This was true both along the St Lawrence valley, which was under French control, and on the east coast of North America which, from the 1670s, was under English control north of Florida, where there was a Spanish presence from the 1560s. The three Anglo-Dutch Wars (1652–4, 1665–6 and 1672–4) led to the loss of New Netherland, New Amsterdam being renamed New York. Earlier, New Netherland had absorbed the Swedish colony in North America.

In contrast, expansion was not a theme that meant much in Florida, nor along the northern frontier of New Spain. The subsequent history of Louisiana as a French colony in the eighteenth century showed the difficulty of developing a significant presence in the absence of a large population, although Louisiana also served as the basis for a wide-ranging trading system in the hinterland. The Spaniards could have established posts along the northern shore of the Gulf of Mexico, but there was no obvious threat to their interests there until the 1680s, and no real incentive for them to act. Moreover, further west, the Spaniards were forced out of the Santa Fé region of New Mexico between 1680 and 1692 by the Pueblo Rebellion, which reflected the pressures created by disease, drought, Spanish fiscal demands, and Apache and Navajo raiding, and which was led by a victim of Spanish attempts to suppress Native religion. Santa Fé itself resisted Native American siege in 1680, but then had to be evacuated. Cultural power was significant, and, when Santa Fé was regained by the Spaniards in 1692, there was a reimposition of Catholic control with Franciscan priests absolving Natives for their apostasy and the Governor serving as godfather for children born to the prominent since 1680.

Coastal Asia

Elsewhere, the European impact overseas was also mixed. The power that had the greatest success for much of the century was the United Provinces. The profits made from shipping spices back to Europe led to the foundation of the United East India Company, which was granted a charter giving it political and military powers, including the right to make war, peace and treaties, and to construct fortresses. Jayakĕrta (Djakarta), where the Dutch had a trading base from 1603, became the centre of Dutch power in the East Indies from 1619 after the town was stormed and the forces of Bantam, the local state, defeated. It was renamed Batavia.

Dutch trading interests and maritime power ensured activity in many parts of the world, and the Dutch pressed hard both against rival European powers, notably the Portuguese, and also against non-Western powers, especially in South-East Asia. The Dutch were even willing to challenge China, although this challenge was much less serious than those from Japan (in Korea) in the 1590s and the Manchu from the 1610s. A Chinese fleet intimidated a Dutch squadron into abandoning the offshore Penghu Islands (Pescadores) in 1604, only for another Dutch fleet in 1622 to occupy the islands and to begin to construct a fort. The Dutch also threatened to attack the Chinese coast unless the Chinese accepted their commercial demands, and a refusal to comply led to Dutch attacks on towns and shipping later that year. In 1623, a compromise reached by local representatives was rejected by their superiors on both sides, and the Dutch tried to capture Chinese ships bound for Manila, the Spanish centre in the Philippines and a major commercial entrepôt. Early in 1624, the Dutch raided the Chinese coast, but the Chinese sent a large force that occupied most of the main island of the archipelago and cut the fort off from its water supplies, which led the Dutch to agree to evacuate the position. They did not subsequently attempt to reverse their loss.

The value of garrison positions and European weaponry in a different context was revealed in 1603 at Manila, when a rebellion against Spanish rule by the large Chinese population who lived outside the city led to an assault on its walls. Reliant on the traditional methods of siege towers and ladders, the untrained Chinese were beaten off by the musket and cannon fire of the garrison, and their towers were destroyed. Subsequently, in the face of Spanish sorties, the Chinese fled, only to be hunted down and about 15,000–25,000 killed. Another Chinese rising in 1639 was brutally suppressed while, in 1662, the danger of Chinese invasion of the Philippines, at a time of vulnerability after the fall of the Dutch bases on Taiwan, led to a fresh massacre.

Military strength was a key guarantor of control, but other factors were also involved: in 1652, the firepower of 150 Dutch musketeers cut short a Chinese rebellion in Taiwan, although the Dutch also benefited from the help of the indigenous population who were opposed to the Chinese immigrants. Indeed, the Dutch ability to play off these two groups while seeking allies among them was important to their success.[17] Fortifications anchored the European presence. In 1628–9, the Dutch base of Batavia on Java survived two sieges by Sultan Agung of Mataram, while Goa, the leading Portuguese base in India, successfully resisted attacks by the Sultanate of Bijapur in 1654 and 1659, and by the Marathas in 1683.

Nevertheless, less well-fortified Portuguese positions fell to Asian attack. Hormuz, which lacked adequate artillery, fell to the Safavids of Persia in 1622 and the Portuguese were also driven from many of their positions in India and the Bay of Bengal. After a siege in 1632, Selim Shah of Arakan forced Portuguese adventurers to abandon their positions on Sandwip Island and at Chittagong and Dianga. The Mughal Governor of Bengal took Hughli. In the 1650s, Sivappa Nayaka of Ikkeri captured the Portuguese positions on the Kanara coast of India – Honawar, Basrur, Gangolli and Mangalore – while, in 1662, Golconda took the Portuguese post at São Tomé. Thus, the Portuguese presence declined nearly as much due to Indian as Dutch and English attacks. The tiny size of the Portuguese garrisons contributed greatly to these losses.

Africa

Such losses reflected the vulnerability of positions that were weakly garrisoned and lacked support from within the balance of local political forces. In addition, there were other important aspects of European military failure. The Portuguese experience in Sri Lanka and Africa revealed the limitations of European land warfare outside its home continent. Their attempts to operate from bases in coastal Sri Lanka into the interior and in Mozambique up the River Zambezi both failed. Portuguese adventurers sought to gain control of the upper Zambezi, but could not prevail against larger forces that were well attuned to fighting in the region. The attempt to exploit the civil wars in Mutapa (modern Zimbabwe) was thwarted in the 1690s, with Changamira of Buta, the head of the Rozwi empire, driving the

Portuguese from the plateau in 1693: they retreated to their base of Tete on the lower Zambezi.

The warfare indicated the extent to which there was no clear distinction between European and non-European forces. The adventurers raised private armies from among their slaves and offered their services as merc- enaries in the civil wars in Mutapa, sometimes with two adventurers serving on opposite sides. In exchange, they were given what amounted to revenue assignments, which they then represented in Portugal as land grants, and they levered their way into having them recognised by the Portuguese crown. The adventurers never really operated independently in the local wars, instead always co-operating with an African ruler whose authority they accepted and recognised, a form of shared power that was typical of Africa and South Asia. Shared power and delegated sovereignty could be means by which European power advanced, as with France and Britain in the eighteenth century, but no such advance resulted from Portuguese initiatives in East Asia.

In Angola, moreover, the Portuguese were effective only in combina- tion with African soldiers. Unlike the nineteenth-century pattern of European-organised units filled with African recruits, the Portuguese in seventeenth-century Angola were all organised together into a single unit with its own command structure, while the Africans, either mercenaries, subject rulers or allies, were separately organised in their own units with their own command structure. It was only at the level of the army as a whole that Portuguese officers had command, providing control for entire operations.

The Portuguese found the Africans well armed, with well-worked iron weapons, as good in some ways as Portuguese steel weaponry, and certainly better than the native wood and obsidian weapons of the New World. Both the slow rate of fire of Portuguese muskets and the openness of African fight- ing formations reduced the effectiveness of the Portuguese firearms; their inability to deploy anything larger than a small force of cavalry ensured that they could not counter this open order; and their cannon had little impact on African earthwork fortifications. As in North America, further- more, firearms were diffused rapidly, and Africans possibly even had them in equal numbers as early as the 1620s; certainly quantities of them were reported in 1626–8 in the first war against the formidable Queen Njinga of Ndongo, who challenged the Portuguese position in Angola.

The value of firearms was limited, especially in the absence of combined forces. The Portuguese victory over the shield-bearing heavy infantry of the kingdom of Kongo at the battle of Mbumbi (1622) was the result of overwhelming numerical superiority, notably due to alliance with the

Imbangala, cannibal mercenaries, and not of weapons superiority, and the Portuguese army withdrew very quickly and even returned captured slaves when the main Kongolese army reached the region. In 1618, the Portuguese had allied with the Imbangala in order to overcome the kingdom of Ndongo, storming its capital in 1619.

When, however, they were left without African light infantry, Portuguese forces could well be destroyed, as by the forces of Queen Njinga at the battle of Ngolomene (1644). In contrast, the combination of Africans and European infantry, with its body armour and swordsmanship as well as firepower, was effective, as in the Portuguese victories over Njinga at Cavanga (1646) and over Antonio I of Kongo at Ambuila (1665). In the latter, the Portuguese deployed 400 Europeans and 4000 African slave soldiers. Antonio was killed during the battle and thousands of Kongo slave soldiers were captured. As a reminder that Europeans enjoyed no monopoly of firearms, Antonio's army included a small force of musketeers, as well as two cannon. The Portuguese victory at Ambuila has attracted attention, but Kongo did not collapse rapidly and, indeed, the Portuguese attempt to intervene in the Kongolese civil war led to a disastrous defeat at Kitombo (1670) which ended the initiative.[18]

In addition, a long series of wars against the kingdom of Ndongo that had begun in 1579 ended in stalemate for the Portuguese in the 1680s. After they took Pungo Andongo in a difficult siege in 1672 (and at considerable cost), the policy of the Portuguese in the African interior shifted away from large-scale wars aimed at conquest, and central Angola was not to be conquered by Portugal until the late nineteenth century. As a reminder of the constant issue of logistics, Portugal would have found it difficult to carry war much further east against any sort of organised and determined resistance because of the need for extended supply lines. The same was true of operations to the north (into Kongo), and the period of quiescence from the 1680s in part reflected acceptance of the fact.

Portuguese weakness in Africa, together with the contrasting strength of rival, non-Western slave powers, was demonstrated in East Africa. Fort Jesus, the mighty Portuguese position in Mombasa built in 1593, fell in 1631 to a surprise storming by Sultan Muhammad Yusuf of Mombasa, and an expedition by the Portuguese from their major Indian base of Goa failed to regain it in 1632, although they were able to return when the Sultan abandoned the fortress under the pressure of Portuguese attack. However, as part of more general problems for the Portuguese around the Indian Ocean,[19] the Portuguese presence then succumbed to a new regional power. The Omani Arabs captured the Portuguese base of Muscat in 1650, and pressed hard on East Africa from the 1660s in a demonstration of the extent to which the dynamic elements were not only European. In 1661, the Omanis sacked Mombasa but avoided Fort Jesus, and in 1670 pillaged the Portuguese base of Mozambique only to be repulsed by the fortress garrison. Fort Jesus finally fell in 1698, but the siege had lasted since 1696 and the Omanis had no siege artillery. The Portuguese, instead, were weakened by beri-beri and other diseases that killed most of the garrison. The Portuguese presence north of Mozambique was thus lost, and a European territorial presence on the Swahili coast of East Africa did not resume until the 1880s when Germany and Britain established bases there.

In part, the contrasting fate of the Portuguese on the eastern and western coasts of Africa was linked to the different size of their respective presences, but there was also a significant contrast between the effective maritime capability and links of their opponents in the Indian Ocean and the very different situation in the Atlantic. This contrast affected slaving, with the Indian Ocean used by Arab slavers who then penetrated into the African interior, a situation that did not pertain in the Atlantic.

The fall of Fort Jesus gives an impression of European weakness, but it is more realistic to see imperial boundaries as in flux, with contrary pressures from other empires and, more commonly, from both sub-regional powers and autonomous interests within the empire. Indeed, further north, Ottoman power in what is now the eastern part of Saudi Arabia, established in 1550, was overthrown in 1670 as a result of the Banu Khalid rebellion in the region of Hasa, and the Ottomans did not regain control of the region until the 1870s. As a reminder that boundaries of control varied, but also overlapped, the Ottomans, in modern Saudi Arabia, did not exercise power in the region of the Najd between Hijaz and Hasa, but, instead, there was a distant hegemonic influence over the tribal confederations and self-governing oases of the area. Producing little agricultural surplus, Najd was unattractive not only to the Ottomans but also to the autonomous regional powers, the Sharifs of Mecca and the Banu Khalid of Hasa, and this issue underlined the limited appeal of extending control over the region. Moreover, Ottoman activity tended to respond to threats, and, in their absence, there was no need for expansion.[20]

Thus, developments in weaponry, tactics and force structures interacted and overlapped with those in often complex political arrangements. This was true for the Western powers and for others. New and extended administrative structures could be more significant for the extension of power than changes in fighting method. This situation was seen with the southward spread of Russian power across the steppe, which was less related to the field army than to the extension of the *voevoda* system of local government which greatly increased the power of the central chancellery over resources at the local level. This power furthered the policy of establishing military colonies near the frontier, and thus of strengthening it and providing a capability to operate beyond, a process that was significant for this southward spread.[21]

Moreover, all powers were affected by the development of new military forms among their opponents. For example, African warfare was changed by the spread of firearms which led to an increasing preponderance of fire-power over hand-to-hand combat. Earlier in West Africa, armies had fought in close order, with javelin-men in the front line and archers behind, provid-ing overhead fire. The javelins could be thrown or used as pikes, and the javelin-men were also equipped with swords, so that they were able to fight as individuals in 'open' order. Shock warfare prevailed. Lacking shields and therefore vulnerable, the archers were essentially support troops, and the bow lacked the prestige of the javelin and sword, which conveyed greater warrior status.

From the mid-seventeenth century on, however, the role of archers increased in Akwamu and Denkyira, inland states of West Africa, and, as firepower became more important, this led to a more open formation and a wider battle frontage, with archers in the front line flanking the javelin-men. Thus, missile tactics came to prevail in West Africa even before the wide-spread use of firearms – the former, as in North America, helping ease the eventual path of the latter. The new emphasis on archers spread in West Africa, for example to the kingdom of Asante (in the interior of modern Ghana) in the 1670s. Javelin-men came to play a tactical role subordinate to that of the bowmen, and, between the 1660s and the 1690s, the javelin was discarded as a weapon, becoming (like the halberd in Europe) essentially ceremonial.

In turn, the bow came to be supplanted by the musket. Firearms came into use in Africa over a long time span, in part because usage was restricted by the limited availability of shot and powder – an instance of the extent to which the regional parameters of warfare were affected by the implications of technological developments, although these parameters could also be shaped by trade. The use of firearms in West Africa was first reported, in the fifteenth century, in Kano (in modern Nigeria), which was one of the Islamic Hausa city-states that traded across the Sahara, although a regular force of musketeers was not organised there until the 1770s. In contrast, on the West African coast, the Asebu army of the 1620s was the first to include a corps of musketeers, their guns being supplied by the Dutch as a means to advance commercial interests; and muskets replaced bows on the coast in the 1650s to 1670s. However, the tactical shift there towards open-order fighting did not come until later: initially, musketeers were used as a shield for the javelin-men, and tactics centred on gunfire were slow to develop in the coastal armies. Firepower, though, did increase in the 1680s and 1690s, as flintlock muskets replaced matchlocks, but bayonets were not used. In the forest interior of West Africa, muskets replaced bows in the 1690s and 1700.[22]

As part of a process of large-scale change in West Africa, the emphasis on missile weapons, bows and, later, muskets, interacted with socio-economic changes and in particular with the transformation of peasants into militarily effective soldiers, a development that led to the formation of mass armies and to wars that lasted longer. Warfare based on earlier shock tactics had been selective in its manpower requirements, but, on the Gold Coast (coastal modern Ghana) and the Slave Coast (coastal modern Togo and Benin, formerly Dahomey), the replacement of shock by missile tactics was linked to a shift from élite forces relying on individual prowess to larger units. In the states of Akwamu and Denkyira, all males fit to bear arms were eligible for conscription, although in Dahomey there was an emphasis on a small standing army. Larger armies increased the numbers that could be captured in conflicts, which took place over much wider areas and which could yield large numbers of slaves, helping fuel the slave trade across the Atlantic to North and South America.

These military changes were related to the rise of the states of Akwamu and Asante on the Gold Coast and Dahomey on the Slave Coast, and perhaps to the late seventeenth-century expansion of Oyo further east. These powerful states were to have a very great impact on European options in West Africa, serving as a reminder that any discussion of the relationships, and specifically military balance, between Western and non-Western powers should not centre simply on initiatives by the former. Indeed, unlike Portugal, other Western powers did not try to make conquests in sub-Saharan Africa, other than of other European bases. Thus, the European presence in West Africa was anchored by coastal forts that served as protected bases for trade, although, in some areas, there were no settlements and the traders operated from their ships. These bases were vulnerable: the Dutch position at Offra and the French one at Glehue were destroyed in 1692, the Danish base at Christiansborg fell in 1693, and the secondary British base at Sekondi in 1694, although the leading British base at Cape Coast Castle was never taken, and was successfully defended against African attack in 1688.

The garrisons of the European forts were very small, and they relied upon the forces of African allies both for their own security and for their capacity to intervene in local conflicts. As a result, the emphasis was on co-operation and not on conquest. For example, the Swedish African Company was able to play a role in the 1650s on the Gold Coast because the Futu élite wanted to balance the influence of the Dutch West India Company, and this military, political and commercial co-operation was crucial to the establishment of new trading posts.[23] The military situation was thus an aspect of the more general character of the slave trade, one in which local co-operation was crucial.[24] Indeed, slavery entailed the interaction of the economic order and the dynamics of African warfare, with the victims of the latter caught in the middle.[25] Moreover, in so far as comparisons can be made, European slave traders did not enjoy coercive advantages in Africa any greater than those of their Arab counterparts on the Indian Ocean coast of Africa, while the coercive advantages of Moroccan and other slave raiders operating across the Sahara Desert, and from the *sahel* belt south of the Sahara into the forested regions further south, were probably superior. The major European advantage rested not on force or superior military capability, but on a purchasing power that derived from the prosperity of plantation economies in the Americas shipping goods back to Europe, and thus on the integrated nature of the Atlantic economy. Purchasing was crucial because, whereas warfare between African powers provided large numbers of slaves, European powers were not able to seize significant numbers.

North Africa

European weakness in Africa was also seen in North Africa, where there was no resumption of the conquest to which Portugal and Spain had devoted much effort in the fifteenth and sixteenth centuries. Positions that had been held or dominated then, such as Algiers, Biserta, Bona, Bougia, Tripoli and Tunis, were no longer under control, Tunis falling to the Ottomans in 1574, although in 1600 Tangier, Ceuta, Melilla and Oran were key points all ruled by Philip III of Spain. The Spaniards launched naval expeditions against the Barbary pirates, including in 1601, 1602 and 1609, but territorial gains were few, although Larache on the Moroccan coast was captured in 1610. Moreover, under Sultan Muley-Ismael (r. 1672–1727), Moroccan pressure drove the Spaniards from bases at La Mamora (1681), Larache (1689) and Arzila (1691), and the English in 1684 from Tangier. The latter had been acquired alongside Bombay as part of the dowry of Charles II's wife, Catherine of Braganza. The contrasting fate of the two bases is instructive, and, in part, reflects the greater determination of the regional power in North Africa, Morocco, to enforce its territorial position, compared to the more porous approach to power and presence in India where the English were able to retain Bombay. The Spaniards held onto

Ceuta despite the lengthy Moroccan siege of 1694–1720, but the siege indicated the direction of pressure.

Major Western powers maintained their ability to project naval strength successfully against North Africa in an attempt to contain its piracy, and in 1682, 1683 and 1688 Algiers was heavily bombarded by the French, as was Tripoli in 1685, while, under the threat of bombardment, Tunis agreed to return all French captives. This pressure, however, was still a long way from the ability to project power successfully on land, and also very different to the situation in the nineteenth century, when the French occupied Algiers and Tunis in 1830 and 1881 respectively. In part, this contrast reflected the earlier commitment of European powers to conflict in Europe, as when Oran was captured in 1708 by the Algerians from a Spain then affected by civil war and foreign intervention in the War of the Spanish Succession. However, it would be mistaken to see conflict in North Africa simply in these terms since Spain, when at peace in Europe, still failed in major attacks on Algiers in 1775 and 1784.

The political dimension

The balance of capability between Western and non-Western forces was complex and cannot be simply read back from the results of campaigns. Instead, a range of political, commercial and military factors were involved, as with the successful pressure by the Mughal ruler Aurangzeb against the English East India Company's base at Bombay in 1686. This pressure, which led the Governor to submit, as well as the English problems in expanding north to Calcutta in 1688–9, are reminders that the narrative is complex and, as a result, an analysis predicated on European capability and development is questionable, Whiggish and teleological, a conclusion for this book that is repeatedly probed from a number of perspectives. The political dimension recurred frequently with alliances proving a key currency of military failure and success, and it is necessary therefore to see both failure and success as shared, rather than as a simple product of European capability. Far from it being a case of the West versus the Rest, European forces were generally explicitly or tacitly allied with a group of native leaders who used their European military connections for their own purposes. Often misunderstood by the Europeans, the use of these connections had very important consequences in the context of local politics.

These connections could be readily seen in the East Indies, modern Indonesia. In 1605, in the Moluccas, Dutch support for the Hituese led the Portuguese to surrender their fort of Ambon, and Sultan Zaide of Ternate received Dutch assistance in driving the Portuguese from their forts on the islands of Ternate and Tidore, although, in 1606, a Spanish expedition defeated the allies and left a garrison on Ternate. The Sultanate of Gowa in Sulawesi (the Celebes) was only subjugated by the Dutch in 1669 after protracted struggles, and Dutch success owed much to the assistance of a local ruler, the Buginese leader Arung Palakka, who handled much of the fighting on land, and whose men inflicted most of the casualties. The Dutch, nevertheless, contributed 600 troops to the attack on the Makassarese citadel and also provided 21 ships that defeated the Makassarese fleet. The final peace awarded the Dutch the Makassarese fort of Ujungpandang, which they renamed Rotterdam.[26] On Java in 1678–81, Dutch forces moved into the interior, but in alliance with Amangkurat II of Mataram against rebels.

The Dutch also relied on local support in South Asia, so that, in southern India in 1639, the Portuguese and Dutch took opposite sides in the conflict among Vijayanagara grandees, while, in Sri Lanka, the Dutch from 1638 allied with Rajasimha II of the inland kingdom of Kandy against the Portuguese who already were under heavy pressure from Kandy. In a striking reminder of the degree to which many battles are neglected, the Portuguese army in Sri Lanka fell victim to an ambush by the Kandyan forces in the battle of Randeniwela in 1630 and the Captain-General was killed. In 1638, there was another defeat and the death of another Captain-General. Allied with the Dutch, Kandy, with Dutch help, took the Portuguese coastal positions of Galle and Negombo in 1640. The Dutch had no such success against Kandy later in the century.

In the Persian Gulf, Shah Abbas had used the English desire to trade with Persia and English rivalry with Spain in order to obtain English support against Hormuz. Deprived of a friendly hinterland after the Safavids over-ran the mainland possessions of the indigenous ruler of Hormuz, and of naval support by English action, Hormuz proved very vulnerable to Persian attack in 1622.

Furthermore, as another instance of the significance of the political dimension, the Europeans could only achieve so much through military success. Relations with land powers that controlled overland communi-cation routes, sources of goods and access to markets were vital to the success of European projects and positions. The role of these Asian powers and the nature of the trading system ensured that much Indian Ocean trade remained outside the reach of European power. When the Europeans gained control of ports they found it difficult to retain their trade, let alone to create a monopoly. Thus, Malacca proved of limited value to the Portuguese, while customs revenue from Goa fell in the early seventeenth century. In turn, these factors affected the ability of the Portuguese to support military activity.

Ottomans and Christians

A Whiggish approach is encouraged, however, by knowledge of eventual Western dominance in the late nineteenth century, with the British, for example, finally overcoming Kandy in 1815 as a result of concerted operations by independently moving columns. Moreover, the perspective of the late eighteenth century is significant, as the relative Western position was indeed stronger then, notably in India, although not yet as far as China was concerned. The emphasis on Western success is encouraged by the major impression created by the serious Ottoman defeat outside Vienna in 1683, a defeat that ended Ottoman advances on that city and one that understandably plays a major role in the literature, not least due to the preference for dramatic episodes and the quest for apparent turning points. This preference is such that scholarly history makes only a modest impact on public perception, and this perception is encouraged by the willingness of popular publishers and the media to focus on this Ottoman defeat and not on Western failures, as in 2008 when a popular account, Andrew Wheatcroft's *The Enemy at the Gate: Habsburgs, Ottomans and the Battle for Europe*, received extensive coverage. The BBC went on to devote one of its *In Our Time* radio programmes to the episode.

In reality, the flow of Ottoman–Western campaigning was more complex, although, by 1700, the Ottoman position was far worse than had been the case in 1600. In the Thirteen Years' War of 1593–1606, the Ottomans had displayed significant resilience, not least as they were also at war with Persia and faced by rebellion (especially in Anatolia), but they were greatly handicapped by political problems in Constantinople. In addition, as with the contemporaneous conflicts in East and South Asia, the political dimension was also important to military operations, as each 'side' proved more porous than any discussion in terms of a 'clash of civilisation' between Christendom and Islam might suggest. For example, the rebellion of a tributary ruler, Prince Michael of Wallachia, posed a particular problem for the Ottomans and, in 1599–1600, he overran first Transylvania and then Moldavia, but Ottoman–Polish action in 1601–5 restored Ottoman suzerainty. While the Austrian forces in the Thirteen Years' War responded to military developments, notably with the speedy rise in the use of muskets,[27] Ottoman war making also saw tactical development, not least with an increase in the infantry in order to deliver more firepower. Moreover, the *janissaries* were able to deliver volley fire by 1605, possibly as a result of the diffusion of Western techniques, though also possibly as a result of their developing the new technique themselves.[28]

The Ottomans were also helped by their ability to draw on wide-ranging imperial resources as well as an effective arms industry.[29] An efficient supply system moved food from Hungary to the front, being helped by the rivers that flow north–south: beyond Belgrade, men, supplies and equipment were transported along the Danube or the Tisza. Troops could march the 600 miles (965 kilometres) from Constantinople to Buda in six weeks, drawing for provisions on 40 depots. Magazines were set up by the army establishment in the conflict zone. The soldiers were well fed, receiving meat regularly, and the pay was not generally in arrears, in contrast to the situation across most of Christendom. Thus, the 'Ottoman road', from Constantinople to Buda and beyond, ensured that Ottoman military administration was more efficient than that of other European powers.[30]

At the same time, it would be mistaken to put the emphasis for Ottoman resilience solely on changes in force structure and the development of administrative mechanisms, because, like other powers, they could not meet the range of military requirements and also faced difficulties in drawing on the resources of a society that was not bureaucratised by late nineteenth century, let alone modern, standards. Moreover, alongside more infantry firepower, the light cavalry provided by the Khan of the Crimean Tatars, a tributary ruler, was particularly significant, not least in the Ottoman–Polish war of 1620–1, a fast-moving conflict involving light cavalry and fortified camps. The political dimension was also important in the successful closing stages of the Thirteen Years' War, in that Ottoman success, under an effective new commander, Lala Mehmed Pasha, in regaining Pest (1604) and capturing Esztergom (Gran) and Visegard (1605), owed much to the extent to which Austrian policies of Catholicisation had prompted resistance, with Ottoman support, in Protestant areas of Hungary and Transylvania.[31]

The Ottomans focused on war with the Persians in the 1620s and 1630s, regaining Baghdad in 1638 after unsuccessful sieges in 1625–6 and 1630. However, in 1645, a major conflict began in the Mediterranean when the Ottomans invaded the Venetian island-colony of Crete, which lay athwart the key grain-supply route from the port of Alexandria in Egypt to the Ottoman capital of Constantinople (Istanbul). This episode provided a classic example of the clash between continental and maritime power, but, in the case of the Ottomans, the continental, army-based empire also had a formidable maritime capability. Sultan Ibrahim assembled a massive force of 348 ships and 51,000 soldiers (7000 *janissaries*, 14,000 *spahis*, 30,000 artillery infantry, sappers and servants) that landed on the island on 23 June 1645. Khania (Canea) was rapidly captured, and in 1646 Apokoroni and Rethymnon followed, but the siege of the capital, Iraklion (Candia), which began in 1647, lasted until 1669. The Venetians sent reinforcements, including 33,000 German mercenaries, while political divisions undermined the Ottoman war effort, which also faced serious logistical problems.

In order to block Ottoman supply links, the Venetians sought to blockade the Dardanelles from 1647 – leading, in 1648, to the overthrow of Sultan Ibrahim – and again from 1650. An Ottoman fleet which evaded the blockade was defeated off the island of Naxos in 1651, while on 26 June 1656, despite the Ottoman fleet having galleons as well, the Venetians largely destroyed it off the Dardanelles, an instance of the importance of maritime choke-points to battle at sea. This was the most serious Ottoman naval defeat since Lepanto in 1571. However, the vigorous Mehmed Köprülü, who became Grand Vizier in the subsequent political crisis, rapidly rebuilt the fleet, and in 1657 the Ottomans were able to resupply their forces in Crete.

Pressure on the Ottomans in another direction resumed in 1661 when Habsburg forces under Raimondo Montecuccoli intervened in Transylvania, a frequently unstable border zone, to assist a rebellion under Janos Kemeny against the Ottomans. This intervention was unsuccessful and provoked Ottoman attacks on Austria. Montecuccoli repelled the 1663 attack, but, in 1664 the Ottomans advanced anew under the Grand Vizier, Fazil Ahmed, the son and successor of Mehmed Köprülü. He was blocked at St Gotthard on 1 August by Montecuccoli, who was supported by German contingents as well as French troops sent by Louis XIV. The Ottoman forces, prevented from advancing across the river Raab, lost their cannon, but avoided a rout. Far, however, from leading to a lengthy struggle, the war was speedily terminated by the Peace of Vasvar (1664), with an Austrian agreement to respect the Ottoman position in Transylvania.

Fazil Ahmed then personally led a renewed effort to take Candia. The Venetians were greatly outnumbered at sea and the Ottoman fleet cut off the flow of reinforcements from Christian Europe. In 1669, a quarrel between the Venetians and their European allies in the garrison led the latter to retire and forced the Venetians to capitulate. All the churches in Candia were destroyed bar four which were transformed into mosques.[32] This lengthy struggle made a great impact in Christian Europe, not least because of the major efforts to support Candia. The publications that discussed the siege, such as Matthäus Merian's *Das lange bestrittene Königreich Candia* (Frankfurt, 1670) and Johann Scheither's *Novissima Praxis Militaris* (Braunschweig, 1672), which contained a detailed account, did not convey any sense of the Ottomans as redundant militarily.

In the 1670s, the Ottomans also successfully advanced against the Poles and the Russians, as all three struggled for dominance of Ukraine. After an impressive resistance by John Sobieski in 1673 and 1675–6, Podolia, part of western Ukraine, was ceded to the Ottomans by Poland as the price of peace in 1676, and, in 1681, Russia agreed to pay an annual tribute to the Khan of the Crimean Tatars as the cost of retaining eastern Ukraine and

Kiev, which had been gained from Poland in the war of 1654–67. Traditional Russian musketeer units, the *streltsy*, fared badly in the Russo-Ottoman War of 1677–81, and the artillery, though numerous, was ill equipped and mismanaged. The war, which focused on control of the fortress of Chigirin, marked a reorientation of Russian policy in Ukraine away from conflict with Poland and towards that with the Ottomans and their allies.

Russian difficulties were in part an aspect of the more general problem of steppe conflict in which the tactical and operational aspects of cavalry warfare had profound effects on the strategic understanding of what constituted victory. In particular, warfare in the steppes, where there were few strongholds (which helped explain the importance of Chotin, in 1621, and Chigirin and Kiev), relied upon very relative degrees of victory: conditions were extremely fluid and the enemy could always ride away, which made it difficult to control the situation militarily, so that often it could only be contained. Neither holding territory nor defeating armies in the field were necessarily viable. Instead, subsidies and genocide were two possibilities, both of which, but especially the former, were employed at times in Chinese relations with their neighbours. The Russians were eventually to overcome the problem of the steppe and indeed, in 1783, to conquer the Crimea; but, in the 1670s, their success was limited, and this gave the Ottomans more options.

A revolt in those parts of Hungary ruled by the Habsburgs encouraged Kara Mustafa, the Grand Vizier, to negotiate peace with Russia in 1681 and to begin aiding the rebels. His support for war with Austria reflected his belief that the prestige to be gained from victory would strengthen his position. At the same time, although the views of individuals, especially Kara Mustafa and Mehmed IV, were important, there were also broader social developments explaining war, notably the synergetical relationship between Ottoman military activity and the interests of the provincial élite. Cultural factors included the focus of opposition to infidels on the Catholic centre of Vienna, which thus gave point to the bellicosity of the Ottoman regime. The possibility that the Hungarian rebels under Imre Thököly would serve as the basis for a Hungarian client state able to protect Ottoman borders seems more rational in modern terms, but would also have lessened the power of the Catholic empire. That the Ottomans believed Austria to be weak can only have encouraged the attack. Known Ottoman sources are limited, but, hopefully, more information will emerge from research.

The siege of Vienna

Worried by the prospect of renewed French attack on the Rhine, Leopold I, the Habsburg ruler, was reluctant to fight the Ottomans, but the preparations and advance of the latter, encouraged by French promises to the Ottomans that they would not help Austria, forced Leopold to action. The main Ottoman force left Adrianople on 31 March 1683, reaching Belgrade on 3 May, and appeared before the Austrian fortress of Győr on 2 July. The heavily outnumbered Austrians retreated, but Kara Mustafa, rather than besieging Győr, which would have been the priority in the Thirteen Years' War, was determined to march directly on Vienna. As panic mounted, Leopold and his court left Vienna on 7 July, which was surrounded by the Ottomans on 16 July. This date, however, was already fairly late in the year for a successful campaign, not least as the defences, ably improved by Georg Rimpler, were not suited for a general assault but required a siege.

While a relief force gathered, the Ottomans began building siegeworks using both bombardment and mines to weaken the defences. The mines were particularly threatening and were designed to create breaches that would prepare the ground for assaults. The garrison suffered heavy casualties in its defence as well as losses from dysentery. In turn, the Ottomans, who were poorly prepared for a siege of such a powerful position with a very deep moat and large ramparts, suffered similarly; but, during August, the city's outer defences, where not covered by water features, steadily succumbed, although the Ottomans, lacking heavy-calibre cannon, were outgunned by the defenders. As a result, the Ottomans relied on undermining the defences, which they did with some success, leading to breaches in which there was bitter fighting. On 4 September, the garrison fired distress rockets to urge the relief army to action.

It built up, first with German contingents and, then, with the crucial addition of a large Polish force of 21,000 troops under the king, John Sobieski, who assumed overall command: the Poles provided about 31 per cent of the relief force. The arrival of the Poles also contributed to the morale of this force. On 9 September, the relief army advanced through the Vienna woods. Though aware of this deployment, Kara Mustafa made little preparation for the attack, which was successfully mounted on 12 September, and this lack of preparation was a key failure of his generalship. The battle involved heavy fighting and the Ottoman centre put up a particularly determined resistance; however, helped by the advantage of height as they advanced from the Vienna woods, as well as by divisions among the Ottoman commanders, the Christian forces on the left and right broke through.

The conquest of Hungary

The crushing Ottoman defeat was very different to Suleiman the Magnificent's failure to take the city in 1529, which had been a check, not a disaster.[33] Instead, defeat in 1683 was followed by a fundamental change in the European balance of power and one that illustrated the ability of armies to deliver decisive results. Unlike in 1664, Austrian success brought military and political consequences. On 1 November 1683, Sobieski captured Gran, a long-contested position, and, the following March, Leopold, Sobieski, Pope Innocent XI and Venice formed a Holy League, which Russia joined in 1686. In practice, co-operation and co-ordination between the allies were limited, but the maintenance of pressure by allies provided an important guarantee of Ottoman weakness. Challenged on several fronts and also suffering from domestic discontent, the Ottomans were in a poor position to resist the Austrian advance, and this factor needs to be underlined when considering the reason for Ottoman defeat.[34]

In 1684, Charles V of Lorraine besieged Buda, the most important point between Vienna and Belgrade and the key to Hungary, but, although an Ottoman relief attempt was blocked, the fortress was a strong one with many cannon, and disease and supply difficulties hampered the four-month siege which was eventually abandoned. In 1685, although financial problems obliged Leopold to cut his army by 20,000 men,[35] Charles defeated an Ottoman force at Gran; Neuhäusel (Ersek Ujvár), a lesser fort which allowed the Ottomans to threaten Moravia, was successfully stormed; and the pro-Ottoman revolt in upper Hungary collapsed. The Ottomans sued for peace, but would not accept the Austrian terms which required their withdrawal from Hungary. In 1685–6, the English envoy in Constantinople, James, 8th Lord Chandos, sought to explain Ottoman failure. Claiming that 'they had no military discipline', Chandos also argued that they were not numerous enough, whereas, in the past, 'their prodigious vast multitudes of men that by the weight of flesh bore down all their enemies before them' showed greater spirit in battle.[36]

In 1686, Buda was again attacked by the Austrians under Charles of Lorraine. A shell landed on the main powder magazine on 22 July, blowing open a breach in the walls; Charles turned back a relief attempt, and repeated assaults then led to the fall of the city on 3 September after a brave defence by the Ottomans under Abdurrahman Pasha. The pressure was sustained. On 12 August 1687, Charles of Lorraine defeated the Grand Vizier at Berg Harsan (Harkány) and captured Esseg, and the cumulative strain of defeat led to a rebellion that drove Mehmed IV from his throne; while, by the end of 1688, Szegedin, Belgrade and the major positions of Transylvania had been captured by the Austrians. The collapse of the Ottoman position in the Balkans and an Austrian advance into the Greek Orthodox world appeared imminent. The Austrians developed links with rebellious elements among the Bulgarians and Serbs and began negotiations with the Prince of

Wallachia, an Ottoman client-ruler. In 1689, Ludwig Wilhelm of Baden had only 24,000 troops with which to face the Ottomans, but he defeated their main force south of Belgrade, and advanced to Nish, despite orders to remain on the defensive. The Austrians pressed on to seize the towns of Vidin, Pristina and Skopje, and to reach Bucharest, and the overthrow of the Ottoman position appeared to be total. In April 1690, indeed, Leopold issued an appeal for the support of all Balkan peoples against the Ottoman empire and promised them liberty, under his rule as King of Hungary.

The Ottomans were also under pressure on other fronts. Russian advances on the Crimea in 1687 and 1689 failed with heavy losses, in part due to serious logistical problems, but the Poles conquered Podolia (southwestern Ukraine) and campaigned against the Ottomans in Moldavia, and the Venetians, in 1685–6, exploited an anti-Ottoman revolt in the Morea (Peloponnese), seizing the key positions. In 1687, the Venetians moved north to capture the towns of Lepanto, Patras and Athens, where the Ottoman magazine in the Parthenon was blown up by a mortar shell.[37]

The late 1680s may have offered the best opportunity for driving the Ottomans from all or most of the Balkans until the nineteenth century, but, from 1688, the Austrians were distracted by the outbreak of war with Louis XIV of France, the Nine Years' War, Charles of Lorraine commanding their forces in the Rhineland in 1689, while the Ottomans proved increasingly resilient. The key role of leadership was shown in 1688 when the new Sultan, Suleiman II (r. 1687–91), crushed rebellion in Constantinople. Moreover, an able Grand Vizier, Fazil Mustafa Köprülü (1689–91), restored order to the army and government. The absence of a united Christian bloc also proved significant. Catholicisation by the Austrians made the Orthodox restless and, in 1690, there was a revolt in Transylvania, while most Austrian troops had to be withdrawn to face France. In July, Fazil Mustafa launched a counter-offensive in which he retook Nish, Semendria and, after a six-day siege, Belgrade: treachery by a French engineer, timorous command, and explosions in the powder magazine have all been blamed. On 9 August 1691, however, Fazil Mustafa's hopes of recapturing Hungary were dashed by Ludwig Wilhelm at Zálankermén, a long, hard-fought battle which left a third of the Imperial army killed or wounded, but the Ottomans routed and Fazil Mustafa dead. This was one of the more important battles of the century and was also indicative of the extent to which the years from 1683 saw a marked increase in the number of battles between Ottomans and Austrians in contrast to earlier wars between the two powers. Sieges remained important but were now less significant than battles in determining the balance of success.

Conflict over the next few years was indecisive and difficult due to the unwillingness of either power to offer acceptable terms and to Austrian commitments against Louis XIV. In the battle zone, fortifications were improved, making progress harder, while local sources of supply were depleted and fighting in marshy, fever-ridden lowlands was difficult. The Austrians recaptured the fortress of Grosswardein in Transylvania in 1692, but in 1693 were forced to raise the siege of Belgrade. Matters came to a climax as a result of the accession of the energetic Mustafa II in February 1695 and of the end of the war in Italy in 1696, which enabled Leopold to transfer more troops and his rising general, Eugene of Savoy, to Hungary. Mustafa had some success, storming Lippa, defeating Count Federico Veterani and relieving the fortress of Temesvár in 1695, while in 1696 he outmanoeuvred the new Imperial commander, Augustus, Elector of Saxony.

However, in 1697, Eugene moved rapidly and attacked Mustafa at Zenta on 11 September, as the Ottoman army was crossing the river Tisza in Hungary. The Ottomans, caught unprepared and divided by the river, were massacred, with the loss of perhaps 30,000 casualties to only 300 in Eugene's army. With their back to the river, and the cavalry on the other bank, the Ottoman infantry was completely destroyed and Mustafa fled, forced to abandon his supplies and artillery, including 6000 camels, 5000 oxen and 9000 baggage carts. The victory made Eugene's reputation and his men went on to raid Bosnia, sacking Sarajevo, although it was too late in the year to attack the major Ottoman fortress-bases of Temesvár and Belgrade. In the following year, the Ottoman forces refused to engage, while Eugene's army was troubled by a mutiny caused by lack of funds. With Leopold keen to end the war in order to concentrate on the disputed succession to the sickly Charles II of Spain – which indeed was to lead, in 1701, to the renewal of conflict with Louis XIV – peace was negotiated at Karlowitz in 1699. Under the treaty, Austria kept Transylvania and most of Hungary, Poland kept Podolia, and Venice the Morea and its gains in Dalmatia. The following year, Peter the Great made peace, retaining Azov, which he had successfully besieged in 1696.

Yet, although important Ottoman territories were conquered by Austria, Poland, Russia and Venice in 1684–1700, Ottoman power in 1700 was not, as far as Christian Europe was concerned, less far-flung territorially than it had been in 1494, which serves as a key qualification of the idea of Ottoman decline. In addition, the important Ottoman conquests made earlier in the Balkans, including Greece, Bulgaria and Serbia, had been retained. Moreover, the Ottoman presence in Asia in 1700 was greater than in 1550, let alone 1490, and the Ottomans had retained the territories in North Africa conquered in the sixteenth century. Attempts had been made to deliver knockout blows at the Ottomans, with the Holy Alliance of the 1680s–1690s seeking a co-operation between Austria, Poland, Russia and Venice that included Venetian operations in the Aegean Sea near the centre of Ottoman power, but they had no more lasting effect than the arrival of a Russian fleet there in 1770. The Venetians, moreover, were easily driven from the Morea in 1715, and the Morea was not to be permanently free of Ottoman power until 1830, a success that required a major commitment of Western naval power, with British, French and Russian squadrons joining against the Ottomans and Egyptians at Cape Navarino in 1827, a battle that proved highly significant for the conflict on land. Meanwhile, Austrian gains at the expense of the Ottomans were made in 1716–18, including Belgrade, but most of these gains, including Belgrade, were lost in 1739.

The balance of advantage has to be assessed with care. There was clearly no equivalence between the defeat at Vienna in 1683 and the Dutch failure in Taiwan, or the Russian loss of the Amur valley, or the English abandonment of Tangier, or French failure in Thailand, because the Vienna campaign involved the main Ottoman army, whereas the other operations were relatively minor. In addition, the warfare between the Christians and the Ottomans in 1683–99 indicated in particular the strength of Christian infantry firepower and the value of its ability to operate in a disciplined fashion on the battlefield, such that Ottoman war making no longer had an edge in battle. However, defeats, for the Ottomans as for others, involved more than relative effectiveness. For example, divisions among the Ottoman commanders, which reflected an absence of common purpose and the lack of a reliable command structure, appear to have played a major role in the Ottoman defeat in 1683. In particular, Murat Giray, Khan of the Crimean Tatars, distrusted the Grand Vizier and did nothing to prevent the build-up of the relief army. Moreover, the Ottoman right flank abandoned the subsequent battle.[38]

Aside from flaws in battle, there was no significant disparity between the two sides in their ability to mobilise and finance forces for major campaigns until improvements in the Austrian (and allied German) military system in the late seventeenth century – and, even then, the Ottoman system remained formidable. As a key capability, the Ottomans continued to be effective in feeding and supplying their troops, a logistical strength that was important to their operational capability. In contrast, Austrian troops frequently lacked food and money, which helped explain the importance of being able to sack the Ottoman camp. The Austrian system, based on the *Proviandhausen* – depots scattered along the marching routes – was less effective than the Ottoman one. Each of the systems was supplied by water, coming down or up the Danube. The Ottomans had an effective river flotilla, whilst the Austrians only developed a good one around 1715.

Moreover, after 1683 the Ottomans were fighting in their own territories, closer to the ordnance and supplies they had previously accumulated.

The first Austrian campaign in the Balkans that had been logistically well organised was that of 1716. Prior to that, every campaign, including all those fought in Italy during the War of the Spanish Succession (1701–14), was logistically unsatisfactory, with the Austrian troops almost starving and deprived of shoes and horses. The Austrians prevailed in Hungary in 1684–99 largely due to the superior quality of their commanders, supported by the divisions between the Ottoman commanders. The significance of this success for the wider balance of military success between Western and non-Western forces is unclear as, in the absence of significant clashes in this period, there is no reason to suggest that Western war making was superior to that of the Manchu, Mughals, Marathas or Safavids.

7 Conflict, 1683–1707

China

The most dramatic clash in the last years of the seventeenth century occurred in East Asia. Earlier, the Rebellion of the Three Feudatories had prevented Chinese opposition to the expansion of a new steppe force, the west Mongolian tribes, known collectively as the Oirats, which had united in the dynamic new Dzhungar Confederation from 1635. They conquered the domain of the last Altan Khan in north-western Mongolia and, in 1670, overcame his former vassals in the western part of the region of Tuva. Under Taishi Galdan Boshughtu (r. 1671–97), the Dzhungars seized the Islamic oases near Mongolia from 1679: Hami and Turfan that year, Kashgar in 1680, and Yarkand soon after. This expansion made the Dzhungars a more serious potential challenge to the Manchu, who were far more concerned about the steppe than the Ming had been. The latter only tended to worry about how steppe politics impinged upon 'Chinese' territory.

China and the Dzhungars were not the sole regional players, but the others were overshadowed and marginalised, including the European power in the region, Russia. Before clashing with the Dzhungars, the Chinese had expelled the Russians from the Amur valley, which they had penetrated in the 1640s. In 1683–9, Chinese forces drove the Russians from both the Amur basin and from lands to the north. The successful siege of the Russian position of Albazin was the key event. By the Treaty of Nerchinsk of 1689, the Russians acknowledged Chinese control of the region, although the Chinese, keen to ensure Russian neutrality in their forthcoming struggle with the Dzhungars, abandoned the idea of pushing the Russians back beyond Lake Baikal.

Meanwhile, in 1687, the Dzhungars had intervened in a struggle between the two khans of the Khalkha regions of (eastern) Mongolia, and defeated the Tushetu khan. As the Khalkhas took refuge in China, many entering the Chinese army, this brought the Dzhungars into direct confrontation with China, which was challenged by the advance of the Dzhungar presence and by the collapse on the steppe of any balance of power for the Chinese to seek to manipulate.

On 3 September 1690, the two armies clashed at Ulan Butong, 320 kilometres north of Beijing. Galdan's defensive tactics, not least sheltering his men behind camels armoured with felt, limited the effectiveness of the Chinese artillery, but the Chinese drove their opponents from the field, although they were unable to mount an effective pursuit due to a shortage of food and because their horses were exhausted, a frequent problem after battles. The Chinese commander was happy to negotiate a truce. Galdan had established a military-industrial complex, although it did not prove particularly impressive. He had Lutheran Swedes casting cannon for him against those of the Chinese, which had been cast by the Jesuits.

In 1696, the Kangxi emperor, a more determined figure than the earlier commander, advanced north across the Gobi Desert with converging columns. This serious test of the logistical resources of the Chinese army led his advisers to urge him to turn back before it starved, but the Chinese coped far better than the Russians had in their advance across the steppes against the Crimean Tatars in 1689. Moreover, on 12 June 1696, Galdan's army was destroyed at Jao Modo, thanks in part to support for the Chinese from Galdan's rebellious nephew, Tsewang Rabdan, prefiguring the betrayal that helped Robert Clive defeat the Nawab of Bengal at Plassey in 1757. After another effective Chinese campaign, the following winter, Galdan died in suspicious circumstances, probably poisoned, and the Chinese benefited by extending their control in Mongolia and intervening in Tibet. The Manchu system had delivered a decisive verdict, despite the difficulty of the terrain, the distance from Chinese sources of supply, and the long months of campaigning. The combination of effective forces and successful logistical and organisational systems made the Manchu army the best in the world, not least because the banner system enabled Mongols, Chinese and Manchu to work together as part of a single military machine. The logistical system ensured that the wealthy agricultural zone of lowland eastern China could be tapped to support campaigns to the north and west closer to the frontier.

By the end of the 1690s, China had its strongest and most advanced northern frontier for centuries. The combination of Chinese and steppe forces and systems ensured that the problems that had beset Ming China had been overcome. The strength of Manchu China owed much to the extent to which the lands that had formed the initial Manchu homeland and the early acquisitions in eastern Mongolia had been the source of intractable problems for the Ming. As a result of ending these problems, the frontier had been overcome, or rather pushed back, a process underlined when settlement was undertaken in conquered areas in order to provide resources to support the army.[1] This war did not end the conflict with the

Dzhungars, which, indeed, was not to be settled finally until the late 1750s, when the Dzhungar heartland was conquered by Kangxi's grandson, the Qianlong emperor, who wiped out most of the Dzhungar population. Nevertheless, Chinese success in the 1690s ranks as a formidable achievement[2] and is therefore deliberately placed first in the chapter.

India

So also with Mughal warfare. Unable to defeat the Marathas in the early 1680s, Aurangzeb turned to conquer the two Deccan sultanates which, having been subjugated in the 1630s, had (benefiting from the civil warfare among the Mughal élite) reasserted their independence in 1657. Division between the sultanates, however, helped the Mughals. Thus, in 1677, Bijapur joined with them in an invasion of Golconda.

Aurangzeb's campaigns, which began in 1684, were large-scale enterprises in which strongly walled positions with substantial garrisons fell to large armies, the supply of which was a formidable undertaking. A long siege of the massive walls of Bijapur ended with its surrender in 1685 when Mughal trenches reached the ramparts. Two years later, the four-mile-long outer wall of the fortress of Golconda was invested by Aurangzeb. In a lengthy siege, two mines were driven under the walls, but they exploded prematurely. The fortress finally fell by betrayal and Mughal forces entered through an opened gateway. The sultanates were annexed. The logistical challenge facing the Mughals was formidable, albeit not as significant as for the Chinese because it was possible to draw on nearby and local agricultural resources. A more significant difference to Kangxi's 1696 campaign was that the latter had no comparable need for sieges.

Aurangzeb thought he had dealt with the Marathas: in 1689, Shivaji's heir, Shambhaji, was captured and killed, the capital, Raigarh, was captured, and the Maratha state was annexed. However, resistance continued under Shambhaji's brother, Rajaram, and subsequently under his young son, Shivaji II. Aurangzeb, indeed, spent his last years combating the Marathas. The latter relied on mobile, lightly armoured horsemen and musketeers who avoided battle and supported themselves by raiding. Their strategy of *bargi-giri* – cutting supply links, launching devastating raids and using hit-and-run tactics – proved highly damaging, and the mobile and decentralised style of the Maratha fighting system was crucial in enabling them to resist Aurangzeb effectively. Thus, the Marathas revealed an important weakness in Mughal warfare: its failure to sustain the mobility of its origins. By the seventeenth century, Mughal armies were large and slow-moving, and their cavalry was preponderantly heavy. The Mughals sought battle, but there was no equivalent to Kangxi's success at Jao Modo. Instead, the Mughals proved vulnerable to an opponent able to focus on mobility. The Mughals, in turn, responded to the Marathas by fielding larger forces, which both exacerbated the problem of lesser mobility and drove up the already high cost of campaigning. The Marathas did not defeat the Mughals in decisive battles, but rather denied the Mughals safe control of territory.

However, the Maratha advantage of mobility was lost when they defended forts, which provided clear targets for the Mughals and their effective siege equipment: the Marathas lacked comparable artillery and their siegecraft was poorly developed. Yet, on both sides, there was only limited comparison with the siegecraft developed in Europe. For example, it was only in Aurangzeb's later years that the Mughals used iron cannon balls in place of the stone ammunition they had earlier employed. Most of the Mughal siege artillery was not particularly sophisticated by European standards, and was made of wrought iron as opposed to the less rigid cast iron of Europe.

The Marathas were swayed by the view that forts were necessary for the symbol and reality of power, a view very much taken by Louis XIV of France, but Aurangzeb was able to conquer a whole series of these forts, most of which were hill fortresses, frequently of considerable antiquity. These hilltop locations reflected the value of topography to the defence, and the massive hill fortress of Jinji held out against Mughal siege until 1698. In contrast, the Vauban-style forts in Europe often lacked the strength brought by height and, instead, the use of planned fire zones by the defence was more significant. The *trace italienne* was introduced to India by the Portuguese, who were also probably responsible for circular bastions in India, but the diffusion of these techniques was limited. The Mughals won successes, but often by exploiting the weaknesses and divisions of their opponents and by their willingness to negotiate. Tanjore was conquered by the Mughals in 1694. In 1699, Aurangzeb launched a systematic attack on the hill fortresses: 13 fell, most after the bribery of their commanders. Maratha armies were not strong enough to relieve the fortresses, and Aurangzeb covered his siege forces with mobile field armies, as Louis XIV did in Europe. Nevertheless, despite his successes, Aurangzeb failed to conquer the Marathas, while the war was costly and the impression of failure it created was damaging.

Aurangzeb also faced other problems. Aside from difficulties against the Marathas, the Mughals were defeated in the Battle of Itakhuli (1682) by the energetic new King of Ahom, Gadadhar Singh, and his river flotillas, and the Mughals had to accept the Manas river as a frontier. There were also problems within the Mughal dominions, in part due to the strain created by the war with the Marathas. A serious revolt in 1696–8 challenged Mughal rule in Bengal, but was eventually suppressed. In responding to these and other problems, the Mughals did not simply rely on the dispatch of punitive expeditions. For example, the Mughal presence in Bengal was strengthened in the 1690s by the construction of an embanked road from Siripur to Alamgirnagar. Further west, from the mid-1680s, there were growing problems with the Jats, a people living south of Delhi, although the situation was temporarily stabilised when their stronghold of Sinsini was captured in the early 1690s. In Rajasthan, there was serious opposition from 1679, especially in the region of Marwar, while there were also rebellions by the Sikhs in Punjab.

Moreover, in terms of weaponry, Indian warfare was not innovative. Adoption of the flintlock musket was slower than in Europe, and the bayonet was not used. Mughal India also failed to keep pace with European advances in artillery, especially in cast iron technology. Thus, there were clear signs of political and military overextension in Aurangzeb's later years. Yet, the ability to maintain dominance of northern India even when Aurangzeb and most of his army were engaged in protracted conflict with the Marathas was significant. This control was important to his success in the south because many of the troops and animals, and much of the supplies and money for the operations, was obtained in the north and then moved south on the royal road from Delhi to Burhanpur. Whatever the deficiencies of the Mughal regime in Aurangzeb's last years, European rulers would have considered themselves very fortunate to wield such power. The range of Mughal sway was impressive and it rested on an effective military infrastructure. Moreover, Aurangzeb's concern to campaign in person, like that of the Kangxi emperor, reflected a determination to prevent the empire rusting away by the nobility losing their inherited nomadic warrior energy.[3] Although there was no comparable nomadic background, Louis XIV, like other European rulers, was also anxious to maintain the military commitment and ability of his nobility, which contributed to the emphasis on their role in command.

Africa

As with the Mughals, though not the Manchu, political and military overextension were also seen in the case of Louis XIV. In each case, there was also the varied relationship between state forms and the political and military drive and capability of individual rulers. The latter factor was particularly apparent in Africa as the state forms there were frequently more transient, although it is important not to primitivise Africa in these terms. In particular, the fate of the Spanish empire both under Charles II (r. 1665–1700) and subsequently after he died without children, thus setting off a war of succession, indicated the dependence of European monarchies on the capabilities of individual rulers and on the stability of the succession. To turn to Africa, in Madagascar, the kingdom of Merina was given cohesion by a sacred monarchy, force by firearms, and purpose by warfare for slaves. In Abyssinia (Ethiopia), the role of the individual ruler was again important. Under Fasiladas (r. 1632–67) in 1642, the army was destroyed by the nomadic Oromo, after which much of the country was raided by them, which helped cause a protracted decline, with the weakness of the monarch ensuring that provincial independence grew. In turn, Iyasu I, who became king in 1682, made a major attempt to reverse the system. He built up the royal bodyguard as a separate army, supported by a treasury, to prevent it from following the militia in becoming overly connected to particular areas. Iyasu also developed a new militia from among loyal Oromo tribes who converted to Christianity. In the 1680s, 1690s and 1700s, Iyasu took the war to the other Oromo, but he found it very difficult to gain lasting success, and was assassinated by domestic opponents in 1706.

Europe

That year, another ruler whose ambitions and energy had come to define his state's activity, Charles XII of Sweden (r. 1697–1718), invaded Central Europe. The Great Northern War (1700–21) usually takes a subordinate place to the later conflicts of Louis XIV and, of course, occurred after the Nine Years' War (1688–97) in which Louis was the leading protagonist. Nevertheless, the Great Northern War, which initially entailed an attack on Charles by Russia, Denmark and Saxony-Poland, and was launched in order to make gains from the Swedish empire, demonstrated that conflict in Christian Europe was not necessarily on a confined scale compared to that in Asia. Indeed, this reiterated theme of variety within Christian Europe also provides a way to look at the Nine Years' War. The latter, notably, included not only naval and colonial warfare but also, on land in Europe, the struggle to establish William III in the British Isles, a struggle that was very different in character to those on France's borders.

At the same time, weaponry and the nature of land battle changed fundamentally. In the European battles of mid-century, such as Naseby (1645), the infantry had been divided between the musketeers, who provided firepower, and the pikemen; however, the pike/musket system was swept away in the 1690s, thanks to the development of an effective bayonet, one of the most important and underrated innovations in military technology. Whereas, with the plug bayonets devised earlier in the seventeenth century that were inserted in the barrel of the musket, it had been necessary to remove the bayonet before firing the musket, the socket bayonet enabled firing with the bayonet in place. The transition to the bayonet in Western Europe was very rapid, with Russia following in the 1700s. All infantry were thus armed with a weapon that combined firepower and steel. However, this did not greatly encourage attacks, because bayonet drills were, for a long time, based on pike drills, with the weapon held high and an emphasis on receiving advances. It was not until the 1750s that a new bayonet drill, with the weapon held waist-high, made it easier for the English infantry to mount attacks; in France, the drills and formations of the age of musket and pike continued into the eighteenth century and tactical changes were slow.[4]

Indeed, while the remark above, 'was swept away', suggests a revolutionary change, in practice the move from the use of the pike was gradual, with the proportion of pikemen decreasing during the century as that of musketeers increased. For example, the percentage of pikemen – which, at the start of the century, formed most of the Austrian infantry – fell during the Thirty Years' War, and, by 1670, their percentage was down to a third. Yet, Montecuccoli retained his belief that pikes were important because he did not think that musketeers alone could repel cavalry attack, and he accordingly deployed his pikemen in six ranks. However, in the 1690s, the Austrians deployed the bayonet and abandoned the pike, a significant step as they fought both the Ottomans and the French that decade.[5] The proportion of pikemen in French infantry units fell from half at the start of the century to a third by 1650, a quarter by 1680, and a fifth by 1690, and formations accordingly became longer and thinner.[6]

As pikes were replaced by muskets equipped with socket bayonets, so matchlock muskets were replaced by flintlocks which were more reliable and fired faster. All the new English regiments raised from 1689 were equipped with flintlocks and in 1699 a French ordinance ordered that the flintlocks be adopted by all, the pike being abandoned in 1703. The new English Land Pattern Musket could be fired at least twice a minute and weighed one pound less than the matchlock previously used. The speed of fire led to new tactical formations, with the infantry deployed first in four ranks and then in three. European armies were not to experience a comparable change in weaponry until the introduction of rifled guns in the nineteenth century.

Since all the Western European armies followed a similar pattern of re-equipment, however, capability gaps between them did not emerge. In contrast, the enhanced weaponry was very useful for conflict overseas against non-Westerners who lacked such weapons, for example in North America, not least because the tactical mobility and flexibility of European troops were increased by the fusion of musketeer and pikemen into a soldier wielding a flintlock carrying a bayonet. Much of the rest of the world did not follow the European pattern of development, with neither China nor South-East Asia (unlike India) moving from matchlocks to flintlocks. Indeed, hand-to-hand weapons remained more important, there and elsewhere, than is frequently appreciated. These weapons were employed not simply by weak or unchanging powers, but also by dynamic powers and people, such as the Nepalese Gurkhas who used swords (*kukris*). In South-East Asia, pikes, swords, spears and daggers, such as the Malay *kris*, were still important, and firearms made scant impact on tactics.

In Europe, the key campaign in the Nine Years' War did not involve a battle. Instead, it set a central alignment for the war. William III of Orange was able to invade southern England from the Netherlands successfully in 1688 despite King James II controlling an undefeated navy and a larger army. Favourable winds gave the Dutch fleet a crucial lead and William was able to stage an unopposed landing at Brixham in Devon, but his route thereafter to London was blocked by James on Salisbury Plain. However, indecision, ill health, and desertion by a series of senior officers, including John Churchill, the future Duke of Marlborough, led James to abandon his army, which weakened the morale of troops already hit by dissension and conspiracy among the officers. As the army retreated towards London along the Thames Valley, it largely dissolved through desertion, before being disbanded on James's orders. William pressed on to seize London, and James's regime collapsed without any battle being fought in England. The campaign, which led to William becoming king in 1689, indicated the degree to which political developments in Britain continued to depend finally on the role of force and the willingness to use it.

Scotland and Ireland did not fall so easily. On 27 July 1689, a Jacobite (pro-James) force of Scottish Highlanders won the battle of Killiecrankie over a far larger Williamite force by charging with their broadsides against static musketeers, but the death in the battle of their commander was followed by poor leadership, an unsuccessful attack on the fortified position of Dunkeld, and the collapse of the Jacobite position in Scotland.

The decisive battles in the struggle for control of the British Isles, battles that were important to the politics and geopolitics of the Western world over the following century and beyond, were fought in Ireland, where James's Catholic supporters were particularly concentrated and which was more accessible than Scotland to the major French naval base of Brest. In 1689, James's supporters controlled most of Ireland, although the town of Derry, fearing massacre by the Catholics, resisted a siege and was relieved by the English fleet on 28 July, after the boom blocking the harbour had been broken. Naval power thus offered William military flexibility and denied James overall control. On 13 August, 10,000 of William's troops, many Huguenots (French Protestants) and Dutch, landed in Ireland near Bangor, County Down. They were under the command of Frederick, Duke of Schomberg, a German Protestant who had left the service of Louis XIV, in which he had risen to the rank of Marshal, when that king in 1685 revoked the Edict of Nantes which had guaranteed Protestant rights. Having captured Carrickfergus after a two-day bombardment, Schomberg marched to Dundalk where he assembled his army in a good defensive position, from which, however, he refused to advance to fight the Jacobites; and both armies then retired to winter quarters. In a clear instance of the damage that could arise from disease, Schomberg lost up to half of his troops that winter, an outcome that indicated the problems created at the strategic and operational levels, by a decision not to fight that might be fully understandable in terms of the dynamics of the potential battlefield.

Critical of Schomberg for having failed to force a battle, William decided that he would have to take command in the 1690 campaign. He built up his new forces, which were well armed with flintlock muskets; his Dutch and Danish troops had bayonets as well. The French also sent reinforcements to James. Louis supported James for legitimist reasons and because of James's Catholicism, but also because he sought to distract William from the conflict with France in the Low Countries, which is a reminder that strategic understanding and planning were present, though not the terminology of strategy. The French advice to their ally was to play a waiting game rather than to risk battle. James was urged to burn Dublin, the Irish capital, to destroy all the food and forage in William's path, and to wait for a French fleet to interrupt his seaborne supply route, and for subsequent privation to demoralise and weaken him. James, in contrast, understood the need to consider political as well as military contexts. Grasping Dublin's symbolic and strategic significance, and fearing that the political and logistical strains of delay would lead the Irish and French forces to waste away before his opponents, James decided to fight. However, he was a poor commander, not least for failing to reconnoitre the battlefield, and he was outmanoeuvred at the Battle of the Boyne on 1 July 1690. The fighting was not militarily decisive, casualties being modest and most of the defeated escaping, but James, in the battle, projected his abiding fear of envelopment onto William's manoeuvres, and his nerve failed. The disintegration of the Franco-Irish army after the battle was based on a collapse of morale stemming from James's flight. As a reminder of a political dimension of conflict, this flight also gave the Williamites a propaganda coup. They could describe William as an exemplar of calm and heroic leadership, a key theme in the presentation of generalship, while James was depicted as a coward. Thus, the Boyne took on a lasting role in political theatre.[7]

The aftermath of the battle was instructive: it indicated the extent to which such success has to be absorbed within a more complex narrative which notes both the benefits that could flow from success and the extent to which problems still remained, so that outcomes could not be readily forced. After the Boyne, Dublin was abandoned by the Jacobites and, having entered it, William advanced to Athlone, a major bridging point over the River Shannon, only to be thwarted when the bridge was broken. Repeatedly in the wars of the century, bridging points emerged as crucial. In part, this reflected the limited number of bridges and the extent to which, with the technology and resources of the period, it was difficult rapidly to produce substitutes in the shape of effective pontoon bridges. Secondly, the nature of supply links was such that bridging points were key nexuses for systems reliant both on crossing rivers and on moving large quantities of supplies along them. The supply of bread was particularly significant, for operational reasons.[8] Thirdly, rivers offered significant defensive positions as well as obstacles. These points, for example, were apparent during the conflict between Portugal and Spain from 1640 to 1668, and also help explain the significance of fortification location and siege targets in the wars on France's north-eastern frontier. The role of bridging points also emerged in the warfare in the Balkans, for example in the location of battles such as St Gotthard and Zenta.

Having failed at Athlone, William then moved downriver to Limerick, a major port at the mouth of the Shannon, although his siege train was badly damaged en route. The fortifications were still largely intact when William unsuccessfully tried to storm Limerick on 27 August 1690, suffering over 2000 casualties, a result that, at the same time, showed the narrow but costly margin between success and failure, and the consequences of attempts to force a rapid close to a campaign so that it could have the desired place within a wider conflict, permitting the movement of troops to other fronts.

In an indication of the potential offered by amphibious operations, a separate expedition under John Churchill, then Earl of Marlborough, was more successful. The port of Cork surrendered in September 1690 after its fortifications were breached by a bombardment from higher ground and the Jacobite outworks were overrun. The following month, James Fort and Charles Fort, which dominated the harbour at Kinsale, were taken. These successes improved British naval capability and made French reinforcement of the Irish more difficult. The contrasting fate of the Irish towns also indicated the operational and strategic consequences of position warfare. Success or failure in the capture of positions took on a disproportionate significance because, aside from the specific benefits (notably in terms of casualties inflicted and transport nodes taken), it gave an impression likely to attract or weaken support. The latter was significant both in civil wars and in those of foreign conquest.

In 1691, William's forces in Ireland were commanded by Godard van Reede de Ginkel, a Dutch general. Athlone fell in June after hard fighting and a very heavy bombardment, with more than 12,000 cannonballs fired. Ginkel was then able to cross the Shannon, and, on 12 July, the two armies met at Aughrim. After a bitter struggle in which the Irish made good use of field boundaries as breastworks, their commander, the Marquis de St Ruth, was killed by a chance cannon shot and the demoralised cavalry on the Irish left retreated. The deaths of commanders reflected the extent to which generals did not hang back to distant command positions, but instead sought, by their presence, to motivate their troops and guide the tempo of the battle, as with that of Fazil Mustafa at Zálankermén, also in 1691. However, aside from long-term consequences, as with the death of Gustavus Adolphus at Lützen in 1632, the results of the death of a commander could be serious in the battle. At Aughrim, the leaderless Irish centre then came under intense pressure and much of the infantry was killed in the retreat. The Irish lost possibly 7000 killed to about 2000 of their opponents dead and wounded. Aughrim was far more decisive than the Boyne. The Irish army was broken and Galway and Limerick both surrendered within three months.[9]

Thus, in a pointed reminder that the campaigns in the Spanish Netherlands did not define the nature of conflict in Western Europe in this period, Irish campaigns were far from static. Bold generalship and success in battle were far more important than the holding of fortified positions. Though Derry, Athlone and Limerick had successfully resisted attack, at least initially, both the Boyne and, even more, Aughrim were followed by the capture of key positions. Each of the major engagements had been won by the attacking force; in both cases, tactical considerations relating to the terrain and to the ability to take advantage of developments had been crucial, and the vulnerability of defending armies to flanking attacks by opponents that retained the initiative had been clearly demonstrated.

The conflict in Ireland also demonstrated the ability to deliver a decisive result as well as the linked strategic dimension of the Nine Years' War. After 1691, there was no significant Jacobite opposition in Ireland and it did not pose a serious strategic challenge to Britain until the unsuccessful 1798 revolution. William's victory consolidated his control over the British Isles and that control anchored a new constitutional, political and governmental order that was to help take Britain to victory in successive wars with France down to 1815. In addition, Ireland was an important source of supplies and, eventually, manpower for Britain, as William realised more clearly than Louis XIV. Moreover, Ireland in British – as opposed to Jacobite – hands was also significant to the naval situation, notably by ending the possibility of hostile warships and, more probably, privateers using Irish bases.

William, however, was less successful in the Spanish Netherlands, where the French army, then well commanded, was at the peak of its capability as well as being the largest force in Western Europe since the days of imperial Rome.[10] The war on the Continent had begun in 1688 when Louis decided to use his army in order to enforce his interests in the Rhineland. Displaying the vulnerability of the areas in dispute, notably the Palatinate, appeared the best way to overawe his opponents. The French army was not prepared for a major conflict but, in October 1688, a large army, under the ostensible command, significantly, of the Dauphin, the heir to the throne, besieged Philippsburg, the major fortress of the Holy Roman Empire in the Middle Rhine. The Dauphin's command was intended to deal with quarrels over precedence between generals, but also to reflect credit on both heir and dynasty. Another force occupied the papal enclave of Avignon in southern France, as Pope Innocent XI opposed Louis's wishes.

Louis, however, was to be proved wrong in his expectation that his attack would lead to a limited, short and successful conflict in which German rulers would desert Leopold I, who would be driven to terms by French triumphs. Instead, Louis found himself in an intractable conflict, like Aurangzeb with the Marathas. Philippsburg and Mannheim, the capital of the Elector Palatine, quickly fell, but German resistance gathered pace. Factors not generally associated with *ancien régime* warfare were seen. First, reflecting a rise in German patriotism, the rulers of Brandenburg, Hanover, Hesse-Cassel and Saxony concluded a treaty in October 1689 for the defence of the Middle Rhine. Secondly, French generals resorted to crude intimidation, devastating much of south-western Germany in 1689. These tactics touched off a guerrilla struggle in the Palatinate and accentuated the anti-French nature of German patriotism which contrasted with the willingness earlier in the century of German rulers to seek French support.

Meanwhile, the war had broadened out, with Louis XIV declaring war on the United Provinces in November 1688, following, in April 1689, with Spain, which had refused to promise to be neutral, and which presented a vulnerable target to France in the Spanish Netherlands, now Belgium. In May, William III, as King of England, declared war on Louis, while an Austro-Bavarian treaty brought Elector Max Emmanuel of Bavaria into the war; and, in 1690, Victor Amadeus II of Savoy-Piedmont, fed up with French tutelage, and eager to dislodge the French from the neighbouring fortresses of Pinerolo and Casale, joined the alliance and built up his army, from 8239 men in 1685 to 24,023 in 1696.[11] The opposition of most of Western Europe was a comment not only on Louis's policies but also on the sense that he was now vulnerable and that he would not determine any reordering of Europe. The politics of the war were reconfigured as princes both opportunistic and vulnerable, and thus keenly aware of shifts in the wind, such as Victor Amadeus and Max Emmanuel, now looked for opportunity at the expense of Louis, as it no longer appeared prudent, or indeed wise, to accommodate Louis's pretensions and goals.

Louis sought to overcome the crisis by a string of victories that would divide his opponents. His generals were successful in the Spanish Netherlands, winning victories at Fleurus (1690), Leuze (1691), Steenkirk (1692) and Neerwinden (1693), and conquering a number of major fortresses including Mons (1691) and Namur (1692). Moreover, Victor Amadeus was defeated at Staffarda (1690) and Marsaglia (1693). The only Allied attacks on France itself, on Dauphiné in 1692 and on French Channel ports, failed. However, Louis was unable to make significant inroads into the Empire or northern Italy, to maintain James II in Ireland, or to sustain the naval success in the English Channel that he won in 1690. Furthermore, French military prestige was damaged in 1695 when Casale fell, a sign of Spanish military resilience, and when Namur was recaptured by William III. Moreover, as a reminder of the role of economic warfare, French trade was greatly harmed by commercial embargoes by England, the Dutch and the Empire. As in the 1670s, French wine exports collapsed, affecting rents and wages.

The mixed fortunes of war encouraged negotiations from 1692, which again was a characteristic of war, not only in Europe, as during the Thirty Years' War in the 1640s, but also more generally. Thus, campaigns were designed to affect the prospects for, or the course of, negotiations. In particular, Louis sought to exploit divisions among the opposing coalition. Thus, in 1695, facing the loss of Casale, Louis, by means of a secret deal with Victor Amadeus, ensured that it did not fall into the hands of Leopold I. In a difficult situation in October 1696, and with his war effort under great pressure, Louis bought off Victor Amadeus in the Peace of Vigevano, at the price of Pinerolo, so that France no longer had any positions in northern Italy. This peace enabled Louis to transfer forces to Catalonia, where Barcelona fell to the French in 1697, encouraging Spain to press for peace. This shift accentuated fears and tensions in the anti-French alliance and brought growing war-weariness among the combatants to a head. Negotiations at Rijswick led to a compromise peace that involved Louis surrendering many gains since 1678, including Luxembourg, although his position in Alsace, including his occupation of Strasbourg in 1681, was recognised. Regaining Luxembourg was a major instance of the continued importance of Spain at the close of a century often seen for Europe as a sequence of the Decline of Spain and the Rise of France. In practice, most of the Spanish empire was still intact on the eve of the death of Charles II in 1700, which triggered the War of the Spanish Succession as the Austrian and French dynasties had rival claims on the inheritance. By 1700, Spain had lost, since 1650, Franche Comté, parts of the Spanish Netherlands, Roussillon, Jamaica and St Domingue, and had acknowledged Portuguese independence, but not only had most of the empire, including Spanish Italy, Catalonia and nearly all of Spanish America been retained (just as the Ottomans had retained most of their empire), but this retention also owed much to the efforts of Spain rather than simply the support of its allies. These efforts reflected the extent to which the Spanish monarchy 'remained a relatively powerful, functioning military structure or "system", a surprisingly integrated and coherent war machine',[12] a definition of military capability that is more generally pertinent.

In addition, Louis suffered during the Nine Years' War both from Leopold I's willingness to focus on his challenge, rather than on the Ottomans, and from William III's ability to devote English resources to a continental commitment against France as well as to a naval war. This ability was a function of the degree of William's political and governmental control of the state that contrasted with the inability of Charles II (r. 1660–85) and James II (r. 1685–8) both to direct policy and to raise the necessary resources. Parliamentary government, in the sense of government that needed Parliament for fiscal reasons, proved a source of strength for England, as it provided the basis for a funded national debt that eventually commanded confidence.

The campaigns of the 1690s are usually rushed through in order to permit a focus on the War of the Spanish Succession (1701–14), in which battles such as Blenheim (1704) and Turin (1706) offer a greater drama and, apparently, decisiveness. Thus, the Nine Years' War appears as a prelude or anticipation in which France's opponents, notably England and Austria, proved unable to devise the victorious methods they were to show the following decade, methods that therefore repay attention. This approach, however, has serious limitations, and one of the attractions of a break at the close of the seventeenth century is that it directs attention to the 1690s, a period in which army numbers increased greatly, notably in France, Austria and Britain, but also elsewhere, for example in many of the German states. The campaigns of that decade brought greater experience with coalition operations[13] and indicated the ability of armies to respond to innovations, notably the bayonet, but also showed the difficulty of creating a capability gap within Western Europe. The latter was to emerge anew from the War of the Spanish Succession, which ended, like the Nine Years' War, in a compromise peace. Each war suggested the same lesson as conflicts earlier and elsewhere during the century, namely the value of experienced troops and capable leaders. In the 1690s, the French benefited from both, with François, Duke of Luxembourg, the victor of Fleurus, Leuze, Steenkirk and Neerwinden, proving particularly important. His sudden death at Versailles on 4 January 1695 was a significant blow, and French generalship thereafter was less adroit. Luxembourg was especially skilled at maintaining control of the flow of the battle, and preparing fresh attacks, as at Fleurus and Neerwinden. Similarly, the extent to which battles lasted for a while placed a premium on the experience and determination of the troops and, more specifically, on their ability to take casualties and go on fighting. Thus, although uniformity might have been the objective of drill that focused on repetitive movements and formulaic tactics,[14] patterned training and battle-field dispositions did not define what, in practice, was a far more varied military experience both in battle and elsewhere.[15] This point is equally valid for military cultures across the world, and thus makes it difficult to establish an inherent characteristic for each that can then apparently serve as the basis for a ready comparison.

Skill in command was eminently shown in the major battles that closed the century, Jao-Modo (1696), Zenta (1697) and Narva (1700), each of which delivered a clear-cut result. In the last, at the end of the first campaigning season in the Great Northern War (1700–21), the Russians besieged a major fortress guarding the Swedish presence in Estonia, only to face a relieving Swedish army under Charles XII, who was very much a hands-on military leader, and had already that year both defeated Augustus II of Saxony-Poland and knocked Denmark out of the war. Charles's ability to seize the initiative was crucial both in strategic terms, in order to disrupt the far stronger opposing coalition, and in operational and tactical terms, not least because the Russian army (like the Ottoman one at Zenta) was far larger. The Swedes advanced rapidly and broke into the Russian entrenchments in two columns. The value of determined and effective troops taking the initiative became apparent as the Swedes rapidly came to hand-to-hand combat and proved adept with their bayonets. A snowstorm blew directly into the defenders' faces, and the Russian positions collapsed as their troops fled or surrendered. The Swedes suffered 2000 dead and wounded while the Russians lost 8000–10,000 men and all their artillery. Just as a Polish–German relief force under John Sobieski had crushed the

Ottoman besieging army at Vienna in 1683, so also Narva demonstrated the vulnerability of a poorly commanded and badly deployed siege army to a relief attempt, not least because the latter enjoyed the initiative while the siege army tended to lack a ready responsiveness.

The defeat at Narva, like the costly failures of Prince Vasilii Golitsyn's campaigns against the Crimean Tatars in 1687 and 1689, and the less costly failure, in 1695, of Peter's first attempt on Azov, led to questions about the effectiveness of the Russian army, when it was possibly more appropriate to focus, for all bar Narva, on the particular problems of operating across the Black Sea steppe.[16] Both these questions and the changes associated with Peter the Great (r. 1689–1725) underline the tendency for commentators to prefer an account of revolutionary change in Russia's military development. In the case of Peter, as earlier with Gustavus Adolphus of Sweden, there is the related preference for the 'great man' approach, with leadership seen to lie not only in decisive generalship but also in an ability to be a man of destiny. In practice, there was a longstanding tendency for Russian leaders to seek to improve their military system and, more specifically, to look to foreign powers for military innovations. In the Middle Ages, there had been both an adoption of the Byzantine preference for heavy cavalry and borrowing from the steppe peoples that had overshadowed Muscovy, but firearms encouraged a shift to borrowing European methods in the sixteenth century. This pattern of borrowing remained the case during the seventeenth century, notably with the costly new formation regiments of Peter's father, Alexei, which had been created in order to fight the Thirteen Years' War with Poland (1654–67) and many of which had foreign officers. In 1689, Golitsyn, the lover and political adviser of Sophia, the Regent for her younger half-brother Peter and his incapable half-brother Ivan, led over 110,000 troops against the Crimea. Most were from the new-style units of the seventeenth century: nearly 50,000 as infantry and nearly 30,000 as cavalry. There were also 17,000 traditional-style troops, both musketeers and cavalry. In search for information that would be useful for future operations, Golitsyn made use of a primitive wagon-mounted odometer and compiled a *versta* or distance-book that was intended to be used to prepare a map. In 1695 and 1696, Peter led expeditions of over 90,000 troops against Azov, including about 16,000 traditional-style troops, 28,000 new-style infantry, and the rest ancillary cavalry units, such as Cossacks and Kalmyks.[17]

Peter, in the 1680s, had already created the basis of a new force when he established several regiments, most of which also had foreign officers. He came to power in 1689, in large part as a reaction against Sophia and Golitsyn, who was seen as a Westerniser and discredited by the failure of his Crimean expeditions. However, if Peter's accession had comparable anti-Western consequences for the army, they were swiftly reversed and, in 1698, he responded to a revolt by the *strel'tsy*, the traditional musketeer units in Moscow, not only with brutal punishments but also by disbanding much of the Moscow garrison and, instead, raising 27 new regiments. It was these forces that defeated Sweden, most prominently at Poltava in 1709. At the same time, as a reminder of the need not to take a Eurocentric approach, Peter benefited from the support of the Kalmyks, the Oirats who left Dzhungaria in 1636 and settled in the Volga. Their alliance with him during the reign of Ayuuki Khan secured the southern frontier from Crimean Tatar and Nogai attacks and allowed Peter to focus more on Europe and, from 1700, his war with Sweden.

Conclusion

Charles's victory over the Russians at Narva was followed by fresh successes, although, in the end, Sweden lost the Great Northern War (1700–21). Nevertheless, this conflict, like William III's conquest of Ireland and the war between the Chinese and the Dzhungars, showed that major and important victories could be secured. The operational range of these armies was impressive and warfare was far from indecisive. Many of the territorial changes that resulted from, and/or were secured by, conflict in the period 1683–1707 lasted for over two centuries and thus helped provide a basis for the international and domestic power politics of this period. Decisiveness in consequences does not, however, explain causes. There was no consistent contrast between the victorious and the defeated in the struggles of the period, and nor was it the case that it is readily possible to explain success in one conflict in a fashion that also accounts for it elsewhere. It would certainly be mistaken to see technology as the key element. Instead, it is necessary to underline the extent to which differing modes of conflict were absorbed within contrasting goals that reflected the very varied politics of particular wars.

8 Naval Capability and Warfare

The Western powers had a clear edge on the oceans as only the major Western European powers controlled fleets of deep-draught vessels able to operate at great distances. Only Western European warships and merchantmen sailed across the Atlantic or Pacific or between the Atlantic and the Indian or Pacific Oceans. Havana, Seville, Goa, Malacca, Manila and Acapulco were all way stations on routes of global exchange controlled by the Western powers, and each offered possibilities for resupplying and repairing warships. Moreover, this network expanded during the century, with the creation of new Western bases, notably Cape Town by the Dutch in 1652, which offered a valuable stopping point between the Atlantic and Indian Oceans, followed for the English by St Helena in 1673, and Batavia (Jayakĕrta/Djakarta), also by the Dutch, in 1619, which centred their presence in the East Indies. The establishment of colonial bases in North America, such as Boston by the English and Quebec by the French; or the West Indies, such as Kingston, Jamaica by the English; or South Asia, such as Pondicherry by the French, also provided naval facilities, notably safe anchorages and supplies.

Nevertheless, non-Western powers could also take an important role at sea. This activity, however, has not been studied systematically and this neglect poses serious problems, not least because there is a tendency to write about these powers only in so far as they clashed with Western naval forces or positions, which leads to a failure to judge the goals and capability of the non-Western powers other than in terms of such a clash. Moreover, research on non-Western naval forces suffers from a teleology that assumes development on the Western model, which, again, is misleading.

Asia

Non-Western naval activity was especially significant in Asian and Pacific waters, although also in African ones. Asian and Pacific waters, of course, cover much of the globe and its coasts, and it is unsurprising that there was a great variety in naval activity, notably in scale and range, but also in purpose and social, economic and political contexts. South and East Asia were important areas for non-Western naval capability, and the Mataram, Aceh, Mughal and Magh fleets all played a local role in South Asian waters. However, in a major clash between such fleets and European power, Sultan Iskandar Muda of Aceh (in northern Sumatra) was defeated when, with his large galley fleet in 1629, he attacked the Portuguese-controlled port-fortress of Malacca, in the strategic Straits of Malacca, a funnel for trade between Malaya and Sumatra, and thus between East and South Asia.[1] Such fortress-bases provided the possibility of choke-points on trade and naval movements. Examples of other such points included Muscat, which the Portuguese held until 1650, and Aden, which they had failed to capture the previous century and which had been incorporated into the Ottoman system in 1538. These bases, however, had many similarities in their capability and usage to strategic fortresses on land frontiers in that they could deny important routes for movement, for instance bridging points, but were most effective when combined with significant forces able to sally forth, notably warships for the naval bases and raiding parties for the strategic fortresses.

Resources were a key factor in South Asia, as elsewhere. Thus, after Sultan Agung of Mataram (r. 1613–46) gained control of the major Javan coastal areas with their timber for shipbuilding, he created a navy to support his conflict with the rival state of Surabaya, although he also, unsuccessfully, sought Dutch naval support. In contrast to the Dutch, Borneo marked the extent of Mataram's naval range. Naval conflict was not necessarily defined by that with or involving Western powers. For example, large squadrons of Mughal riverboats, carrying cannon, played a major role in defeating the fleet of Arakan in 1666, although the expansion of Mughal power against Arakan also owed much to operations on land, particularly road-building.

Nevertheless, there was no conflict between non-Western powers on the scale of that involving China, Japan and Korea in the 1590s. In large part, this absence reflected a different balance of opportunity and need to that of the 1590s, particularly the lack of any need for large-scale naval warfare on the part of China. Although the Chinese deployed warships against Taiwan and/or nearby islands, notably in the 1620s, 1660s and 1680s, this was a limited commitment and there was no need for any long-range naval activity. The major conflicts were those between Manchu and Ming, followed by the Rebellion of the Three Feudatories, and the war with the Dzhungars. These were all struggles waged on land, with the naval dimension being modest and principally brown-water (riverine). Modest is not the same as non-existent, and greater attention to the brown-water and coastal operations would encourage a realisation of the range and scale of naval operations,[2] with the same being true for South-East Asia, India and Africa. Nevertheless, there was no repetition in East Asia of the naval warfare of the 1590s and the fleets used in that warfare declined as China focused on other challenges. In particular, the quiescence of Japan proved a key element as it removed a sense of maritime challenge not only to Chinese interests but also to the related prestige and pre-eminence of China's rulers. Korea was lost to the Ming system when it was conquered overland by the Manchu, a conquest that could not be resisted at sea, and there was no repetition of the naval challenge to Korea from the Japanese.

The Manchu conquest of Ming China itself disrupted administrative structures and political links underpinning Chinese naval power. Moreover, the military culture and goals of the Manchu very much focused on land power and challenges. Thus, although the Manchu were finally to capture Taiwan, this represented a peripheral goal essentially linked to the control and pacification of south-eastern China, rather than an aspect of maritime power projection, still less such projection at a distance.

The Europeans also proved beneficiaries of this lack of sustained East Asian naval activity. From its stronghold in Manila in the Philippines, Spain established bases on Taiwan, at Keelung in 1626 and Tamsui in 1629, in between which Philip IV of Spain claimed the island in 1627. In turn, while they failed to overrun these positions in 1641, next year a Dutch expedition of eight warships and 690 men – and not a Chinese one – forced the vulnerable Spanish positions to surrender by placing cannon on commanding positions.[3] Their capture was part of the global Dutch assault on the Hispanic world, an assault that greatly contributed to the widespread crisis that affected the latter while also being a product of a longer-lasting situation of wide-ranging commitments and vulnerabilities on the part of Spain and Portugal, and of the potential for naval power projection, amphibious operations and profitable long-distance maritime commerce developed by the Dutch. This assault also testified to the geopolitical possibilities for offshore European activity that were accentuated by China's own mid-seventeenth-century crisis in the shape of the decline, and then collapse, of Ming power.

In the face of attack from China (see p. 81), the Dutch presence on Taiwan was not sustained, but, further from East Asia, the Europeans were successful in establishing a strong presence – the Dutch in the East Indies and the Spaniards in the Western Pacific – in so far as a strong presence can be used to describe, particularly in the latter case, a position in such vast bodies of water. Moreover, the Dutch role in the East Indies rested in large part on a willingness by the local powers to trade, a willingness in which coercion played a part but alongside mutual profit and also the use by local powers of the Dutch presence in order to advance their own interests. The Spanish position in the Philippines proved far more secure than that in Taiwan. A Chinese expedition from there to the Philippines in 1673 failed, while, although the Japanese considered an attack on Manila, none was launched. Moreover, the Spaniards were able to extend their position in the Philippine archipelago, for example capturing Zamboanga on the coast of Mindanao in 1635. A strong fortress was then constructed there under the direction of the Jesuit missionary-engineer Melchor de Vera. In the Western Pacific, Spanish power was established in the Mariana Islands in 1668 and in the Caroline Islands in 1696. More significantly, trans-Pacific trade developed between Manila and Acapulco on the Pacific coast of Mexico to the extent that, although the trade was relatively small scale in volume, Mexican silver dollars became the international currency of the region and had a major impact on the economies of China and Japan.

The seventeenth century saw Japan withdraw from all long-distance maritime activity. Domestic political developments were highly significant to this withdrawal, as groups that had maritime interests appeared a threat to Ieyasu, who founded the Tokugawa shōgunate in 1603. Shimazu, of the powerful Satsuma clan, had obtained permission to restore the profitable trade with China via the Ryukyu Islands, but his invasion of the latter in 1609 in order to impose Satsuma suzerainty was seen as a threat by Ieyasu and he ordered the destruction of all large ships in south-west Japan. Moreover, there was a more widespread restriction on the military activities of Japanese adventurers. As a result, there was no repetition of the rogue attempt to conquer Taiwan in 1616. Mounted by a merchant-adventurer, this was a failure: 13 junks filled with warriors were wrecked by a storm, only one ship reached Taiwan, and the local population killed the crew. In contrast, adventurers were given more leeway by European rulers in the first half of the century, and were, indeed, crucial to the system of military entrepreneurship by which troops were raised. In Japan, the Shogun's fear was in part also of domestic disorder fuelled by the contending rivalries of the recently arrived European missionaries and traders. By the 1630s, these were mostly expelled, as were the Portuguese in 1639. Links with the Dutch were curtailed in 1641. Although the Japanese had traded with South-East Asia in the sixteenth century, in the 1630s they were forbidden to travel overseas.

Japan's quiescence was in part a matter of policy choices, but there was also a broader cultural significance reflecting the situation in East Asia. There was no equivalent to the unique Western experience of creating a distinctive type of interaction between economy, technology and state formation, one in which there were important links between rulers and private entrepreneurs in mobilising resources. This interaction provided a key aspect of the impact of society on military capability and conflict.[4] In contrast, in China, Korea and Japan there was an ability to build large ships and manufacture guns, but there was hardly any interaction in these states between economy, technology and state formation, in so far as creating maritime effectiveness was concerned. Instead, their conception of power, like that of Mughal and Maratha India, was based on, and defined by, territorial control of land. This was a matter of ideas about appropriate roles as well as of the interests represented by landlord control and revenues, and the impact on policy was clear. Thus, the Manchu did not attempt at sea anything equivalent in difficulty to their operations against Kandahar and across the Hindu Kush, nor the Manchu anything similar to solving the logistical problems central to managing steppe warfare, which was considered the supreme strategic threat by all Chinese dynasties.

Islamic naval powers

In contrast to the Manchu, Mughals and Marathas, the Omani Arabs were successful in becoming a regional power for whom naval capability and maritime range were the key modes of operation. The Omanis under Sultan Ibn Saif al-Ya'rubi captured the Portuguese base of Muscat in 1650 and, on the basis of the ships they seized and the hybrid culture they took over, created a formidable navy with well-gunned warships. It was the largest fleet in the western part of the Indian Ocean. Far from that ocean being an area of clear divides between clashing civilisations, there was a willingness to hire and serve across ethnic and religious divides. Benefiting from the use of European mariners, and from the assistance of Dutch and English navigators, guns and arms supplies, the Omanis were also helped by the degree to which the extensive Portuguese overseas empire had already been weakened by persistent Dutch attacks. The Portuguese had only a small military presence on the East African coast; they were short of men, ships and money. The Omanis also pressed the Portuguese in India, attacking their bases (Bombay in 1661–2, Diu in 1668 and 1676, Bassein in 1674) as well as their trade, as aspects of a military policy focused on brigandage as both a way to secure resources and an exemplary form of male activity.[5]

Yet, the Omanis did not match the naval range of the Western Europeans, any more than did the Barbary states of North Africa, Tripoli, Tunis, Algiers and Morocco. Barbary raiders, seeking slaves and other loot, raided the coasts of Mediterranean Europe and the British Isles and Iceland, and there were naval attempts by the Christian powers to constrain them, including attacks on Barbary bases as well as attempts to protect trade, but neither proved particularly effective. Instead, although it proved possible to bribe and/or intimidate the Barbary privateers into leaving the ships of particular powers alone, there was no long-term settlement to the issue until North Africa was conquered by the Western powers. However, there was no repetition of the serious challenge to the Christian position in the Mediterranean mounted by Algiers and the Ottomans from the 1520s to 1570s – notably with the unsuccessful Ottoman attack on Malta in 1565 – let alone any recurrence of the Arab sway over much of the Mediterranean in the ninth century. In part, the situation in the seventeenth century reflected the absence of Ottoman action in the western and central Mediterranean, while the fragmented nature of the Barbary states and their limited industrial and fiscal base did not provide a foundation for the use of naval power in order to expand territorial strength or support commercial penetration.

The major Islamic empires, Mughal India, Safavid Persia and Ottoman Turkey, were all primarily land powers and the shift in Ottoman naval power was particularly notable. In the first 45 years of the seventeenth century, at a time when most of the *Kapudan Pashas*, admirals of the Ottoman Mediterranean fleet, were landsmen, the prime Ottoman naval task was not offensive but defensive, aimed at protecting the Black Sea from Cossacks based on the Rivers Don and Dnieper. Prominent instances of Cossack pressure included raids on Sinope in 1614 and on Yeniköy on the Bosporus in 1623,[6] and the occupation of Azov from 1637 to 1641. In response, the Ottoman fleet engaged in both defensive patrols and mounted expeditions. However, the Cossack *shaykas*, with their flat bottoms and no keel, had a shallower draft than the Ottoman galleys, and were therefore difficult to pursue, as the Ottoman Black Sea fleet discovered in 1615 when it ran aground while in pursuit. In turn, as an instance of the action–reaction cycle of military capability, the Ottomans developed flat-bottomed rowing boats of their own from the 1630s and used them with success against the Cossacks in the Strait of Kerch in 1639.

In the Mediterranean, the Ottomans were able to project force against the Venetian colony of Crete from 1645 to 1669, as they had done success-fully against the Venetian colony of Cyprus in 1570–1, but the challenge from Venice to their naval power in the Aegean from 1648 to 1657 was greater than it had been in the sixteenth century. Moreover, whereas Genoa was no longer a significant maritime power[7] and made no attempt to recreate its once far-flung maritime empire, the Venetians returned to the attack on the Ottomans from 1686. They were unsuccessful in attacks on the Aegean island of Euboea on 1689 and on Crete in 1692, and, although they captured the island of Chios in 1694, the unpopularity of their rule led to an uprising and their expulsion the following year. Nevertheless, these were Venetian attacks in the Aegean, and not Ottoman attacks in the Western and Central Mediterranean. In August 1676, the English agent in Holland reported, 'They are much alarmed at Amsterdam by news come thither of a great Turkish fleet of thirty men of war and fifty galleys besides many other vessels appearing between Sicily and Italy, who, some advices say, have already taken possession of the Faro of Messina.'[8] In reality, such speculations were of another age, and it was the Dutch, French and Spanish fleets that contested Sicilian waters. Indeed, this contest helped ensure a focus of the French navy on the Mediterranean rather than the Atlantic in the late 1670s.

The nature of Mediterranean naval power also changed. Improvements in armaments, rigging and sail patterns helped to ensure that sailing ships (galleons), rather than galleys, became far more important in Mediterranean warfare, although galleys continued to have a role until 1814 when they were discarded by the Royal Sardinian Navy. With their reduced demand for manpower and, thus, water and food, and their greater storage capacity, galleons were less dependent on local bases. The English and Dutch vessels that introduced new methods into Mediterranean naval warfare were copied by the Mediterranean powers, including, first, the North African Barbary states, which adapted Atlantic naval technology in the late sixteenth century through the intermediary of English and Dutch privateers.

The Ottomans were not confronted by the example, challenge and threat until later, the key intermediary being Venice, which adopted galleon construction in response to the threat from the Western European and Barbary states, before using these ships against the Ottomans following the latter's invasion of Crete in 1645. Venetian attempts to blockade the Dardanelles in 1647–8 deprived the army on Crete and the population in Constantinople of food, helping lead to the overthrow of Sultan Ibrahim in 1648, while the *Kapudan Pasha*, Ammarzade, was executed. The crisis continued and, in 1656, the Ottoman fleet was destroyed at the Dardanelles. In response, the Ottomans began to construct galleons (10 being built in 1650), although the galleon only became the standard Ottoman warship in 1682. The limitations of the Ottoman fleet helped explain the time taken to conquer Crete, but, alongside the use of flat-bottomed boats in the Black Sea, this development of a galleon force indicated the variety of means seen as appropriate to success. Even then, however, the Ottomans continued to lack good gunners and skilled crews.[9]

The potential for Ottoman naval power in the Indian Ocean that had existed from the conquest of Egypt (1517) and Iraq (1534) was not sustained. The bases of Suez, Aden and Basra, from which the Ottomans had exerted pressure on the Portuguese, notably between 1538 and 1554, remained in Ottoman hands, but they were no longer the bases for long-range activity. In 1568, an expedition had been sent to help Sultan Alauddin Riayat Syah al-Kahhar of Aceh in northern Sumatra against the Portuguese base of Malacca, but, from the mid-1570s, a rough division between areas of naval hegemony developed, with the Ottomans largely confined to the Red Sea. Moreover, the Portuguese and Safavids were able to neutralise the Ottoman presence in the Persian Gulf. This situation did not change in the seventeenth century, and it was the Omani Arabs, not the Ottomans, that challenged the Portuguese on the Swahili coast of East Africa. Whereas most of the cities on the latter between Mogadishu and Kilwa had recognised Ottoman supremacy after naval expeditions in 1585 and 1588, this pressure was not maintained.

An emphasis on the Omanis, moreover, cannot disguise the fact that it was the Dutch who proved a more formidable threat to the Portuguese, conquering their principal bases in the Moluccas from 1605, as well as Malacca in 1641, the bases in coastal Ceylon in 1638–58, and those on the Malabar coast of India, Quilon, Cranganore and Cochin, in 1661–3.[10] Much of the fighting took place on land, but naval capability was a crucial prerequisite. In the Indian Ocean a nominal Dutch protectorate was established, replacing Portuguese influence, and the Dutch were also able to use their naval power against non-Western powers. Prior to Russian pressure from the 1720s, the Western impact on Persia was restricted to the Persian Gulf where, in 1684, a blockade by a Dutch East India Company squadron was part of a process by which Western commercial interests were defended, rather than an attempt to create a network of bases. The Dutch captured the island position of Qishm, but restored it to Persian control in 1685 in order to forward negotiations. The Portuguese had similarly used a naval force in 1674 to secure their share of toll revenue.

Naval tasking

The deployment of naval power in the Persian Gulf serves as a reminder that battle was not the sole definition of such power, no more than it was on land. Indeed, part of the problem with discussion of naval power arises from the tendency to see it in later terms of control of the sea. In practice, such control was not really viable given the resources and technology of the period, while the concepts of naval power were different to those advanced by A. T. Mahan and other writers of the late nineteenth century. Factors other than just resources and technology played a role as there was also a contrast in goals. In particular, the shared sovereignty and overlapping powers that were so important to government and politics round much of the world in the seventeenth century were not readily equated with the late nineteenth-century idea of control of the sea. Instead, in the seventeenth century, it was common to find vague talk of mastery over the sea combined with the focus on protocol and precedence that encouraged the enforcement of showing respect to the flag.

The range of naval activities in the seventeenth century included battle as well as smaller-scale engagements, blockades, attacks on trade – by both warships and privateers[11] – and, in particular, the support of amphibious operations or opposition to them. The latter, indeed, were the most important naval activity, but, as has often been the fate of combined operations across history, have been underplayed by those more interested in a single-'service' approach, namely those of armies or navies. In practice, many of the naval battles of the period were linked to these operations and/or to blockades, rather than to some less 'fixed' and more general notion of control of the sea. This linkage of battles at sea to amphibious operations serves as a parallel to those of battles on land and sieges. To take, for example, the most prominent naval conflicts of the century, the three Anglo-Dutch wars of 1652–4, 1665–7 and 1672–4, this linkage was an important element in the third war. Thus, in 1672, the English and French sought to destroy the Dutch fleet, the most impressive in Europe and, therefore, the world, in order to assist the French land invasion of the United Provinces. In response, De Ruyter surprised the English fleet in Southwold Bay, inflicting much damage and delaying a planned attack on the Dutch coast. In 1673, De Ruyter skilfully fought off a larger Anglo-French fleet in defensive actions at Schooneveld and the Texel. Dutch successes were significant operationally and strategically: they prevented attack on the Dutch coast and helped deny the quick victory necessary to keep Charles II of England in the war.[12]

Earlier, in 1639, a Spanish attempt to strengthen their presence in the Low Countries by sea, in a form of strategic relief that reflected the closure of the land route from Spanish Italy, led to the Battle of the Downs as the Dutch successfully intercepted the fleet. This was one of the more significant battles of the century, not only because of the heavy losses suffered by Spain, but also because the battle, between major forces, established a clear impression of Spanish weakness and Dutch strength at sea, an impression that then became normative.

As another instance of the naval–amphibious nexus, French intervention in support of a rising in 1674 in Messina in Sicily against Spanish rule led to the deployment of over 11,000 troops and to a number of naval battles in Sicilian waters in 1675–6. These battles involved Dutch, French and Spanish squadrons which sought to affect the operations on land. Composed of sailing ships, the French squadron carried more cannon than the opposing Spanish galleys and therefore raised the Spanish siege of Messina in 1675, only for the Dutch, in response, to send a fleet of their own sailing ships.[13] Blockading by sea a fortress that was being besieged was a key way to help ensure its fall, not only by cutting off supplies but also by demonstrating the strength of the attacking power.

In 1688 the English navy, although large and undefeated, failed, as a result of contrary winds and divided leadership with differing political views, to block the Dutch invasion of England; there was no naval battle in what was one of the most successful amphibious operations of the century. In contrast, in 1689, French intervention in Ireland and, in 1692, preparations for a French invasion of England led to battles respectively at Bantry Bay and Barfleur.[14] Naval clashes in the Baltic were also linked to expeditions and to challenges to maritime routes, notably those between Sweden and its possessions on the southern shore of the Baltic, routes repeatedly attacked by the Danes.

The use of naval power in support of amphibious operations was a key theme for conflict between Europeans outside Europe, although the ratio of naval power to distance was such that there was less of a risk there of clashes between warships and, still less, between appreciable forces of warships. Moreover, for logistical reasons, most warships could not sail far from their bases without resupply and, anyway, the bulk of European warships were designed primarily to fight in home waters.

This factor became more apparent with the development of line-ahead tactics from mid-century: although not always easy to execute in practice, these tactics involved ships sailing in a line and firing broadsides at close range at a line of opposing warships who would presumably be doing the same. As a result of this tactical possibility, the importance of heavily gunned ships of the line greatly increased, and, in the 1660s, large two-deckers – ships displacing 1100–1600 tons (1117–1625 tonnes) armed with 24-pounders (11 kg) – were constructed in great numbers in Europe. Naval success in part reflected the ability to benefit from these changes, whereas, conversely, a failure to adapt spelled trouble. Less heavily gunned vessels, such as those of the Dutch in the First Anglo-Dutch War of 1652–4, were rendered obsolete. Firepower was enhanced by the replacement of bronze cannon, as advances in cast iron produced cheaper and more dependable heavy guns. These large ships drove up the cost and prestige of being a major naval power and also encouraged a naval race between the Dutch, France and England, each of which, in turn, had the largest navy in the world.[15] A shift to heavily gunned vessels encouraged the focus on purpose-built warships with strong hulls, rather than converted merchantmen, and this shift led to a professionalisation of naval officership, senior ratings and infrastructure.

Victory at sea required fixing opponents for combat, which, however, was not easy given the dependence of ships on the wind, and the fact that it blew in the same direction for all combatants so that ships that sought to avoid conflict had a good chance of doing so.[16] Like conflict on land, victory at sea requires an understanding that success is not necessarily measured in terms of the ratio of casualties. Indeed, given the difficulty of sinking wooden ships (unless they caught fire after gunpowder on them was ignited), battles sometimes did not result in any ships being sunk. Such battles, however, were not necessarily indecisive, and victory can best be understood in terms of the combatants' goals, particularly when fleets were being employed for specific missions such as supporting or preventing expeditions, rather than simply searching for triumph in battle.

The large, heavy ship-batterers with their substantial crews were not suitable for transoceanic voyages, and, instead, it was less heavily gunned warships, which had better lines for speed and required a smaller crew, that supported attacks on the bases of other powers. These attacks were crucial to transoceanic conflict because European colonies largely rested on their maritime links. Most of the conflict in the colonies was not across land frontiers, as was increasingly to be the case between the English and French in North America and India from the mid-eighteenth century, but, instead, focused on these bases: for example Québec in Canada, which was the target of English attack on several occasions, only falling once in the seventeenth century, in 1629; it was returned to the French in 1632 as part of the peace settlement. The forces involved in transoceanic conflict, for example in the English occupation of the Dutch position of New Amsterdam (New York) in 1664, were generally far smaller than those committed for conflict in Europe. Thus, in 1642, a Dutch force of 591 men took Keelung, the Spanish base on Taiwan, which had a garrison of only 115 Spaniards and 155 Filipinos, being an outlier of the Spanish colony on the Philippines. When such small forces were involved, there was a premium on experience, morale and command that was at once bold and skilful.

Naval operations were particularly important to conflict centred on islands, notably in the Caribbean, but also, for example, off the coast of West Africa. Thus, as a central aspect of their assault on the Hispanic world,[17] the Dutch attacked island bases, including São Tomé and the Portuguese bases on Sri Lanka, their gains including Trincomalee in 1639, Galle and Negombo in 1640, Colombo in 1656 and Jaffna in 1658. In the Dutch War (1672–8), the French recaptured the Caribbean islands of St Martin (1676) and Tobago (1677) after Jean, Count of Estrées, defeated a Dutch squadron off the latter island; but an expedition sent to the Dutch colony of Curaçao in 1678 ran aground in May on the Isle of Aves off the coast of Venezuela with the loss of seven ships of the line. The Dutch, in turn, were unable to capture Martinique in 1674.

These islands produced plantation goods, particularly sugar, coffee and cocoa, that were a major source of revenue for the governments of colonial powers, with profit gained from selling into domestic markets as well as from re-exports. Moreover, the value of this trade was enhanced as loans could be raised on the basis of anticipated customs revenue. Thus, naval power can be seen as part of a benign administrative cycle, securing colonial trade that produced revenues that, in turn, could be invested in naval strength that offered not only protection but a means of harming the rival systems of opposing states and thus transferring revenues. The French sent six expeditions to the Caribbean in 1689–97 during the Nine Years' War with England and the Dutch. The English, in turn, made major efforts, although they failed to capture Guadeloupe in 1691, Martinique in 1693 and St Domingue in 1694.

Naval expeditions were also important against 'land islands', bases on land that had scant contact with a hostile, or at least unsupportive, hinterland, such as the European bases in West Africa and on the Guiana and Brazilian coasts of South America. Thus, despite significant and often successful resistance, the Dutch conquered the northern provinces of Brazil from Portugal from the 1620s, capturing the major port of Recife in 1630, only to fail in Brazil from 1645 and be driven out in 1654 when Recife was recaptured. The port was important not least because the value of a colony derived in large part from its ability to trade.[18] In 1676, the Dutch recaptured Cayenne (French Guiana) from the French, only for it to be taken back later that year.

In West Africa, the Dutch captured the Portuguese slaving bases of Luanda, Beneguela and São Tomé in 1641, but in 1648 a Portuguese fleet from Brazil recaptured them, which provided the basis for a marked revival of the integrated Portuguese slave and sugar economy in the South Atlantic: slaves were shipped to Brazil from Angola and West Africa. In part, this process reflected the relative economy of force, in that the labour from the sugar plantation economy of Brazil had initially derived largely from slaving raids against the native population. However, although this method continued, it had become less significant due to the exhaustion of nearby sources of labour, to effective resistance by more distant tribes in the heavily forested interior, and to the cost of transporting slaves over-land. In contrast, it proved easier and more profitable to move slaves by sea across the South Atlantic, having purchased them from African rulers who had gained them through warfare in Africa, which is an example of the multiple relationships between different types of conflict and power. The Portuguese South Atlantic remained an important politico-economic zone until the 1820s when Brazil fought off Portuguese control, but in the seventeenth century the Portuguese were to be much less successful in resisting Dutch (and local) pressure in South Asia. More generally, wars revealed the vulnerability of isolated bases. Thus in 1658, the Danes seized the Swedish positions in West Africa, which were then sold to the Dutch West Africa Company. Also in West Africa, the French took the slave trade bases of Gorée (1677) and Arquin (1678) from the Dutch, ruining their trade.

In Asia, as on the coast of West Africa, co-operation with the local rulers was far more important than in South America, and a failure of co-operation helps explain why French attacks on the Dutch in Sri Lanka and southern India during the Dutch War (1672–8) failed. The French established a base at Trincomalee on Sri Lanka in the spring of 1672 and made approaches to Sinha II, ruler of the interior kingdom of Kandy, then at war with the Dutch. He was willing to negotiate an alliance, but French inaction led to a failure to co-operate and, in July 1672, the base capitulated to a Dutch fleet. That month, the French captured São Tomé on the Coromandel coast of India, a Dutch base within the dominions of Golconda, but the pressure of France's European commitments led to a failure to send necessary reinforcements, and in 1674 an alliance of Golconda and the Dutch forced the French to surrender. No French fleet of comparable size was sent to the Indian Ocean during the rest of the century.[19] The attitude of local powers was often crucial. Thus, in the East Indies, the Dutch took control of the Makassarese fort of Ujungpandang on the island of Sulawesi in 1669, but only in combination with a local ally, the Buginese. Moreover, as a reminder of the relative severity of threats, and thus of the prioritisation that helped determine strategy, military structures and doctrine, the French were far less significant to Golconda than the Mughals, and the Coromandel coast, while economically valuable, was strategically peripheral in terms of Golconda's relations with the latter.

Any move from the water meant that Western military advantages were greatly lessened. For example, the Dutch had no success in conflict with the kingdom of Kandy, while in the Javan interior in 1678–81 they faced problems due to logistics, terrain, the number of their opponents and the unreliability of their allies. Such a character to power projection anticipates some aspects of Western military power at present.

Knowledge and Western naval power

At the same time, the Western powers proved distinctive in their ability to obtain information on distant waters and apply it on a global scale. The inventions discussed by William Barlow in *The Navigators Supply* (London, 1597) offered a range of possibilities. They included the hemisphere, a portable globe aiding calculations on site, the pantometer for measuring the vertical and horizontal angles of terrestrial and celestial objects, the traverse board which facilitated calculation of speed and course, and the traveller's jewel, an equinoctial sundial for calculating the correct time at any point of latitude. In his *L'Architecture navale* (Paris, 1677), the Sieur de Dassié included not only details of vessel construction and preparation but also tables of longitude, latitude and tides, details of the major ports of the world and of sailing routes to the East and West Indies, and information on sailing seasons. Colbert, the key figure in developing French naval power, was the dedicatee in 1666 of *L'Art de Naviger*, an attempt to discover the variation between different magnetic measuring instruments, by one of his protégés, Guillaume Denys, who had opened a school of hydrography in Dieppe the previous year. Other aspects of naval activity were also covered by European writers. For example, John Smith published *An Accidence or the Path-Way to Experience necessary for all Young Seamen* (London, 1626), which appeared as the expanded *A Sea Grammar* the following year, providing printed information on seamanship and naval gunnery. Another edition appeared in 1699.

Moreover, during the century there were clear signs of improvement in knowledge, notably in the mapping of coasts and waters which were seen to be important for warfare and defence. It was generally the case that more ships were sunk as a result of running aground than due to losses in battle, and knowledge of inshore waters was therefore highly significant to both amphibious operations and blockades. Established commercial chart publishers were called on to meet official needs for charts, as with the activities of the Blaeu dynasty in connection with the Dutch East and West India Companies,[20] and with the publication of the *Neptune François* and the Dutch pirate version in the early 1690s. In a direct, and ultimately successful, challenge to Dutch hegemony over the sea-chart market, the initial issue of *The English Pilot* was published in London in 1689 and eventually ran to four books encompassing the whole globe. Although many of the maps were derivatives of earlier Dutch charts, the work proved enormously popular, not least due to the charts' accompaniment of sailing directions written in English.

Naval operations were heavily dependent on maps, and mapping spread and improved. For example, the Swedish navy used Dutch maps of the Baltic Sea until 1645 when the first Swedish map was published by the navy's Senior Master Pilot, Johan Månsson. This map was heavily dependent on the Dutch maps. A much better map was published by Petter Gedda in 1695 after extensive surveying operations, and, from then, the navy continually surveyed and updated maps of the Baltic and the Swedish coast. This was significant to the ability to project power swiftly so as to support Swedish territories on the eastern and southern shores of the Baltic, providing an effective strategic response to the problems posed by the threat from a number of powers each able to take the initiative on land, notably Russia, but also Poland, Prussia and Denmark. Moreover, in 1696, Peter the Great's second campaign against Azov saw the mapping of the coastline as part of a successful effort to prevent the Ottomans from resupplying the fortress as they had done the previous year. More generally, the sea was both a highway for reinforcement but also a space that had to be overcome swiftly and safely; and knowledge, both learned on the job and prepared information, was valuable for the latter.

Western navies and state power

Transoceanic power projection was important to the economies of the Western European states, helping precipitate a capitalism able to generate per capita wealth greater than that in Asia, as well as leading to greater social integration between 'the old military-agrarian extractive elite' and those linked to commerce.[21] In turn, these economies enhanced the capacity to create and sustain navies, which were expensive, notably because of the capital and running costs of the ships and equipment, and of the infrastructure necessary to support them. As a result of the difficulties both of financing these capital and running costs, but also, more generally, of creating the very systems that would lead to such forces, navies were an important aspect of the degree to which war, or more specifically military capability, increasingly became a matter of the intersection of capitalism and the state. This intersection was central to the ability to marshal resources, although care is needed before assuming that navies were necessarily the expression of freedom or, at least, liberal tendencies, which is a view often advanced today, drawing on the later examples of the naval power of Britain and the USA. Instead, slaves were used as rowers for some European galley fleets, notably France[22] and Tuscany, while Peter the Great conscripted serfs for his fleet.

Moreover, under Louis XIV, who was less liberal than his Dutch and English opponents, French naval power overtook that of the Dutch before, in the 1690s, Louis's decision to focus on the army[23] helped the English shipbuilding programme to lead to a larger fleet than that of France. French naval strength was also underwritten by large-scale work on developing an infrastructure of bases which were also strongly fortified against attack. Brest and Toulon were the key bases under Louis XIV.

The intersection of capitalism and the state was focused and symbolised in institutions such as the Bank of England, which was founded in London in 1694. Thus, the military-financial combination of the early-modern period preceded the military-industrial complexes of the nineteenth and twentieth centuries, although the latter were also necessary in the seventeenth century, not least to produce firearms as well as warships. The study of such complexes in the seventeenth century is only patchy (although Guy Rowlands is working on firearms production in France), and does not readily permit precise comparative judgements. Nevertheless, a measure is provided by the naval facilities of the period, which were some of the most impressive constructions of the age, used for the process of naval change seen with the building of numerous large-deckers from the 1660s. Like line-ahead tactics, this building reflected the ability of naval systems to develop a capability in which resources, organisation and the pressure of conflict combined.

The role of each was seen in the development of Dutch naval operations which, in the first half of the century, were affected by the autonomous nature of the five Dutch admiralties. In contrast, in the second half, as a result of war with England and France, naval activities and administration were better co-ordinated. The Dutch navy was then well manned: the supply of seamen on the labour market and the regulations during wartime were such that all available and required men-of-war could always sail and could be commanded by qualified and motivated officers. The protection of economic interests and the hostile political situation in Europe constantly compelled the Dutch ruling class to ensure that it had a strong navy, and it did so.[24] Although no longer, from mid-century, the leading navy even, arguably, by 1690 in qualitative terms,[25] the Dutch navy remained a major one and its co-operation with that of England was highly significant to the naval dimension of the Nine Years' War (1688–97). As a result of this co-operation, the French navy was outnumbered in the English Channel, which provided a useful margin both in battle and in responding to any possible French naval action, although success was not thereby guaranteed. Moreover, the strength of the Anglo-Dutch position in the Channel made possible a safer force projection into the Mediterranean and the Caribbean.[26] Thus, the maintenance of the Dutch navy as an effective force gave the allies an important strategic capability which was significant for retaining the appeal of the alliance in the Mediterranean.

Naval construction involved complex issues of procurement, specialisation and integration that played an important role in the development of modern industrial processes. Any single account of the reasons why industrialisation of the sophistication and scale termed the Industrial

Revolution began in Britain would be simplistic, but the creation of the world's foremost ship-construction industry was significant, notably for the experience it provided in large-scale manufacturing processes and because it helped secure the country's maritime and commercial position. The transition of skills was particularly apparent to commercial shipbuilding. Moreover, the procurement of necessary raw materials, such as wood (of certain specifications), hemp, tar and iron, and their manufacture into ships and cannon, involved wide-ranging supply networks, and these tested commercial and financial capabilities. In particular, these networks linked the Baltic sources of naval supplies to shipyards in Western Europe, although there were many other links, for example between Balkan timber supplies and Mediterranean shipyards, notably in Toulon and Venice.

These networks helped explain the strategic importance of particular areas, and, due to their place in manufacturing, they had a different role to that of areas producing food surpluses, which, instead, were primarily of operational significance for armies. Nevertheless, food supplies were also of strategic importance, and thus their interruption and safeguarding were important, as in 1694 in the North Sea when a fleet of grain ships en route from the Baltic to provide Paris with much-needed food after two years of poor harvests was captured by a Dutch squadron, only to be regained by the French, under Jan Bart, who was himself of Dutch origins.

Only certain states were able to draw on the wide-ranging supply networks of naval stores seen as important to English naval power by Thomas Hale,[27] and that helps explain the differing character of naval power and activity across the world. In Africa, as in most of the non-European world, military capability was largely a matter of land power, although there was also a series of coastal polities that controlled flotillas operating in inshore, estuarine, deltaic and riverine waters. These boats were shallow in draught and therefore enjoyed a range denied European warships. Their crews usually fought with missile weapons. Fleets of outrigger canoes were developed in some areas, including Madagascar as well as in the Pacific, in New Zealand and in Pacific North America. The divide between the hunting of animals and conflict with humans was not too great at this level of weapon technology and military organisation.

A fleet of Pacific canoes involved an impressive degree of organisation, as perceptive European observers noted in the eighteenth century, but this organisation did not conform to the commercial-industrial requirements of the large ships of the line produced in only a relatively few centres. Yet, a link between state development and military potential was provided not only by large-scale, long-range navies but also by the need for political-administrative structures capable of mobilising large numbers of men in order to sustain firepower tactics based on large forces. This situation was definitely true of European states that created substantial armies in the second half of the seventeenth century, but was not a demonstration of European exceptionalism since it was also the case elsewhere, for example on the Gold and Slave Coasts in West Africa. These points need to be borne in mind alongside the commonplace observation that the choice between land and sea power had political and governmental consequences that influenced socio-economic develop-ments,[28] as well as helping to secure a certain type of state, a point made by those who note that navies do not stage coups because they lack the authoritarian culture, context and consequences of armies.

In considering these and related issues, it is worth underlining a simple historiographical point, namely the dependence of historical scholarship on a very small number of individuals. This is particularly true of naval history, which attracts less attention than its land counterpart, with most of the scholarship devoted to individual navies, especially to the English navy by anglophone scholars. There is little comparative work and the only comparative scholar of note to address conceptual issues with any thoroughness, the Swedish academic Jan Glete, died relatively young in 2009. No other scholar has yet taken his place, and that suggests that this aspect of the subject will not be taken forward. The particular problem is that Glete was subtle in probing the degree to which navies required (and armies as well[29]) not simply state support but also a grounding in particular socio-economic contexts, and that the nature of naval force reflected in many respects the character of this context. This approach offers a qualification to the commonplace account of naval development in terms of state action, with themes of bureaucratisation and government control pushed to the fore. Instead, it might be more appropriate to emphasise a consensual approach to naval power, with this approach seen not simply or solely as a contrast to more authoritarian army systems but, instead, as sharing with armies in a pattern of joint control between state and society – with both state and society, in practice, proving abstractions the activities of which were mediated by the roles of the social élite in governance and by patronage. The death of Glete suggests that the empirical basis for such an approach will not be tested for a while.

Moreover, naval warfare was not a struggle in the abstract but, instead, a carefully honed process in which particular goals were pursued. These objectives varied by state and conflict, and their variations provide a key element that is ignored when the literature's emphasis is on uniformity and focuses either on change, for example technological development, or on continuity, such as the nature of conflict. The challenge of relating naval warfare to goals is one that has been inadequately pursued. Instead, a goals-based approach to early-modern naval history remains in its infancy, particularly for non-Western European states. The need to locate the study of this history in the specific political contexts of particular states remains a pressing one.

9 Warfare, Social Contexts and State Development

War and state development

The early-modern period is generally given a major role to play in works on the development of states.[1] A classic account of this period argues that newly developed technology, in the shape of cannon and firearms, helped strengthen the military potential of the state and also acted as its cutting arm, supposedly enabling central government to overcome local particu-larism in the shape of the castle walls of powerful aristocrats and the town walls of independent cities. Indeed, the terms of the surrender of the Huguenot stronghold of La Rochelle in 1628 included the demolition of its fortifications, and, in 1629, Cardinal Richelieu oversaw personally the destruction of the walls of Huguenot towns in the rebellious province of Languedoc. Thus, at Montauban, which submitted under the threat of a siege, Richelieu both celebrated a *Te Deum*, an affirmation of Catholic triumph, and watched as the first stone was removed from the town ramparts. In 1632, the castle and ramparts of Les Baux-de-Provence, long a centre of aristocratic opposition to royal control, were demolished. Military capability and the consequences of internal conflict were linked, in the classic account of military-political developments, to a newfound political cohesion that served as the basis for the early-modern state, distinguishing it from medieval predecessors. Furthermore, it was argued that the pressures of external conflict, in particular its cost, helped lead to this new situation. In short, a form of social Darwinism (competition resulting in the survival of the fittest) focused on military capability and employed war as its process: conflict serving as cause, course and consequence of state development.[2]

At the systemic and abstract levels, the analysis outlined above has considerable force, but, aside from the specific problems in applying a gunpowder-based approach to comparative power and state building,[3] explaining why some states did better than others, this analysis also suffers from its schematic character. The abstraction of 'the state' is a particular problem, and there is a misleading tendency to treat 'the state' as an essentially bureaucratic entity automatically seeking greater power. This account fails to assess the multiple divisions within what is termed 'the state', and their close interrelationship with social dynamics,[4] not least the relationship between court and aristocratic factionalism and the impact of this relationship on government.

There is also a highly misleading tendency to modernise the nature of decision making and the rationale of power and goals, a tendency that can be seen as a corollary to the emphasis on rationalism and efficiency in the literature on the Military Revolution. In practice, the ambitions of the rulers were the key element, and these ambitions frequently focused on dynastic honour and personal glory, each of which were goals in their own right as well as characteristics that greatly affected the interpretation and pursuit of other goals. This situation was true of monarchs in China, India and Persia as much as Europe, but, similarly, the Iroquois in North America were concerned with glory, honour and revenge, rather than economic issues.[5] The sense that monarchs had of their own reputation played a major role in the choices they made, not least in resolving conflicting priorities. War, indeed, served to win prestige and glory, and to assert and affirm rank and privilege – and notably those of rulers struggling to establish their own position and those of new dynasties, such as the Bourbon and Romanov in early seventeenth-century France and Russia respectively, and the Braganza in Portugal and Manchu in China later in the century. Many rulers led their forces on campaign and into battle, Tsar Alexei taking a major role at the siege of Smolensk in 1654. This number included those not noted as war leaders, such as Philip IV of Spain, who, in 1642, joined the forces that unsuccessfully sought to suppress the Catalan rising.

War as a means to win prestige and glory and to affirm rank and privilege was also true for social élites, whether or not their position was expressed, as in Europe, as an hereditary aristocracy. Indeed, these factors helped explain both the attitudes of ministers and generals in the service of their own rulers and their concern for their personal *gloire* or, in Spanish, *reputacion*.

These factors also explained the willingness to serve 'foreign' rulers, which was common, not least as the ties of service were largely personal, with personal honour proving a key concept in such circumstances. Moreover, this personal relationship worked both ways, leading to rulers, such as the Austrian Habsburgs and Russian Romanovs, being happy to have many commanders and officers who were not, at least by birth, subjects. In turn, the reward of service created mutual obligations that helped make these individuals subjects, and notably if they received land, which was the case for many who served the Austrian Habsburgs, especially as the suppression of the Bohemian revolt in 1620 was followed by the expropriation of much of the Protestant aristocracy. Lands confiscated from Protestant nobles who resisted Ferdinand II in the Bohemian Rising were conferred on Ferdinand's generals, creating the basis for a political system that lasted until the First World War.[6]

Patronage was a fundamental practice of government and politics, and the extension of patronage networks served to provide an important strengthening of political influence, as well as to consolidate control in conquered regions. This was an aspect of the nuanced relationship between rulers and the socially prominent, one seen in China and India as much as Europe.[7] Military service was a central cause, means and consequence of patronage.

Alongside the habitual tendency to treat states as entities inherently seeking greater power, it is necessary to emphasise the multiple pressures they encountered. These pressures greatly increased from the early sixteenth century, in large part due to the highly disruptive consequences of the Protestant Reformation and the Catholic Counter-Reformation, consequences not matched in China or India, although rivalry between Islam and Hinduism could be important in the latter. The Reformation and Counter-Reformation ensured that many rulers faced sustained opposition to their attempts to secure religious uniformity, opposition that challenged not just the reality, but the very legitimacy, of their rule. Disruption also stemmed from the Safavid takeover of Persia in the sixteenth century, as the Safavids were not only Shi'is but also claimed quasi-divine status, both of which challenged the Ottomans, notably in Anatolia where there were many Shi'is and also more generally in the Muslim world.

In Europe, there was no sense of church and state as separate, and thus a challenge to the church was seen as one to the ruler and one that required prompt action in order to prevent the dissolution of the state. Much of the resulting dynamic of conflict lasted from the mid-sixteenth century to the mid-seventeenth, notably with the Dutch Revolt of the 1560s, which finally ended when Spain in effect acknowledged Dutch independence in 1648. The crisis in France similarly began in the 1560s, although it ended with the suppression of Huguenot military power and political independence in 1629, the two being crucially linked but only secured as a result of successful campaigning by royal forces. In Germany and the Habsburg hereditary lands, notably what is now Austria and the Czech Republic, the Peace of Westphalia of 1648 also resolved most of the political tensions arising from the Reformation, tensions that had led to the Schmalkaldic War in Germany in the 1540s and to the rebellion in Bohemia against Habsburg rule in 1618.

However, in many parts of Europe, the divide between Protestantism and Catholicism continued to be important in helping cause civil conflict, notably in the parts of Hungary under Habsburg control, where Protestant nobles resisted Catholicisation, and also in Ireland, where William III's conquest in 1690–2 was, for many, a new iteration of the wars of religion. Other elements of domestic opposition to rulers, such as aristocratic factionalism in France, focused in part on religious divisions, although the opposition there of Catholic aristocrats, such as the Guise, to Catholic rulers indicated that more was involved.

From the perspective of these and other domestic restraints and opposition, the military capability of the central government was often a matter of bold pretensions but, in reality, also of desperate shifts and expedients in the face of criticism and factional interests. Rather than seeing the state as a powerful player able to impose its will on society, the state, instead, emerges as a product of social dynamics and political factionalism and with only a limited ability to mould either – an ability, moreover, in which circumstances, notably the personality and skill of rulers and the nature of international challenges, bulked large.

Moreover, these social dynamics included towns which had their own politics that were different to those of rural areas, although rarely separate from them. These urban spaces provided capital and skills but also required management. Townspeople were also significant in fostering the demand for information about war. For example, urban public interest encouraged the production of maps showing regions of contention and hostilities. In 1635, a map published in The Hague depicted recent Dutch operations in Brazil and Curaçao, providing both details of particular sites, such as Recife (captured by the Dutch in 1630), and a large-scale map of Brazil on which the general campaign could be followed.

Religious division heightened the bitterness of conflict, providing another dimension to the relationship between war and society. This is still a field in which work is somewhat limited, but it is clear that the enhancement of military capability, or at least the frequency of conflict, had a major impact on both social mores and the fabric of life.[8] Most of the work on the cultural aspects of the relationship between war and social mores relates to the élite, and not to the bulk of the population, but the latter were highly vulnerable to the disruption brought by war. This vulnerability was a matter not only of the direct devastation wrought by conflict and the passage of troops but also of the extent to which warfare hit trade and led to demands for food and manpower.

In turn, the impact of society on military capability and conflict was important not simply due to functional issues, such as ease of recruitment and financial support, but also with reference to the social norms affecting the pursuit of war and the nature of conflict, norms that greatly influenced the choice of commanders, and also extended to operational issues. The widespread nature of violence in society, moreover, was a factor in setting the context within which warfare was considered,[9] and reflected the extent to which ownership of arms and experience in their use were far more common than today. This had functional as well as cultural consequences for warfare, namely in making it easier across the world to find men able and willing to take part in conflict.

Recruitment

There were two main forms of military service: that for pay in which there was a degree of volition, and service that was compulsory. The latter might be rewarded with money, but the cash nexus was not the main rationale explaining service. Compulsory military service was generally for the ruler of the state or his representative. Such service was therefore 'national', although that is to employ a terminology that was anachronistic for most of history. Furthermore, service from foreign captives could be significant, and included slaves from abroad (often an important source of manpower) as well as combatants captured in war. The latter practice continued to be important in the seventeenth century, with such service not necessarily being unwelcome to those captured. A separate, and more significant, form of compulsory service was that for landlords. The position of leaders within kinship networks added another element.

Voluntary service for pay was of the essence of mercenary payment, but it has been redefined across history in order to ensure that such service is seen as virtuous if for one's own state/country/people/lord, and very much not so if for someone else's. This construction means much in the modern world, and helps locate private military service in an ambiguous light, but the situation is far less secure in terms of the historical judgement of the seventeenth century. Thus, a distinction of troops serving as mercenaries for pay, rather than for reasons of patriotism or ideology, does not capture the nature of military service across most of history because it rests on a social politics that is largely true for the modern world ('modern' understood as essentially beginning with the French Revolution), but not earlier. Moreover, the modern stigma of fighting for a foreign ruler meant less when foreignness was not such a clear concept as in the subsequent age of nationalism that was also part of this modernity.

As in southern India, the large number of weak states in medieval and early-modern Europe encouraged the use of mercenaries, although they were also associated with particular areas. As a reminder of the difficulty of locating developments, mercenaries can be seen as an instance of 'sub-feudal' warfare, and yet also as evidence of the onset of capitalism, both of which were important elements in the seventeenth-century economy and, with the onset of capitalism, regarded as a modernising perspective. In the case of 'sub-feudal' warfare, the presence of mercenaries reflected the ability of prominent individuals (and most leaders of mercenary forces were from the social élite) to recruit troops. Indeed, the distinction between such units and those raised by members of the social élite for the service of their sovereign was not always as clear as the use of the term 'mercenary' might imply, and this overlap continued to be important throughout the seventeenth century. For example, although money is generally seen as the prime nexus of mercenary activity, this ignores the extent to which commanders were frequently rewarded with land and the social status that went with it. This practice was seen, for example, in the Thirty Years' War (1618–48), but was also the case in India.

Similarly, the fact that soldiers (and their commanders) were serving for money was not inherently incompatible with feudalism, a socio-military system that had linked the provision of military service to the receipt from the sovereign of land and other feudal rights. This system is usually seen as European, but was also common elsewhere, as with the Ottoman allocation of a *timar*, usually a village or group of villages, to a cavalryman in return for military service. Far from being static, feudalism had proved an adaptable system that had responded to the spread of the money economy in the medieval period and subsequently. Although the formal character of feudal military service declined, feudal concepts of position in return for service continued to influence aristocratic attitudes and thus the armies, which drew heavily on aristocratic forces. Indeed, the notion of reciprocal relationship was akin to that of the mercenary. The common result was that entrepreneurs were contracted to raise and maintain units and could also take a role in directing policy.

Whether as feudal levies, militia, mercenaries or permanent armed forces, recruited voluntarily or by conscription, the social dimension of war included an assumption that soldiers and sailors would serve at the behest and under the control of their social superiors. Although there was dissatisfaction and mutiny, the soldiery were not consulted about their conditions or instructions. At the same time, soldiers were not reduced to unthinking ciphers, and officers had to take steps to maintain morale. The latter element was particularly important given the significance of experienced troops for ensuring military capability. Thus, despite being slaves, the Ottoman *janissaries* were able to force attention to their wishes by staging mutinies, as in 1622 when Shah Osman was forced to turn back from a journey the *janissaries* believed was intended to lead to his collecting an army in order to disband them. In 1606, an expedition sent into Anatolia had been abandoned when the unpaid troops mutinied.[10] Slave soldiers were common in the Islamic world and were also found in large numbers in sub-Saharan Africa.[11]

Across the world, efforts to maintain military morale included not only ensuring pay and supplies, but also particular efforts at moments of conflict. Thus, when attempts were made to storm fortresses, the soldiers were promised spoils, including a blind eye turned to pillage, rape and murder; and there were often offers of money for the first to storm the walls, which was a hazardous role. Mercenaries tended to have a fearsome reputation for depredations on civilians. During the Ottoman–Austrian Thirteen Years' War of 1593–1606, the German, Bohemian, Italian, Hungarian and Walloon mercenaries of the Emperor Rudolf II, the Wallachian and Serbian mercenaries of Prince Michael of Wallachia, and the Ottomans and their tributary allies, the Crimean Tatars, all inflicted terrible damage. Mercenaries were also responsible for considerable cruelty to civilians during the Thirty Years' War (1618–48) in Germany,[12] and this cruelty helped typecast them for subsequent generations.

Mercenaries in the seventeenth century came from across Europe. The Italian states were an important source of mercenaries, with Italians serving not only in the forces of the Habsburg rulers and overlords of much of Italy, but also for non-Habsburg rulers across Europe.[13] They had particular expertise in fortification engineering. Germans were also an important part of the military labour market.[14] Although this practice was less significant for the Ottoman and Chinese empires, there were important military labour markets in some areas outside Europe, notably India.[15] Thus, in 1662, the southern Indian territory of Tanjore was conquered for Muhammad 'Ali II of Bijapur by Marathas led by Venkājī, who, in turn, seized control for himself in 1678.

There was considerable variety in the mercenary trade, and it was engaged in by rulers who provided units to other rulers for pay, not only to secure financial gain but also to obtain political benefits, including support. Mercenary activity, therefore, could be an aspect of alliance diplomacy. In the early-modern period, the pursuit of dynastic and territorial ambitions was frequently an objective when providing mercenary units, and thus they were units in the complex and nuanced world of patronage, its pursuit and provision. This was particularly the case with the supply by lesser German and Italian rulers of mercenary units to more prominent rulers.[16] This process was also important to obtaining foreign subsidies and was thus part of a continuum of means of negotiating support and maintaining military power. Such subsidies could play a major role in forwarding domestic political agenda.[17]

In the early-modern period, the loyalty – or lack thereof – of mercenary units frequently led to concern, although the 'changing of sides' has to take note of the porosity and mutability of the 'sides'. For example, Danish-born Heinrich Holk (1599–1633) served Christian IV of Denmark and held the important fortress of Stralsund against the Austrian general Albrecht Wallenstein, Prince of Friedland, only for Holk to change over to the Austrian army when Christian left the war in 1629 and to fight under Wallenstein who, as the leading military entrepreneur, offered a better guarantee of employment. Mercenary leaders and units, indeed, could be unreliable both politically and on the battlefield. A spectacular and decisive example of betrayal by mercenaries switching sides in mid-battle occurred at Klushino in 1610 when Tsar Vasilii Shuiskii of Russia was betrayed by De la Gardie's Swedes, whose pay was in arrears. The battle threw open the road to Moscow for the victorious Poles. The Swedes had provided mercenaries from 1609 in return for an alliance against Poland and an agreement to surrender claims to the Swedish-ruled province of Livonia. As another drawback, mercenaries were frequently recruited at a distance from the zone of hostilities, which caused delay in starting operations and also created the problems of having to fight their way through and of being reluctant to move so far that it made a return home difficult.

Yet, it is important to understand the questionable nature of the nationalist and teleological assumptions that have made mercenaries appear poor soldiers,[18] and, instead, not simply to dwell frequently upon the deficiencies of mercenary service, since it is necessary to explain why recourse was had to mercenaries. They could, for example, provide loyal service. The large number of Scots in the service of Sweden and Russia generally proved loyal. Modern mercenaries are often typecast as social, political and economic marginals, the three characteristics seen as mutually reinforcing, and also as helping to locate mercenary activity as something outside the purlieus of civil society, indeed as semi-criminous behaviour by semi-criminals, if not criminous behaviour by criminals. This, however, is a view that requires revision. A recent study of English and Welsh mercenaries serving with the army of the States General (Netherlands) in the Dutch Revolt of the late sixteenth century against Spanish rule has concluded that 'contrary to the impression given by most historians, the majority of the rank and file … were not press-ganged criminals, vagabonds, but, instead, were raised by gentlemen and drawn from their traditional connections – from clients, retainers, and tenants'.[19] Furthermore, when considering mutinies, for example those of the Spanish Army of Flanders, it is useful to appreciate the extent to which they could be formulaic and formal. Indeed, such mutinies were aspects of negotiation and part of the process of consensus searching that characterised early-modern government, including the governance of military activity, rather than irreparable breakdowns in military systems, although the latter also occurred. Similar points could be made about plundering.

Mercenaries were accustomed to war and had the group cohesion and experience that was crucial to success in combat. It required training and experience to employ a pike or an arquebus effectively,[20] and steps were taken to ensure procurement of such troops, notably the habit of hiring experienced men from units that were being disbanded. Such men expected better pay than new recruits, while the latter were 'trained' by a process of osmosis: being exposed to more experienced men. Aside from inexperience, new recruits also deserted more readily than experienced soldiers, although desertion was a serious problem at every stage. Desertion was particularly serious among the unpaid and lowly paid, but it was exacerbated by a willingness by other recruiters to sign up deserters. This willingness reflected the desire of many deserters to get a recruitment bounty, and also the difficulty of readjusting to civilian society. For armies and governments, signing up deserters, like recruiting mercenaries, at least ensured experienced men. This point underlines the problem with assuming, as is often done, that mercenary service was inherently less effective and anachronistic. Indeed, in some respects, the opposite was the case.

In contrast, militias as well as other forces recruited at the outbreak of hostilities were regarded as less combat-ready, in terms of both experience and training. When tested on campaign, militia repeatedly lacked the skill of professionals. Nevertheless, despite the greater experience of mercenaries, there were important advantages to be found in using alternatives. A reliance on militia ensured larger forces, as the soldiers raised from conscription were less expensive than mercenaries and were less likely to transfer allegiance. The issue of relative cost played a role in the Swedish reliance on militia from the 1540s. The men were increasingly given peacetime training by the king's officers. By the 1550s this militia had become an operational army that could defend any part of the country. Moreover, in the 1560s, it proved possible for Sweden to deploy larger forces than Denmark, which, instead, relied on professionals.[21] Yet, mercenaries were also used by the Swedes, notably by Gustavus Adolphus. An emphasis on local militia-type forces was particularly seen when invasions were faced. The French town of Saint-Jean-de-Losne on the banks of the River Saône resisted a siege by Austrian forces in 1636 and was rewarded with tax exemptions.

More generally, Western rulers in the sixteenth century sought to move towards professional standing armies that combined the experience of mercenaries with the reliability of subjects, although, in wartime, as in the early seventeenth century, these armies tended to be supplemented by both militia and foreign mercenaries. The administrative capability, in terms of information, local officials and police enforcement, that systems of conscription could call on with considerable success from the late seventeenth and eighteenth centuries was less in evidence earlier on, and rulers tended to create standing forces by drawing on mercenaries, as well as by using the important and longstanding 'sub-feudal' pattern of encouraging aristocratic officers to recruit from their own connections and tenants, the latter being particularly favoured in France.

It would be mistaken, however, to adopt too schematic an approach to recruitment, not least because armed forces varied greatly, not only between peace and war, but also within individual years of peace or war. A complex interaction of opportunity and motivation, involving factors such as the reliability of pay, the season, and the proximity of the harvest, encouraged recruitment or desertion, and the size of units could vary very greatly. If this situation encouraged a reliance on paid professionals, the variation in the size of armed forces could also be accentuated by their use.

Across the world, mercenaries offered specific expertise. Moreover, artillerymen and cannon founders were frequently mercenaries. Mercenaries thereby served to ensure the diffusion of expertise and, crucially, new techniques, although it was not necessary to rely on private markets and contractors to ensure such diffusion, as it could be provided by allied states. Indeed, military assistance of this type was common within – and, in part, was a constituent of – alliances and imperial systems, and the echo can be seen in modern practices of international military training and advice. Such assistance was a key means by which states exercised influence, but, alongside this strand in state assistance, and overlapping with it, came the private strands arising from the activities of entrepreneurs and from the desire by local rulers and groups for military assistance from those who could provide it.

The diffusion of firearms provided many instances of these processes, as it helped alter the balance of military advantage between states, peoples and areas. Possession of, and expertise in, firearms became the first priority in the struggle for military predominance, or even survival. Some of the provision was by states to allies, as when the Portuguese sent 400 musketeers to help Ethiopia in 1541, but this episode indicated the extent to which it was not easy to draw a distinction between public and private, or state and mercenary, a situation that may also pertain in the future. The Ethiopians rewarded Portuguese musketeers with land in the 1540s in order to retain their services, and these musketeers (and their descendants) continued to play an important military role into the following century.

More distantly from public provision, there were probably several thousand European renegades in South and East Asia by the early seventeenth century, some of whom forged cannon for local rulers.[22] The role of mercenaries overlapped with that of adventurers, for, in a world being recast through force, there seemed great opportunities for those who deployed force and this situation replicated that of the *condottiere* in later-medieval Italy, mercenaries several of whom had taken over states. Spanish-supported adventurers, led by a Portuguese mercenary, Diego Veloso, attempted to take over Cambodia in the 1590s, and in 1597 their candidate was proclaimed king. This endeavour came to an end in 1599, when the greatly outnumbered Spaniards were killed in a rebellion, but, the same year, Philip de Brito, a Portuguese adventurer in the service of the ruler of Arakan, was given charge by the ruler of the port of Syriam in Pegu. The Portuguese crown recognised de Brito's position by granting him the captaincy of Syriam. However, he lacked the resources of a European state or trading company and, in 1613, the Burmese ruler, Anaukeptlun, was able to capture Syriam after a long siege. Accounts vary, but de Brito was crucified or impaled. Significantly, the Portuguese and Eurasian inhabitants of Syriam were enslaved and employed as gunners, a different form of ensuring expertise.

The military and social politics

The issue of mercenaries has been discussed at length as it underlines the problems of judging modernity and modernisation, and also the complexity of the relationship between war and state building. Military capability was a key product of political effectiveness and, in part, this effectiveness was a matter of governmental development, seen as the creation and use of bureaucratic bodies – what indeed has been termed the bureaucratic revolution.[23] However, the capacity of, and reliance upon, bureaucratic systems has frequently been exaggerated. For example, the Kangxi emperor favoured his commanders at the expense of bureaucratic rules.[24] In Europe, the ability to win and use political support, specifically the backing of major landowners and the merchant oligarchs who dominated towns, was more crucial than bureaucratic systems. As a consequence of the major role of political support, the relationship between war and state development was most acute in times of civil war because this warfare reflected the loss of such support and, in turn, greatly reduced the resources available to cope with this loss. Civil warfare often reflected key issues of political legitimacy and related divisions over the nature of political consent, as in the Russian Time of Troubles,[25] the Thirty Years' War, the British Civil Wars and the Chinese Rebellion of the Three Feudatories. Separatism within composite states was also an issue, for example in the Bohemian Revolt in 1618, the Bishops' Wars in Scotland in 1639–40, and in the Catalan, Portuguese and Neapolitan rebellions against Spanish Habsburg rule in the 1640s. In turn, political support, namely élite backing for the government, which was the norm sought by both, permitted action against those identified as opponents of this political alignment. Thus, troops were used against striking workers and in opposition to peasants and others rebelling in order to secure a different rural settlement, a quest bluntly presented when nobles were slaughtered alongside officials, as in Stenka Razin's rising in the Volga region in 1670. The social politics of using the military has received insufficient attention in military history, but it was important and became more so in the absence of effective police forces. As a result of the latter point, troops were employed for a range of activities that today are associated with the police, such as guarding official buildings, figures and prisoners; escorting money shipments; keeping an eye on markets; and responding to demonstrations, which could lead to firing on rioting crowds. Troops employed for such purposes were not armed differently to those used for warfare. In rural areas across the world, troops were deployed against brigands, smugglers and others seeking to challenge the state's authority and profits, and military action against them helped strengthen this authority, especially in frontier regions and other areas where the state could appear marginal, for example heavily forested districts. By the end of the seventeenth century, certainly in Western Europe and in large part thanks to an improvement in crown–élite relations, there was a shift in norms, with a greater assumption that regular forces would be present, ready and able to enforce the government's requirements.

An emphasis on state building[26] and other functional aspects of military capability and goals of war can lead to an underplaying of different aspects, notably the culture of power, which concerned questions of honour and prestige that were greatly bound up in the successful use of force, as well as such related issues as insecure and provoked masculinities. These human frailties played a role in decisions for war.[27] The cultural dimension also extended to the aesthetics of warfare, with rulers placing particular value on a good-looking army. This preference played a role in recruitment, encouraging the acceptance of tall men over short ones. Furthermore, rulers took an interest in their soldiers' uniforms, notably those of élite guard units, with an emphasis on having the army look good. These aesthetic factors could also be significant in functional terms, as well-presented forces appeared more formidable. Rulers' direction of their forces' appearance became more common in Europe in the second half of the seventeenth century with the growth in standing forces and the receding – with the end between 1648 and 1668 of a series of lengthy conflicts – of the immediate exigencies of conflict. This direction was an aspect of the top-down command structure that was the general case around the world. More democratic military structures were unusual and generally tribal in character or composed of outsiders, such as brigands and pirates, although in these cases there were also authoritarian structures. More generally, armies and navies conformed to a hierarchical model, with officers, drawn from the social élite, who directed troops in a harsh disciplinary fashion.

Yet, there were also important variations, both formal and informal. The formal, hierarchical model of authoritarian-style military service focused on conscription, for military service was generally less harsh and more conditional when troops were volunteers. Conscription was taken further in the case of slave soldiers, who were uncommon in Christendom, other than with the case of galley slaves. Elsewhere, however, slave soldiers were more common, notably, but not only, in Islamic societies. The *janissaries* were the élite force in the Ottoman army, largely recruited as slaves from a levy on non-Muslim households, while Abbas I of Persia based his army on *ghulams*, Caucasian military slaves.[28] Such forces provided a key element of central control, lessening the need to rely on tribal or feudal levies. Another instance of a centrally controlled slave force was the corps of black slaves, personally attached to the Sultan, created in Morocco by Mawlay Isma'il (r. 1672–1727), who wanted to be free of local political pressure. Slave children were trained in horsemanship and the use of spears and firearms, and then married to slave girls to produce more slaves, while slave raids were also mounted south into the Sahara in order both to recruit more soldiers and to enforce power over a very vague frontier zone. However, under his successor, the slave corps became a force for chaos, trying, like the Praetorian Guard of Imperial Rome, to sell its political support.

Such independence also became a key problem with the *janissaries*, one that ensured that a military agenda focused on their management became central to the internal stability of the state. Indeed, the role of the *janissaries* indicated the extent to which the state came to serve the military, or at least military purposes, rather than vice versa. On the whole, the *janissaries* wanted war as they could obtain loot and other benefits from campaigning. Moreover, the response of the *janissaries* to changing circumstances indicated the extent to which the varieties in recruitment and military discipline across the world overlapped with the significant informal variations in military service seen in contrasting practices of obedience. Aside from seeking to sell political support, some units responded to what were seen as unreasonable conditions by resorting to passive disobedience, strike action or even mutiny, as with the seizure of power in Tunis in 1591 by the rank and file of the *janissary* garrison. Such diversity in response needs to be emphasised because it subverts attempts to present troops as automatons. That uniformity might have been the objective of drill that focused on repetitive movement and formulaic tactics, but patterned battlefield behaviour did not define what was a more varied military experience.

Social stability and the military

Nevertheless, rather than facing disobedience from their soldiers, most rulers had, instead, generally to fear an unwillingness from their subjects to provide the necessary resources. This domestic response, however, could have a direct military consequence overlapping with disobedience, as officers and commanders were generally members of the social élite, and an overlap between domestic disaffection and problems with the military could be an issue. This, for example, rose to a crisis in France during the *Frondes* in 1648–52, and, more generally, was in the background to French military patronage and politics during the century.

A different question was posed if the regime reflected a military that was divorced from the socially powerful, which was the situation in Interregnum England, from 1649 to 1660. The social and ideological politics of the New Model Army ensured that it was impossible to demobilise and return to what struck most of the population as normal governance. In 1655 the unpopularity of the army, as an autocratic and expropriatory force, was accentuated when, largely in response to an unsuccessful Royalist rising, authority in the localities was entrusted to major generals, instructed to preserve security and to create a godly and efficient country. They took authority away from the traditional gentry families, and were unpopular not only with Royalists but also with many republicans.[29]

The military dominance of English politics was only ended by the implosion of the revolutionary regime in 1659–60, with criticism and suspicion of the army becoming more potent in Parliament, leading, in October 1659, first to the army being put under commission, followed by the army resorting to force.[30] However, significantly, the overthrow of the bitterly divided Interregnum regime required military action in the shape of the march into England of the Scotland garrison force under George Monck. This action led to the restoration of the Stuarts in the person of Charles II, the eldest son of Charles I who had been executed in 1649, largely at the behest of the military leadership. Anxious about the army, Charles II disbanded it and sought to create a new force under royal control. However, in a reaction against the use of force, the Restoration of royal power was followed by a rejection of the idea of a large standing (permanent) army. Thus, the creation of a 'modern' military in the shape of the New Model Army did not lead to a lasting governmental or military development.

The case of England also indicates the importance of grounding new regimes in terms of existing social networks. This process sounds consensual when, in practice, there was often a high degree of intimidation and coercion involved, not least because these regimes were frequently the product of conquest or civil war. Yet, the force used to secure the possibility of such coercion in turn produced a socio-political system that helped ensure the support of existing military units, and the availability of additional ones. Alongside the use of coercion to advance change, there was the widespread practice of force and conflict as means to prevent it, both in terms of changes in territorial power and with reference to prevailing political, social and ideological practices and norms. Armies thus suppressed rebellions and maintained or strengthened social and spatial patterns of control, as in 1670 when the peasant-Cossack army of Stenka Razin, a Don Cossack who had rebelled against the social politics of the Tsarist regime, especially the control over the serfs, was destroyed by regular Russian forces.

The reality of socio-political control and the anger felt when it was challenged can be glimpsed in a diplomatic report of 1676 that also provides an insight into the problems created by supporting units during the winter in wartime, as the demobilisation of peacetime was not an option when trying to retain forces for the next campaigning season. Roger Meredith reported from The Hague on 14 January:

> The government of Arensberg a place in the diocese of Cologne, having lately driven out two Osnabruck and one Celle regiment that had taken quarters in their territory, which they did by six thousand peasants whom they raised upon them on a sudden; an agent from the Duke of Celle here tells me that this affront is highly resented by those dukes and that they have given out orders to some new forces to march into the same quarters who it is supposed will severely revenge the disgrace put upon their companions.[31]

However, the social politics of war varied greatly. That summer, John Ellis, visiting William III's forces besieging Maastricht, noted peasants building defences and bringing in forage and wood, 'as to a mart'. In short, the financial strength of the Dutch helped ensure supplies, while William's willingness and ability to provide protection for the surrounding country 'makes provisions plentiful'. Such activity broadened out the nature of recruitment, as did the large number of women in the camp, 'many arriving every day to look after the persons they are most concerned for, and that not only mean people, but of very good quality'.[32]

In turn, opposition to states varied in character. The principal challenge faced by the Kangxi emperor came from the Rebellion of the Three Feudatories, while, in so far as it can be seen as a rebellion, that by the Marathas was the most serious challenge confronting Aurangzeb. The difficulty of classifying the two challenges serves as a reminder of the problems of defining war. As the Rebellion of the Three Feudatories showed, rebellions could be on a greater scale than many conflicts between sovereign rulers.

In Western Europe, states came by the second half of the century to monopolise organised, large-scale violence; the situation, however, was different in much of Eastern Europe, including Poland, Hungary, Ukraine and Moldavia. Nevertheless, the rulers of Western Europe only did so with the co-operation of their social élites who dominated command positions, crucially those of individual units which were run under a facade of centralised royal control. Under Louis XIV, the reality of the 'state commission army'[33] was that officers could buy and sell their units, which gave them an incentive to keep them in good order.[34] Leading rulers increased the size of their armies, that of Austria rising from about 20,000 around 1650 to over 100,000 regulars a half-century later,[35] while minor rulers, especially in Germany, raised permanent forces of their own. In the early 1660s, Duke Charles Emmanuel III of Savoy-Piedmont declared six infantry regiments as standing or permanent, thus ensuring that the military establishment created for the wars earlier in the century was sustained. In contrast, in 1617, Charles Emmanuel I had raised an army of 5000 mercenaries under General Ernst von Mansfeld. Both major and lesser rulers in the second half of the century thus provided a focus for aristocratic loyalty and honourable service, at the same time as the development of the notion of rank based on service, for example in 1671 in Denmark (where the obligation on nobles to provide soldiers ended in 1679[36]), furthered this process.

This socio-institutional change, which was a crucial part of a broader pattern of crown–élite co-operation,[37] was more important than developments in weaponry and tactics, and was not dependent on them. Instead, the growth of militia-type forces under a degree of royal direction made it easier to implement tactical changes than had been the case when there was a stronger emphasis on frequently autonomous mercenaries. As organised drill was a matter of duty imposed by rulers, mercenaries could reject the idea. This situation restricted the options for Gustavus Adolphus, and, on the whole, ensured that the principles of the changes introduced in the Untied Provinces largely gained traction only in the second half of the century.

More generally, developments in warfare were mediated through existing social and political structures, such that, in some areas, they contributed to a strengthening of the authority of the ruler, in others to its lessening, and, in the majority, to the need for the partnership between rulers and élite to confront new challenges. For example, the capture of the Huguenot stronghold of La Rochelle in 1628 was an important date that marked the shift towards a situation in Western Europe in which military developments worked to the advantage of central governments, but these developments generally only did so if it was possible to win local co-operation, and usually only in the absence of sustained external intervention. Thus, within states, the effectiveness of force was dependent on a range of political factors. For example, international intervention was important to the attempts by Ferdinand of Bavaria, Prince Bishop of Liège from 1612 to 1650, to control the city of Liège, and he was only able to use troops to do so in 1649, when his former opponents had changed position or policy: France was convulsed by the *Frondes*, the Dutch had negotiated peace with Spain, and France and Sweden had ceased attacks on Bavaria. The conflict in Liège reflected the range of factors at play, especially the international context, which arose from the bishopric's strategic position in the Meuse valley bisecting the Spanish Netherlands, and the important role of Liège and Huy as bridging points over the river, as well as the continued vitality of urban independence in the politics of the period. More generally, however, cities were vulnerable to state pressure since they provided clear sites of wealth that could be readily coerced. This situation also encouraged pressure on independent city-states, as with the unsuccessful attempts by the rulers of Denmark and Savoy-Piedmont to take control of Hamburg and Genoa respectively, Charles Emmanuel II attacking Genoa in 1672.

Conclusion

As part of a system of public–private partnership, to use a modern terminology that does not capture the personal links and cultural assumptions of the period, Western European élites were willing to co-operate with military change, including the organisation of armies around a state-directed structure and, to a greater extent than elsewhere, the downgrading of cavalry, processes that élites in other areas were more reluctant to accept. A monopolisation of large-scale, organised violence by states proved harder to sustain in the Ottoman and Mughal empires than in the Manchu empire or Western Europe; but comparison with the situation in individual European states has to make allowance for the very great difference in scale. Looking at Christian Europe as a whole, it was more violent and wracked by as much, if not more, warfare in 1580–1609, 1618–67, 1672–9 and 1688–1714 than was the case with the Ottoman and Mughal empires. However, the multi-polar nature of Europe ensured that this warfare was largely controlled by reasonably well-established states, rather than directed to their overthrow.

The forces deployed by these states changed, both on land and at sea. Scale, weapons and organisation all altered. As with all statements about war, and the nature and rate of change, comments about the scale of activities can be hedged with caveats and qualifications, and, indeed, there has been an important debate about army sizes and the Military Revolution, a debate particularly focusing on the consequences of *trace italienne* fortifications for the size of besieging forces and armies as a whole. Automatic equations of greater scale have been queried.[38] Moreover, detailed work has indicated a decline in average army size in the latter stages of the Thirty Years' War, in so far as campaigning forces in particular theatres were concerned; and this is a major qualification of Roberts's definition of the Military Revolution, to which army size was important. Qualifications relate not only to the earlier use of specific examples, but also to the very value to be attached to the size of armies.

Nevertheless, despite these caveats, a substantive development was apparent in many cases in the institutional character of military activity, notably from the mid-seventeenth century, with permanent forces becoming a prominent feature both on land and at sea in Europe, while in China banner units were integrated by the Kangxi emperor into an effective army joining Manchu and Ming traditions of war fighting. In Europe, the armies and navies of the later decades of the century required, and made possible, a practice of war in which, in many cases – but by no means all – the characteristics of consistency, regularity and uniformity were more pronounced than in earlier centuries, or at least were presented in terms that accorded more clearly with nineteenth- and twentieth-century Western definitions of these characteristics.

10 Conclusions: Beyond the Military Revolution

War was central to the international and domestic politics of the period, to its culture and confessional development, and to social experience and that of many individuals across the century. There is no doubt of the political, demographic, social, economic and cultural importance of military preparedness and conflict, although causal relationships can be obscure, ambiguous and controversial. The problematic definition and usage of the concept of an early-modern Military Revolution suggests, while noting the great and continuing advances made by scholars deploying this thesis, that it would be helpful now to consider approaching the period without employing an idea that also has serious conceptual, methodological and historiographical deficiencies and baggage. There is, more generally, a need for a new set of intellectual strategies (and operational concepts) for approaching both military history and the early-modern period. In particular, in emphasising the protean character of war and the military, and in arguing that any argument that proposes a clear shape for developments is misleading, it is necessary nevertheless, while avoiding teleology, to provide a sense of more than one thing after the other.

Accepting that, it is still the case that allowing for differences between contrasting approaches underlines the tentative nature of each, and thus confirms the open nature of the subject. If history entails an acceptance of the limitations of the evidence and the difficulties of advancing firm conclusions, and thus inculcates a humane scepticism about overarching interpretations, there is no reason why military history should be excluded from this mental world and operational historiography. Indeed, given that military historians bewail frequently that they are ignored by the remainder of the profession and their subject slighted, it would be helpful if more of them were chary of the teleologies that have been challenged and largely discarded in other branches of the subject.

Querying teleology does not mean that the role and extent of change, and the significance of change-based analytical approaches, should be slighted, but there is room for pursuing greater analytical openness by noting different developmental accounts. Rather than, for example, putting the focus, as is conventionally done, primarily on weaponry, it is possible to probe the value of pursuing a developmental model centred on information, which, indeed, is crucial to military capability and war. In particular, the need for information increased in the seventeenth century as the scale of conflict rose or, at least, remained high, which proved increasingly the case for both the range of operations and the number of combatants.

Information and the military

Information was a key aspect of the shift towards consistency, regularity and uniformity in European forces as it encoded these characteristics and replicated them, which was a particular feature of the culture of print. Publications about war had begun in Europe, with the introduction of printing there during the fifteenth-century Renaissance, but the role of print and the appearance of these publications became more frequent with time. Printing made it possible to disseminate reports, knowledge and opinion, rapidly and at great distance.

Philological work and the Printing Revolution were also followed by the widespread 'rediscovery' and availability of Classical texts, and this return to the past served to validate new emphases.[1] The military reformers in the Netherlands and Germany linked to the House of Nassau consciously used Classical models, alongside those of the modern world, notably German models, for their efforts to improve military organisations. This usage was important because of the authority of Classical texts, which were frequently reprinted, as with Justus Lipsius's *De militia Romana libri quinque commentarius ad Polybium* (Antwerp, 1630). This reprinting was not the case simply in the early decades of the century. For example, the *Ars Tactica* of Flavius Arrianus (*c*.96–175) was published in Amsterdam in 1683, and the *Strategematum* of Polyaenus (fl. *c*.163) at Leiden in 1691. Works also appeared in translation, as with Julius Caesar's *Commentaries*, for example in London in 1682 and 1694, and Frontinus's *The Stratagems of War* (London, 1686). The authority of Antiquity extended to Byzantium, the Eastern Roman Empire, as with an edition of the Emperor Leo VI's *Tactica* (Leiden, 1612), and a translation of Procopius's *The History of the Warres of the Emperor Justinian* (London, 1653).

Printed information was most apparent in drill manuals, with their depiction of troops operating in a predictable fashion, for example William Barriffe's *Military Discipline: or the Young Artillery Man. Wherein is Discoursed and Showne the Postures both of Musket and Pike the Exactest Way*, a lengthy work of which the second edition appeared in 1639, the same year as his

Mars, his Triumph. Or, the Description of an Exercise performed the 18 of October 1638 in the Merchant-Taylor's Hall. John Cruso's *Militarie Instructions for the Cavallrie* had been published in 1632. Moreover, fortification diagrams and manuals were also at once descriptive, programmatic and predictive, if not prescriptive. Like drill manuals with their diagrammatic depiction of military formations, these fortification diagrams captured the spatial characteristic of force – that is, the deployment of power and its operation, whether for defence or offence, in terms of controlling space.

At the same time, the more general shift towards both the use of written instructions and, more widely, the culture of print in military discussion ensured that the practical value of publications and depictions – namely the utilitarian drive towards recording and showing information – was just one aspect of print's more normative use. An emphasis on the importance of the normative character of developments, rather than the stage of initial innovations, is significant in considering how best to consider their chronological dimension. For example, to take information, the period 1450–1600 saw the dissemination of printing, the work of the printers Johannes Gutenberg and William Caxton and the mapmakers Mercator and Ortelius, as well as European exploration and the related challenges of the discussion and depiction of this 'new-found' world. As far as warfare is concerned, this age witnessed the rise of the first transoceanic empires and, therefore, issues in considering how best not only to understand, discuss and depict new colonies but also how to allocate and use military resources on an unprecedented scale. The conventional literature on military history accords with this focus by seeing the period *c.*1490–*c.*1660 in terms of a military revolution. Yet, as this book has sought to demonstrate, the nature and extent of military change in the period 1550–1660 has been exaggerated, and this point can be amplified by drawing attention to the tendency to underplay continuity with fifteenth-century and earlier circumstances and developments. There is also the issue of the subsequent period, usually seen as 1660 to the outbreak of the French Revolutionary wars in 1792 – or, in some accounts, the American Revolution in 1775 – a period, labelled *ancien régime*, that has generally been discussed in terms of limited change, if not stasis, an approach that rested on a non-continual account of change. In contrast, however, to this standard account, it can be argued, first, that the period 1660–1792 is highly significant because it saw the implementation of earlier change and the process by which it became normative. The application of printing to military topics can be considered in this light. Secondly, and not necessarily in complete contrast, there has been a failure to appreciate the nature and scale of change in the 1660–1790 era, which provides not only a fundamental critique of the conventional

Military Revolution thesis, but also a way to approach the publications of this period. They do not need to be seen only in terms of implementing earlier developments, but can also be regarded as important in their own right.

Contemporary writings on war reflected the sense that not only were there lessons to be learned but that they needed learning. For example, there was an increased use of battlefield artillery, as with the Swedish crossing of the River Lech in 1632, and the development and application of knowledge reflected this. In particular, there was greater knowledge available in print on the composition and use of gunpowder, as with Joseph Furttenbach's *Halintro-Pyrobolia* (Ulm, 1627) which subsequently appeared as the revised and enlarged *Büchsenmeisterey-Schul* (Augsburg, 1643). For artillery, there was also a process of mathematisation, through an engagement with ballistics,[2] although the interest in mathematics was longstanding, reflecting as it did the increased use of quantification in European society for the understanding of space and time,[3] and the concern with regularity, harmony and precision seen from the Renaissance. This concern lent itself to a mathematical interest in tactical formations[4] and fortifications.

Mathematicians played a major role, as with the case of Simon Stevin (1548–1620), who was Quartermaster-General of the United Provinces and tutor of Prince Maurice of Orange. Aside from introducing the use of decimals, he wrote on fortifications, including a work on the use of sluices to flood areas, *Nouvelle Maniere de fortification par escluss* (Leiden, 1618). That year, he also published a second edition of his work on castrametation – the laying out of camps – according to Prince Maurice's model. In 1606, Galileo published *Operations of the Geometric and Military Compass*, in which he discussed such problems as how best to calibrate guns for cannonballs of different materials and weight, and also how to deploy armies with unequal fronts and flanks. His *Discorsi* (1638) demonstrated the parabolic trajectory of projectiles and provided a complete table of ranges. Samuel Marolois's *Fortification ou Architecture Militaire* (Amsterdam, 1628) was first published in 1614 as part of his *Oeuvres Mathématiques*, while an English edition, translated by Henry Hexham, appeared in 1638. Christoph Nottnagel, the Professor of Mathematics at the University of Wittenberg, published a *Manuale Fortificatorium* (Wittenberg, 1659).

This interest was taken forward with the greater commitment to ballistics. Ernst Braun, Captain of Artillery in the city of Danzig (Gdansk), published in 1682 a work on the most up-to-date foundations and practice of artillery, *Novissimum fundamentum und praxis artilleriae*. His stress on novelty indicated a more general concern to be current in writings on war, both in what was written and in how it was presented. Thus, the authority of the old, which had been a feature of the use of Classical works from the Renaissance, became less important, although, like modern citation of Sun Tzu or Clausewitz, they continued to be pillaged in order to provide a gleam of authority and verisimilitude for otherwise more present-minded accounts. Andreas Cellarius's *Architectura Militaris* (Amsterdam, 1645), the second edition of which appeared in 1656, included engraved plates showing the use of Classical techniques: the Roman testudo and the battering ram. The continued practice of comparison was shown by the publication in London in 1678 of Louis de Gaya's *Treatise of the Arms and Engines of War … both Ancient and Modern* and in Wilhelm Dilich's *Krieges-Schule* (Frankfurt, 1689).

The relative decline of the authority of the old was related to a process of theoretical consideration and empirical trial and error focused on the new. In particular, mathematical advances and Newtonian science were linked to military engineering, artillery and military thought. Theoretical and empirical advances greatly increased the predictive power of ballistics, and helped turn gunnery from a craft into a science that could and should be taught. The same was true of naval shipbuilding, on which there was a growing literature.[5] Flintlock muskets and bayonets also provided instances of the process of trial and error not least as far as related tactical deployments were concerned. In place of the standard chronology of the Military Revolution, with its emphasis on change in the period closing in the mid-seventeenth century, a visual exemplar of the possibility of a different chronological model is provided by the very Classical echoes that link the squares of pikemen in the Thirty Years' War to the Macedonian phalanxes of Antiquity, while, in contrast, the shallower, more linear deployments of musketeers by the end of the century appear radically different.

A second Danzig edition of Braun in 1687 demonstrated the market's demand for work on artillery, as did the publication in Nuremburg in 1685 of Johann Buchner's *Theoria et Praxis Artilleriae*. Moreover, this activity was not limited to Northern European writers. Thus, *L'Artiglieria* by Pietro Sardi was published in Venice in 1621. The importance of translation also showed the extent of interest, as with the *Traité des Armes* (Paris, 1678) by Louis de Gaya which appeared in 1685 in an English translation, and the treatise on fortification by Menno van Coehorn, the Dutch Vauban both for fortification and for siegecraft – published in Dutch and French in 1685, it was swiftly translated into other languages, including English in 1705. Appearing as *Le Maistre du Camp général* in Frankfurt in 1617, Giorgio Basta's book was first published in Italian in 1606. *Artis Magnae Artilleriae*, a work by Kasimierz Siemienowicz, Lieutenant-General of Ordnance for Wladyslaw IV of Poland, appeared in French (1651), German (1676) and English (1729) translations.

Fortification was a longstanding subject for publications that were designed to be educational, as in Jean Errard's *La fortification demonstree et reduite en art* (Paris, 1620), Jean Fabre's *Les practiques ... sur l'ordre et regle de fortifier, garder, attaquer, et deffendre les places. Avec sun facile moyen pour lever toutes sortes de plans, tant de places et des bastimens, que de la campagne pour les cartes* (Paris, 1629), Joseph Furttenbach's *Architectura martialis* (Ulm, 1630), Gerard Melder's *Korte en Klare Instructie van Regulare en Irregulare Fortificatie* (Amsterdam, 1664), Allain Manesson-Mallet's *Les travaux de Mars, ou la fortification nouvelle* (Paris, 1672) and Johonnes Teyler's *Architectura Militaris* (Rotterdam, 1697). References in titles to modern and new are also indicative, as with Matthias Dögen's *Architectura Militaris Moderna* (Amsterdam, 1647).

Printed manuals on gunnery, tactics, drill, fortification and siegecraft spread techniques far more rapidly than word of mouth or manuscript, and through translation provided a key means of accurate transmission. *Uchenie I Khitrost' ratnogo stroeniya pekhotnykh lyudei*, the first Russian printed book on military matters, was published in 1647. An infantry manual, it emphasised training and included a large number of sketches and plans to teach drill. Aside from specifics, manuals emphasised the very value of military education, and, crucially, associated military skill with a knowledge that could not simply be gained through conflict, as with the Sieur de Birac's *Les Fonctions du Capitaine de Cavalerie* (The Hague, 1693). Manuals also permitted and made possible a degree of standardisation that both helped to increase military effectiveness and was important for the utilisation of military resources.

Literacy and printing had other values as well, fostering discussion of military organisation and methods, and encouraging a sense of system. Literacy and printing were important to command and control, and to military administration, not least because it was now less difficult to survey the quantity and state of military resources as military statistics became more accessible. The official report of the Russian Ordnance, *Kniga Pushkarskogo prikaza, za skrepoyu d'yaka Volkova* (*Book of the Gunners' Chancellery, with the certification of secretary Volkov, 1680*), listed all arms and ammunition as well as current production. The number of cannon located in Russian towns was revealed to be 3575 pieces, while another 400–500 field guns were probably available for the field army. Literacy and printing also aided the positive interaction of resources and requirements of different military branches, in particular localities, and of forces that were in different locations.

As with other aspects of military change, early developments may have been more significant than a greater rate of change later, but it is also possible to argue the opposite, which indicates the interrelated methodological and conceptual problems of establishing an agreed analytical framework. At any rate, an acceleration in scientific innovation and application occurred from the later seventeenth century, rather than in the conventional earlier period of the Military Revolution. This acceleration can be related to the European Scientific Revolution of these years, which was certainly important for ballistics.

Publications, moreover, reflected public interest in war, as with the appearance in London in 1647 of Joshua Sprigge's *Anglia Rediviva*, an account of the operations of the New Model Army, in Amsterdam in 1667 of a history of the recent Second Anglo-Dutch War, and in London in 1671 of the *Observations Upon Military and Political Affairs* by George Monck, a former English general. The appetite was not only for the most recent campaigns. For example, Charles de Croy's book on the campaigns in the Low Countries in 1600–6 was published in 1619, with a second edition appearing in 1642. War, therefore, was part of the knowledge economy, both public and institutional. Rulers, for example, aimed to accumulate knowledge on zones of combat by acquiring maps, plans – for example those in Nicolas de Fer's *L'Introduction à la Fortification* (Paris, 1695) – charts and other data. Louis XIV showed one of his generals in 1678 'a list he had received and had then in his hand of all the English officers as well generals as colonels; and gave a character to each'.[6]

Yet, having argued the danger of a teleological approach in other fields, it is important not to abandon caution and caveats here. For example, it is unclear that the far greater availability of printed material, which was anyway only the case in Europe, had a major impact on operations, in part because the selection of commanders put more of an emphasis on birth than education. Across the world, military education itself was largely 'on the job', and there were few military academies.

More significant, possibly, was the difficulty of producing information that was readily usable for operational and tactical purposes. In part, this was a reflection of technical points, such as the lack of a system for providing and displaying accurate contour information in a systematic fashion. As a result, commanders had to rely on their own eye to understand the lay of the land and, in particular, to sight lines of fire for guns. More generally, despite developments in certain states, such as France and Sweden, in each of which mapping and land surveys were pursued, there was not yet the institutional basis across much of the world for accumulating necessary information on the terrain that might be used for operations. There was also a vital lack of real-time information on the situation in other states and armies. Indeed, Intelligence as the basis for operational planning was poorly developed, and, in this important sphere, the term Military Revolution appears particularly inappropriate.

The centrality of variety

Whatever the continued value of the concept of an early-modern military revolution, alternative themes can be advanced. They need to be tentative because considerable work needs to be done, even for much-studied states such as Spain.[7] The situation is much more serious outside Europe, notably for South-East Asia and the Horn of Africa. Yet, much valuable work has appeared over the last two decades, in part as military history has become significant for national histories, such as China, where it had earlier been underplayed.[8] As a result of the extent of recent work, the aggregation of conclusions on the world scale may seem out of place, which indeed is the most important conclusion: an awareness that this is not a fixed topic and that assessments are by their very nature tentative. There is also a greater awareness of the diversity of military practice across Christian Europe than was the case 20 years ago, although the far greater diversity of the non-West has not attracted comparable attention. A degree of autonomy in European military cultures that have been studied, such as Gaelic Ireland[9] and Russia,[10] encourages attention to the degree of autonomy elsewhere.

Autonomy, nevertheless, did not preclude interaction with other military traditions and, indeed, borrowings from them, a process facilitated by the use of foreign experts, notably fortress designers and engineers, as well as mercenaries more generally. For example, Scots played a very important role in Sweden and Russia.[11] A process of borrowing certainly lessened the distinctiveness of Russian warfare, and this borrowing was embarked on in a deliberate fashion in order to ensure, initially, a closure of a perceived capability gap and, subsequently, a self-conscious military transformation to conform to Western models and practices.[12]

However, such borrowing was not necessarily a sign of inferiority, nor of the obvious superiority of Western European powers, nor that there was a clear best practice. Indeed, the paradigm-diffusion model, which proposes that there was an ideal model of military activity and that its methods spread accordingly, has serious problems, not least because it argues a clear ranking of military powers. Instead, borrowing, where it occurred, was often only effective because it fitted in with, or could be made to appear to fit in with, existing practices and force structures. This is an important qualification to the paradigm-diffusion model, not least because a process of fitting in encouraged a borrowing of totemic aspects of foreign practices, rather than a transformation of the military system comparable to that seen in Japan in the late nineteenth century. For example, the Chinese use of European artillery experts, notably Jesuits such as Ferdinand Verbiest, in the seventeenth century provided effective cannon,[13] but was essentially an add-on, and did not transform the nature of Chinese war making. The Manchu commitment to cavalry remained more important. Add-ons were the most common aspect of diffusion, and it is necessary to make this distinction.

The theme of variety rests on the diversity of military environments, needs and opportunities, a diversity that many contemporaries and some later commentators were reluctant to grasp. Thus, William Holloway's *A Relation of the Late Siege and taking of the City of Babylon*, published in 1639, depicted the 'Turkish Army' on the cover as if it was an army of the Thirty Years' Wars with squares of pikemen and European-style cannon. The diversity of environments, needs, opportunities and responses suggests not only that any one narrative of military development is inappropriate, but also that any one account of how improvement, whether revolutionary or not, could have been obtained is inaccurate. As such, variety subverts the thesis of the Military Revolution, although those who support this thesis can reply that variety simply leads to differences in the implementation of this revolution, a reply that rests on a neo-Platonic method that assumes a perfect or essential model for change. In addition or alternatively, variety can be seen in terms of a failure of implementation that established a capability gap with those who embarked on the revolutionary path, a gap that ultimately led to the success of the latter.

The global dimension is a useful perspective if it is not deployed in terms of an account, triumphalist or other, of the rise of Western power, an account that has meaning by 1850 but far less by 1750, let alone 1700. Instead, the comparative possibilities of world history are instructive. They throw much light on the uniqueness of Western long-distance naval capability, but indicate that the situation on land offers more similarities, in capability or, at least, effectiveness, and is best approached without any sense of Western superiority. The value of experienced troops, the continuation of other fighting methods alongside firepower, and the importance of leadership, tactics and unit cohesion all emerge clearly as significant factors, not least in permitting an adaptation to the circumstances of the day, notably terrain and weather, as well as to the moves of opponents. For example, in the early seventeenth century, the Ottomans suffered their greatest military humiliations not at the hands of Austria or Poland, but from Persia, which did not enjoy any structural, material or tactical superiority but, rather, the military and political skill of Shah Abbas.[14]

Logistics was another significant factor in explaining success and failure. In part, logistics was a matter of administrative capability, such as the system of bread contracts that reflected the sophistication of Dutch government, and, in part, it was the expression of the nature of the fiscal context.

Armies, however, often rested on limited, and far from predictable, systems of support, in both peace and war. This situation hindered operational planning and helped ensure a widespread reliance on raiding, not only to deny support to opponents, but also in order to seize goods. Such a practice was on a continuum, via contributions from occupied 'foreign' lands, to systems of taxation or forced supplies from often unwilling 'national' or 'state' territory. The common theme was a need, in often hostile environmental circumstances, to rely on force, or the threat of force, in order to ensure consent and raise supplies, and often, indeed, to recruit soldiers and sailors, so that one of the major objectives of the military became its own support. At one level, this situation compromised the ability of armies to achieve operational, let alone strategic, goals, or rather altered them, while, at another level, this need ensured that logistics was heavily politicised. Indeed, the issue of how best to support forces financially helped cause political crises in England and Catalonia in 1640, and, in turn, these crises, respectively, transformed the situation as far as the confrontation with Scotland was concerned and, in the second case, greatly affected the situation in the Franco-Spanish War. These interrelated issues contributed greatly to the deficiencies of armies and navies, and were therefore a significant guide to battlefield capabilities and issues, an approach that is instructive for those who work today on understanding war in terms of the 'Face of Battle', the very experience of conflict. Indeed, the apparently contrasting approaches of 'War and Society' and 'Face of Battle' are linked by this approach.

Returning to the theme of variety underlines the extent to which contrasting circumstances created problems for military systems. Thus, between 1630 and 1690, the opponents of the Mughals included the Ahom, Persians, Uzbeks, Marathas, the Deccan Sultanates, the Portuguese and the English, and these conflicts involved very different physical and military environments, the latter being understood to encompass political circumstances. Due to their scale, most empires and many states faced the problem of reconciling capabilities developed for 'symmetrical' warfare, that with similarly armed opponents, with the issues posed by 'asymmetrical' warfare. In Western Europe, warfare with similar forces was the prime focus, but this emphasis proved a poor preparation for conflict with non-Western forces and with domestic opponents. This situation was exacerbated when training for commanders was limited, on the job, and without any real doctrinal consideration of other types of conflict. Yet, as a further instance of variety, the Chinese military under the Ming dynasty was, in accordance with the longstanding practice of Chinese strategic culture, principally prepared for asymmetrical warfare with steppe attackers, a formidable challenge, although that preparation did not prevent an ability to cope with the Japanese in Korea in the 1590s, a more unexpected and also formidable, but symmetrical, challenge. In turn, Chinese capabilities changed after the Manchu takeover.

Approaching variety from another direction, there are also the differences between developments on land and at sea. Military organisation is an exercise in the control, deployment and sustaining of force, and the situation at sea was obviously different to that on land, not least as the force projection and cost of European warships rose markedly during the century. Professionalisation, specialisation, machinisation and state control all became more evident in Western navies. Moreover, cohesion and state control of the officer class were greater at sea than on land, in large part because military entrepreneurship played a smaller role at sea, especially if the commerce raiding of privateering was secondary. In addition, greater professionalism was expected at sea (compared to on land), and was, indeed, necessary. This was true of sailing skills, fire control, logistics and the maintenance of fighting quality and unit cohesion. In some respects, line-ahead tactics might seem to lessen the requirement for such skills since the independence of individual ships was lessened, and, indeed, such tactics have been linked to the use at sea of commanders with experience of land combat with its pronounced degree of regimentation as far as battle deployments and combat were concerned.[15] Yet, line-ahead tactics still required considerable sailing skills, and notably so if sailing positions were to be maintained.

Conclusions

If a common pattern is discerned alongside variety, it is one of a continuity with earlier circumstances, albeit with important national variations, most clearly the move in Japan from conflict abroad and sustained civil warfare to a marked degree of passivity, a development that was total, abrupt, and a political transformation with profound military consequences for that country but not for others. If a military revolution means an abrupt change and a fundamental shift in capabilities, organisation, or goals, then none occurred in the seventeenth century, either on land or at sea. Instead, there were significant continuities in capability and war making, for example the dependence for movement on human and animal calories or the wind, the restricted speed of command and control practices, the need to mass troops for both shock and firepower, and, more generally, the powerful resource constraints of economies primarily based on relatively low-efficiency agriculture.

Military revolutions are much less common than is frequently argued. Rather, it is more usual for change to occur incrementally, not least in response to the pressure of circumstances, both external and internal. Partly as a consequence, it is foolish to neglect periods that did not apparently have military revolutions and to focus on those that apparently did. Instead, if periods with military revolutions are in fact infrequent and assume some of their meaning in terms of longer-lasting circumstances and developments, then these conditions deserve more attention.

In 2006, Christopher Duffy, a leading specialist on the armies and warfare of eighteenth-century Europe, claimed that 'the notion of a "Military Revolution" … distorted the study of early modern military history for decades from the 1950s'.[16] Duffy did not develop his remark, and his denunciation takes matters too far. The Military Revolution thesis and debate in fact helped greatly in research and discussion of the period; but now it is time, alongside continual valuable work based on this approach,[17] to advance new concepts.

In particular, the cultural rather than the technological dimensions of military service, organisation and conflict repay further study. Cultural dimensions relate to the variety of cultural systems in the world and to their impact on understanding of war, victory, suffering and death, as well as to the significance of social issues, including gender ones such as the gendering of war as a way of life. As an instance of differing cultural systems, Western Europe continued to uphold the Augustinian pattern of rigidly differentiating between peace and war in the sense of arguing that they were opposites. In East Asia, in contrast, peace and war were perceived as unopposed in the sense that warriors were expected to preserve peace by demonstrating the readiness and capability to fight, with the implication that war was understood to result from the lack of warrior capability to preserve peace without fighting.

A key similarity was that of the willingness of leaders and combatants across much of the world not only to kill large numbers but also to accept heavy casualties, and this willingness was also part of an important continuity with preceding and subsequent centuries. This attitude contrasts with much, although by no means all, current and recent warfare, certainly in so far as regular forces are concerned. A functional explanation of this contrast can be advanced based on the cost of training modern troops and their relatively limited numbers, both of which encourage operational and tactical methods designed to minimise casualties. However, social, cultural and ideological factors are more significant, not least of which is the difference between modern individualism and hedonism and, on the other hand, the earlier concepts of duty and fatalism in a much harsher working environment.

This acceptance of casualties was crucial to the bellicosity of the seventeenth century, notably the rulers' willingness to gain glory and to pursue interests through war. Whereas ordinary soldiers are individually commemorated today, in the seventeenth century their corpses were thrown into common graves or picked clean to the bone by carrion animals. Criticism of war as a pointless and even dishonourable blood-lust existed in the seventeenth century, but it was uncommon, and these views had scant impact on the goals and means of waging war. Instead, the continued normative character of resorting to warfare rested on the belief that wars were not only necessary but also, in at least some respects, desirable. This conviction provided a key context for this period, and for those that preceded and followed. There was no revolution here.

Selected Further Reading

The notes of this book and of the books listed here provide details of other relevant works.

General

Black, J. *Rethinking Military History* (2004)
Chase, K. *Firearms: A Global History to 1700* (2003)
Parker, G. *The Military Revolution: Military Innovation and the Rise of the West, 1500–1800* (2nd edn, 1996)

Asia

Gommans, J. *Mughal Warfare* (2002)
Lorge, P. *The Asian Military Revolution* (2008)
Murphey, R. *Ottoman Warfare* (2000)

Africa

Thornton, J. *Warfare in Atlantic Africa, 1500–1800* (1999)

America

Starkey, A. *European and Native American Warfare, 1675–1815* (1998)

Europe

Davies, B. L. *Warfare, State and Society on the Black Sea Steppe, 1500–1700* (2007)
Glete, J. *War and the State in Early Modern Europe* (2001)

Naval

Harding, R. *Seapower and Naval Warfare, 1650–1830* (1999)

Notes

1: Introduction

1. J. A. Lynn, 'The Evolution of Army Style in the Modern West, 800–2000', *International History Review*, 18 (1990), pp. 505–45.
2. G. Parker, *The Military Revolution* (2nd edn, Cambridge, 1996), pp. 24, 26, 29, 32, 37–8.
3. M. Roberts, *The Military Revolution, 1560–1660* (Belfast, 1956).
4. G. Parker, 'Random Thoughts of a Hedgehog', *Historically Speaking*, 4, no. 4 (Apr. 2003), p. 13. See also, in same issue, 'Military Revolutions, Past and Present', pp. 2–7, and Parker, 'The "Military Revolution", 1955–2005: From Belfast to Barcelona and The Hague', *Journal of Military History*, 69 (2005), pp. 205–10.
5. M. Roberts, *The Military Revolution, 1560–1660* (Belfast, 1956), reprinted in Roberts (ed.), *Essays in Swedish History* (London, 1967), pp. 195–225. See also, in the same, 'Gustav Adolf and the Art of War', pp. 56–81; G. Parker, 'Michael Roberts, 1908–1996', *Proceedings of the British Academy: Biographical Memoirs of Fellows*, 115 (2002), pp. 333–54.
6. G. Parker, 'The Limits of Revolutions in Military Affairs: Maurice of Nassau, the Battle of Nieuwpoort (1600), and the Legacy', *Journal of Military History*, 71 (2007), pp. 331–47.
7. R. Frost, 'The Polish–Lithuanian Commonwealth and the "Military Revolution"', in M. B. Biskupski and J. S. Pula (eds), *Poland and Europe: Historical Dimensions* (New York, 1993); G. Phillips, *The Anglo-Scots Wars, 1513–1550* (Woodbridge, 1999).
8. G. Perjés, 'Army Provisioning, Logistics and Strategy in the Second Half of the 17th Century', *Acta Historica Academiae Scientiarum Hungaricae*, 16 (1970), pp. 1–52; J. Lynn (ed.), *Feeding Mars: Logistics in Western Warfare from the Middle Ages to the Present* (Boulder, Colorado, 1993).
9. C. Rogers (ed.), *The Military Revolution Debate: Readings on the Military Transformation of Early Modern Europe* (Boulder, Colorado, 1995); Rogers, 'Military Revolutions and "Revolutions in Military Affairs": A Historian's Perspective', in T. Gongora and H. von Riekhof (eds), *Towards a Revolution*

in Military Affairs? Defense and Security at the Dawn of the Twenty-First Century (Westport, Connecticut, 2000), pp. 21–35; D. Showalter, 'Thinking About Military Revolution', *Historically Speaking*, 4, no. 4 (2003), pp. 9–10.

10. E.g., J. Stone, 'Technology, Society, and the Infantry Revolution of the Fourteenth Century', *Journal of Military History*, 68 (2004), pp. 361–80.

11. For a useful critique, D. Parrott, 'The Military Revolution of Early Modern Europe', *History Today*, 42/12 (Dec. 1992), pp. 21–7.

12. For continuities see A. Ayton and J. Price (eds), *The Medieval Military Revolution: State, Society and Military Change in Medieval and Early Modern Europe* (London, 1998), C. J. Rogers, 'The Medieval Legacy', in G. Mortimer (ed.), *Early Modern Military History, 1450–1815* (Basingstoke, 2004), pp. 6–24, and F. Tallett and D. J. B. Trim (eds), *European Warfare, 1350–1750* (Cambridge, 2010).

13. N. A. M. Rodger, 'The Development of Broadside Gunnery, 1450–1650', *Mariner's Mirror*, 82 (1996), pp. 301–24.

14. For a bold attempt that ignores most of the world, R. Chickering, 'Introduction: A Tale of Two Tales: Grand Narratives of War in the Age of Revolution', in Chickering and S. Förster (eds), *War in an Age of Revolution, 1775–1815* (New York, 2010), pp. 1–11.

15. T. Aston (ed.), *Crisis in Europe, 1560–1660* (London, 1965); G. Parker and L. M. Smith (eds), *The General Crisis of the Seventeenth Century* (London, 1978).

16. W. Cook, *The Hundred Years War for Morocco: Gunpowder and the Military Revolution in the Early Modern Muslim World* (Boulder, Colorado, 1994); M. Dorigny and B. Gainot, *Atlas des esclavages* (Paris, 2006), p. 30.

17. P. Lorge, *The Asian Military Revolution: From Gunpowder to the Bomb* (Cambridge, 2008), p. 180.

18. London, National Archives, State Papers (hereafter NA. SP.) 84/200 fol. 114.

19. P. Boucher, *Cannibal Encounters: Europeans and Island Caribs, 1492–1763* (Baltimore, Maryland, 1993).

20. J. A. Lynn, *Women, Armies, and Warfare in Early Modern Europe* (Cambridge, 2008), pp. 150–9.

21. Sir Leoline Jenkins, English plenipotentiary at the Congress of Nijmegen, to Sir Joseph Williamson, Secretary of State, 5 July 1676, NA. SP. 84/202 fol. 15.

22. NA. SP. 84/202 fol. 128. Ellis was Jenkins's secretary.

2: Sixteenth-Century Background

1. R. Murphey, *Ottoman Warfare* (London, 2000).

2. J. Gommans, *Mughal Warfare: Indian Frontiers and High Roads to Empire, 1500–1700* (London, 2002).

3. M. G. S. Hodgson, *The Venture of Islam, III: The Gunpowder Empires and Modern Times* (Chicago, Illinois, 1974); W. H. McNeill, *The Age of Gunpowder Empires, 1450–1800* (Washington, 1989); K. Chase, *Firearms: A Global History to 1700* (Cambridge, 2003).

4. S. Gordon, *Marathas, Marauders and State Formation in Eighteenth-Century India* (Oxford, 1994), p. 188.

5. K. Roy, *The Oxford Companion to Modern Warfare in India* (Oxford, 2009), pp. 23–4.

6. I have benefited from discussing this point with Mark Stevens.

7. V. T. B. Hui, *War and State Formation in Ancient China and Early Modern Europe* (Cambridge, 2005).

8. S. Pepper, 'Firepower and the Design of Renaissance Fortification', *Fort*, 10 (1982), pp. 92–104, and *Firearms and Fortifications: Military Architecture and Siege Warfare in Sixteenth-Century Siena* (Chicago, Illinois, 1986).

9. R. Knecht, *The French Civil Wars, 1562–1598* (Harlow, 2000).

10. C. Finkel, 'The Cost of Ottoman Warfare and Defence', *Byzantinische Forschungen*, 16 (1990), pp. 91–103.

11. J. M. Wilson (ed.), *From the Beginning: The Archaeology of the Maori* (Auckland, 1987).

12. A. P. Vayda, *Maori Warfare* (Wellington, 1960); A. Taylor, *The Maori Warrior* (Laie, Hawai'i, 1998); N. B. Dukas, *A Military History of Sovereign Hawai'i* (Honolulu, Hawai'i, 2004), pp. 2–26.

13. G. Knaap, 'Headhunting, Carnage and Armed Peace in Ambonia, 1500–1700', *Journal of the Economic and Social History of the Orient*, 46 (2003), pp. 165–92.

14. J. Bergin, *The Rise of Richelieu* (New Haven, Connecticut, 1991).

15. W. H. McNeill, *The Pursuit of Power: Technology, Armed Force, and Society since AD 1000* (Oxford, 1983).

16. J. Black, *War Since 1990* (London, 2009).

3: Conflict, 1590–1615

1. E. W. Bovil, *The Battle of Alcazar* (London, 1952).

2. S. Morillo, 'Guns and Government: A Comparative Study of Europe and Japan', *Journal of World History* 6 (1995), pp. 75–106.

3. M. E. Berry, *Hideyoshi* (Cambridge, Massachusetts, 1982).

4. K. M. Swope, 'Deceit, Disguise, and Dependence: China, Japan, and the Future of the Tributary System, 1592–1596', *International History Review*, 24 (2002), pp. 757–1008.

5. S. Turnbull, *Samurai Invasion: Japan's Korean War, 1592–1598* (London, 2002).

6. The numbers given for both sides vary considerably.

7. J. W. Hall (ed.), *The Cambridge History of Japan. IV: Early Modern Japan* (Cambridge, 1991); E. Ikegami, *The Taming of the Samurai: Honorific Individualism and the Making of Modern Japan* (Cambridge, Massachusetts, 1995).

8. G. Ágoston, 'Habsburgs and Ottomans: Military Changes and Shifts in Power', *Ottoman Studies Association Bulletin*, 22 (1998), pp. 126–41.

9. C. Keyvanian, 'Maps and Wars: Charting the Mediterranean in the Sixteenth Century', in B. Kolluoğlu and M. Toksöz (eds), *Cities of the Mediterranean: From the Ottomans to the Present Day* (London, 2010), p. 60.

10. G. Ágoston, 'Ottoman Artillery and European Military Technology in the Fifteenth and Sixteenth Centuries', *Acta Orientalia Academiae Scientarum Hungaricae*, 47 (1994), pp. 32–47, and 'Gunpowder for the Sultan's Army', *Turcica*, 25 (1993), pp. 75–96.

11. C. Dunning, *Russia's First Civil War: The Time of Troubles and the Founding of the Romanov Dynasty* (University Park, Pennsylvania, 2001).

12. J. P. Puype, 'Victory at Nieuwpoort', in M. van der Hoeven (ed.), *Exercise of Arms: Warfare in the Netherlands, 1568–1648* (Leiden, 1997), pp. 69–112.

13. P. C. Allen, *Philip III and the Pax Hispanica, 1598–1621: The Failure of Grand Strategy* (New Haven, Connecticut, 2000).

14. G. Parker, *The Grand Strategy of Philip II* (New Haven, Connecticut, 1998).

15. G. Parker, *The World Is Not Enough: The Imperial Vision of Philip II of Spain* (Waco, Texas, 2001), and *Success Is Never Final: Empire, War, and Faith in Early Modern Europe* (New York, 2002).

16. A. C. S. Peacock, 'The Ottoman Empire and Its Frontiers', in Peacock (ed.), *The Frontiers of the Ottoman World* (London, 2009), p. 16.

17. E. B. Monshi, *History of Shah Abbas the Great* (Boulder, Colorado, 1978); M. Haneda, 'The Evolution of the Safavid Royal Guard', *Iranian Studies*, 21 (1989), pp. 57–86.

18. R. Matthee, 'The Politics of Protection. Iberian Missionaries in Safavid Iran under Shāh 'Abbās I, 1587–1629', in C. Adang and S. Schmidtke (eds), *Contacts and Controversies between Muslims, Jews and Christians in the Ottoman Empire and Pre-Modern Iran* (Würzburg, 2010), pp. 245–71.

19. R. Mathee, 'Unwalled Cities and Restless Nomads: Firearms and Artillery in Safavid Iran', in C. Melville (ed.), *Safavid Persia. The History and Politics of an Islamic Society* (London, 1996), pp. 409–10.

20. C. Desplat, 'Louis XIII and the Union of Béarn to France', in M. Greengrass (ed.), *Conquest and Coalescence* (London, 1991), pp. 68–83.

4: Conflict, 1616–1650

1. N. Di Cosmo (ed.), *Military Culture in Imperial China* (Cambridge, Massachusetts, 2009).

2. R. Huang, 'The Liao-tung Campaign of 1619', *Oriens Extremus*, 28 (1981), pp. 30–54; T. J. Barfield, *The Perilous Frontier: Nomadic Empires and China, 221 BC to AD 1757* (Oxford, 1989), pp. 251–7.

3. J. B. Parsons, *Peasant Rebellions of the Late Ming Dynasty* (Tuscon, Arizona, 1970).

4. W. J. Griswold, *The Great Anatolian Rebellion, 1000–1020/1591–1611* (Berlin, 1983).

5. M. Rossabi (ed.), *China among Equals: The Middle Kingdom and Its Neighbors, 10th to 14th Centuries* (Berkeley, California, 1983).

6. J. Spence and J. Wills (eds), *From Ming to Ch'ing: Conquest, Region and Continuity in Seventeenth Century China* (New Haven, Connecticut, 1979); F. Wakeman, *The Great Enterprise: The Manchu Reconstruction of Imperial Order in Seventeenth-Century China* (Berkeley, California, 1985).

7. P. H. Wilson, *Europe's Tragedy. A History of the Thirty Years War* (London, 2009), p. 623.

8. J. A. Gross, 'Approaches to the Problem of Identity Formation', in Gross (ed.), *Muslims in Central Asia: Expressions of Identity and Change* (Durham, North Carolina, 1992), p. 17.

9. J. Gommans and D. H. A. Kolff (eds), *Warfare and Weaponry in South Asia, 1000–1800* (New Delhi, 2001).

10. D. P. Marston, *Phoenix from the Ashes: The Indian Army in the Burma Campaign* (Westport, Connecticut, 2004).

11. R. Matthee, 'Was Safavid Iran an Empire?', *Journal of the Economic and Social History of the Orient*, 53 (2010), p. 261.

12. J. F. Richards, *The Mughal Empire* (Cambridge, 1993), p. 139; J. Sarkar, *The Military Despatches of a Seventeenth Century Indian General* (Calcutta, 1969).

13. W. Irvine, *The Army of the Indian Moghuls: Its Organisation and Administration* (Delhi, 1962), pp. 113–59.

14. D. Lombard, *Le Sultanat d'Atjéh au temps d'Iskandar Muda, 1603–1636* (Paris, 1967).

15. The best short introduction is R. G. Asch, *The Thirty Years War: The Holy Roman Empire and Europe, 1618–1648* (Basingstoke, 1997). Wilson, *Europe's Tragedy*, supersedes earlier work but is lengthy. See also G. Parker et al., *The Thirty Years' War* (2nd edn, London, 1997).

16. O. Chaline, *La Bataille de la Montagne Blanche 8 Novembre 1620: Un mystique chez les Guerriers* (Paris, 2000).

17. P. Brightwell, 'Spain and Bohemia: The Decision to Intervene, 1619', and 'Spain, Bohemia and Europe, 1619–21', *European Studies Review*, 12 (1982), pp. 117–41, 331–99.

18. G. Mann, *Wallenstein* (London, 1976).
19. P. Lockhart, *Denmark in the Thirty Years' War, 1618–1848* (Selinsgrove, Pennsylvania, 1996).
20. E. Ringmar, *Identity, Interest and Action: A Cultural Explanation of Sweden's Intervention in the Thirty Years War* (Cambridge, 1996).
21. M. Roberts, *The Military Revolution, 1560–1660* (Belfast, 1956).
22. Amblard, Vicomte de Noailles, *Bernhard de Saxe-Weimar* (Paris, 1908).
23. A. Lopes Pires Nunes, 'Les guerres hollandaises au Bresil', in *Atti del XVIII Congresso internazionale di Storia Militaire*, (Rome, 1993), pp. 459–60.
24. J. Theibault, *German Villages in Crisis: Rural Life in Hesse-Kassel and the Thirty Years' War, 1580–1720* (Atlantic Highlands, New Jersey, 1995); T. McIntosh, *Urban Decline in Early Modern Germany: Schwäbisch Hall and Its Region, 1650–1750* (Chapel Hill, North Carolina, 1997).
25. R. J. Knecht, *The French Civil Wars* (Harlow, 2000), p. 287.
26. D. Croxton, '"The Prosperity of Arms Is Never Continual": Military Intelligence, Surprise, and Diplomacy in 1640s Germany', *Journal of Military History*, 64 (2000), pp. 981–1004, esp. pp. 991, 1001, and *Peacemaking in Early-Modern Europe: Cardinal Mazarin and the Congress of Westphalia, 1643–1648* (Selinsgrove, Pennsylvania, 1999).
27. For an English abridgement of the terms, G. Symcox (ed.), *War, Diplomacy and Imperialism, 1618–1763* (London, 1974), pp. 39–62.
28. D. Croxton, 'The Peace of Westphalia and the Origins of Sovereignty', *International History Review*, 21 (1999), pp. 569–91.
29. J. H. Elliott, *The Revolt of the Catalans* (Cambridge, 1963).
30. F. González de León, *The Road to Rocroi: Class, Culture and Command in the Spanish Army of Flanders, 1567–1659* (Leiden, 2008).
31. R. A. Stradling, *Spain's Struggle for Europe* (London, 1994), pp. 197–212.
32. O. Ranum, *The Fronde: A French Revolution, 1648–1652* (New York, 1993).
33. R. I. Frost, *The Northern Wars, 1558–1721* (London, 2000), pp. 310–12; W. Majewski, 'The Polish Art of War in the Sixteenth and Seventeenth Centuries', in J. K. Fedorowicz (ed.), *A Republic of Nobles: Studies in Polish History to 1864* (Cambridge, 1982), pp. 179–97.
34. M. T. Poe, *'A People Born to Slavery'. Russia in Early Modern European Ethnography, 1475–1748* (Ithaca, New York, 2001).
35. O. Subtelny, *Domination of Eastern Europe: Native Nobilities and Foreign Absolutism, 1500–1715* (Gloucester, 1986).
36. L. White, 'Strategic Geography and the Spanish Habsburg Monarchy's Failure to Recover Portugal, 1640–1668', *Journal of Military History*, 71 (2007), pp. 373–409.
37. M. Fissell, *The Bishops' Wars: Charles I's Campaigns Against Scotland, 1638–40* (Cambridge, 1994).

38. W. S. Brockington (ed.), *Monro: His Expedition with the Worthy Scots Regiment Called Mackeys* (Westport, Connecticut, 1999).
39. G. Parker, 'States Make War But Wars Also Break States', *Journal of Military History*, 74 (2010), pp. 11–34, esp. pp. 17–20.
40. I. Gentles, *The English Revolution and the Wars in the Three Kingdoms, 1638–1652* (London, 2007).
41. J. Morrill, *Revolt in the Provinces: The People of England and the Tragedies of War, 1630–1648* (2nd edn, Harlow, 1999).
42. M. Wanklyn and F. Jones, *A Military History of the English Civil War* (London, 2005), pp. 92–4.
43. M. Griffin, *Regulating Religion and Morality in the King's Armies, 1639–1646* (Leiden, 2004).
44. I. Gentles, *The New Model Army in England, Ireland and Scotland, 1645–1653* (Oxford, 1992).
45. R. B. Manning, 'Styles of Command in Seventeenth-Century English Armies', *Journal of Military History*, 71 (2007), pp. 671–99, quote p. 673.
46. J. S. Wheeler, *Cromwell in Ireland* (Dublin, 1999).
47. M. Wanklyn, *The Warrior Generals: Winning the British Civil Wars, 1642–1652* (New Haven, Connecticut, 2010), p. 231.
48. B. Donaghan, *War in England, 1642–1649* (Oxford, 2008), p. 89.
49. S. Bull, *The Furie of the Ordnance: Artillery in the English Civil Wars* (Woodbridge, 2008).

5: Conflict, 1650–1683

1. L. A. Struve, *The Southern Ming, 1644–1662* (New Haven, Connecticut, 1984).
2. F. Wakeman, *The Great Enterprise: The Manchu Reconstruction of Imperial Order in Seventeenth-Century China* (Berkeley, California, 1985), II, 1047.
3. C. Boxer, 'The Siege of Fort Zeelandia and the capture of Formosa from the Dutch, 1661–2', *Transactions and Proceedings of the Japan Society of London*, 24 (1926–7), pp. 16–47.
4. R. B. Oxnam, *Ruling from Horseback: Manchu Politics in the Oboi Regency, 1661–1669* (Chicago, Illinois, 1970).
5. N. Di Cosmo (ed.), *The Diary of a Manchu Soldier in Seventeenth-Century China: 'My Service in the Army', by Dzengseo* (London, 2006).
6. L. D. Kessler, *K'ang-Hsi and the Consolidation of Ch'ing Rule, 1661–1684* (Chicago, Illinois, 1976).
7. T. V. Mahalingam, *Readings in South Indian History* (Delhi, 1977), p. 154; M. Alam, *The Crisis of Empire in Mughal North India: Awadh and the Punjab, 1707–1748* (Delhi, 1986).

8. R. Stradling, 'Seventeenth Century Spain: Decline or Survival?', *European Studies Review*, 9 (1979), pp. 157–94.

9. J. Ohlmeyer (ed.), *Ireland from Independence to Occupation, 1638–1660* (Cambridge, 1995), and 'The Wars of Religion, 1603–1660', in T. Bartlett and K. Jeffery (eds), *A Military History of Ireland* (Cambridge, 1996), pp. 163–87; P. Lenihan (ed.), *Conquest and Resistance: War in Seventeenth-Century Ireland* (Leiden, 2001).

10. D. Farr, *Henry Ireton and the English Revolution* (Woodbridge, 2006).

11. J. Basarab, *Pereiaslav 1654* (Edmonton, 1982).

12. R. I. Frost, *After the Deluge: Poland-Lithuania and the Second Northern War* (Cambridge, 1993).

13. J. Inglis-Jones, 'The Battle of the Dunes, 1658: Condé, War and Power Politics', *War in History*, 1 (1994), pp. 249–77.

14. C. O'Brien, *Muscovy and Ukraine: From the Pereiaslav Agreement to the Truce of Andrusovo, 1654–1667* (Berkeley, California, 1963).

15. De Bacquoy to Williamson, 26 July 1664, NA. SP. 84/171.

16. NA. SP. 80/15 fol. 122.

17. NA. SP. 80/16 fol. 6.

18. D. McKay, *The Great Elector* (London, 2001), pp. 220–4.

19. Report of 17 July 1676, NA. SP. 84/202.

20. G. Satterfield, *Princes, Posts and Partisans: The Army of Louis XIV and Partisan Warfare in the Netherlands, 1673–1678* (Leiden, 2003), pp. 272, 213.

21. L. White, 'Strategic Geography and the Spanish Habsburg Monarchy's Failure to Recover Portugal, 1640–1668', *Journal of Military History*, 71 (2007), p. 390.

22. C. Pencemaille, 'La guerre de Hollande dans le programme icono-graphique de la grande galleries de Versailles', *Histoire, Economie et Société*, 4 (1985), pp. 313–33; C. Mukerji, *Territorial Ambitions and the Gardens of Versailles* (Cambridge, 1997).

23. K. Friedrich and S. Smart (eds), *The Cultivation of Monarchy and the Rise of Berlin: Brandenburg-Prussia 1700* (Farnham, 2010), p. 57.

24. NA. SP. 84/202 fols 73, 126, 84/207 fol. 124.

25. J. A. Lynn, 'Food, Funds, and Fortresses: Resources Mobilization and Positional Warfare in the Campaigns of Louis XIV', in Lynn (ed.), *Feeding Mars: Logistics in Western Warfare from the Middle Ages to the Present* (Boulder, Colorado, 1993), pp. 137–60, *Giant of the Grand Siècle: The French Army, 1619–1715* (Cambridge, 1997), *The Wars of Louis XIV* (Harlow 1999), 'Forging the Western Army in Seventeenth-Century France', in M. Knox and W. Murray (eds), *The Dynamics of Military Revolution, 1300–2050* (Cambridge, 2001), pp. 35–56, and 'Revisiting the Great Fact of War and Bourbon Absolutism: The Growth of the French Army During the *Grand*

Siècle', in E .G. Harnán and D. Maffi (eds), *Guerra y Sociedad en la Monarquá Hispánica: Politica, estrategia y cultura en la Europa moderna, 1500–1700* (Madrid, 2006), pp. 49–74.

26. G. Rowlands, 'Louis XIV, Aristocratic Power, and the Elite Units of the French Army', *French History*, 13 (1999), pp. 303–31, 'Louis XIV, Vittorio Amedeo II, and French Military Failure in Italy, 1689–96', *English Historical Review*, 115 (2000), pp. 534–69, and *The Dynastic State and the Army Under Louis XIV: Royal Service and Private Interest, 1661–1701* (Cambridge, 2002).

27. D. Parrott, *Richelieu's Army: War, Government and Society in France, 1624–1642* (Cambridge, 2002).

28. NA. SP. 78/142 fol. 289.

29. A. James, *The Navy and Government in Early Modern France, 1572–1661* (Woodbridge, 2004).

30. N. Henshall, *The Myth of Absolutism: Change and Continuity in Early Modern European History* (London, 1992).

31. T. M. Barker, *Army, Aristocracy, Monarchy: Essays on War, Society and Government in Austria, 1618–1780* (New York, 1982).

32. J. A. Harrison, *Japan's Northern Frontier* (Gainesville, Florida, 1953), pp. 7, 10.

6: The Expansion of Europe

1. A. J. Smithers, *The Tangier Campaign: The Birth of the British Army* (Stroud, 2003).

2. P. de Brito, 'Knights, Squires and Foot Soldiers in Portugal during the Sixteenth-century Military Revolution', *Mediterranean Studies*, 17 (2008), pp. 118–47.

3. G. Parker, *The Military Revolution: Military Innovation and the Rise of the West, 1500–1800* (Cambridge, 1988).

4. J. Black, *European Warfare, 1494–1660* (London, 2002), p. 197; G. Ágoston, 'Where Environmental and Frontier Studies Meet: Rivers, Forests, Marshes and Forts along the Ottoman–Hapsburg Frontier in Hungary', in A. C. S. Peacock (ed.), *The Frontiers of the Ottoman World* (London, 2009), p. 71.

5. J. Black, *War: A Short History* (London, 2009).

6. N. Salat and T. Sarmant (eds), *Lettres de Louvois à Louis XIV: Politique, guerre et fortification au Grand Siècle* (Paris, 2007).

7. J. Black, *European Warfare in a Global Context, 1660–1815* (Abingdon, 2007).

8. For a valuable approach from a different background, P. Lorge, *The Asian Military Revolution: From Gunpowder to the Bomb* (Cambridge, 2008).

9. D. Van der Cruyse, *Louis XIV et le Siam* (Paris, 1991).

10. A. J. Smithers, *The Tangier Campaign* (Stroud, 2003).

11. M. Mancall, *Russia and China: Their Diplomatic Relations to 1728* (Cambridge, 1971).

12. J. Forsyth, *A History of the Peoples of Siberia* (Cambridge, 1992).

13. D. Worster and T. F. Schlitz, 'The Spread of Firearms among the Indians of the Anglo-French Frontier', *American Indian Quarterly*, 8 (1984), pp. 103–15.

14. P. M. Malone, *The Skulking Way of War: Technology and Tactics among the New England Indians* (Lanham, Maryland, 1991).

15. L. V. Eid, 'The Cardinal Principle of Northeast Woodland Indian War', in W. Cowan (ed.), *Papers of the Thirteenth Alonquian Conference* (Ottawa, 1982), pp. 243–50.

16. A. Hirsch, 'The Collision of Military Cultures in Seventeenth-Century New England', and R. D. Karr, '"Why Should You Be So Ferocious?": The Violence of the Pequot War', *Journal of American History*, 74 (1988), pp. 1187–1212, 85 (1999), pp. 876–909.

17. T. Andrade, *How Taiwan Became Chinese: Dutch, Spanish, and Han Colonization in the Seventeenth Century* (New York, 2008).

18. J. Thornton, *The Kingdom of Kongo: Civil War and Transition* (Madison, Wisconsin, 1983).

19. G. Ames, *Renascent Empire? The House of Braganza and the Quest for Stability in Portuguese Monsoon Asia, c. 1640–1683* (Amsterdam, 2000).

20. A. C. S. Peacock, 'The Ottoman Empire and Its Frontiers', in Peacock (ed.), *Frontiers*, p. 16.

21. B. Davies, *Warfare, State and Society on the Black Sea Steppe, 1500–1700* (Abingdon, 2007), p. 205.

22. R. A. Kea, 'Firearms and Warfare on the Gold and Slave Coasts', *Journal of African History*, 12 (1971), pp. 185–213; J. Thornton, *Warfare in Atlantic Africa, 1500–1800* (London, 1999).

23. G. Nováky, *Handelskompanier och kompanihandel. Svenska Afrikakompaniet, 1649–1663* (Uppsala, 1990), English summary, pp. 241, 244.

24. R. Law and K. Mann, 'West Africa in the Atlantic Community: The Case of the Slave Coast', *William and Mary Quarterly*, 56 (1999), pp. 307–34.

25. K. Y. Daaku, *Trade and Politics on the Gold Coast, 1600–1700* (Oxford, 1970), pp. 96–114.

26. L. Y. Andaya, *The Heritage of Arung Palakka: A History of South Sulawesi in the Seventeenth Century* (The Hague, 1981), pp. 76–8, 130–3.

27. J. Kelenik, 'The Military Revolution in Hungary', in G. Dávid and P. Fodor (eds), *Ottomans, Hungarians, and Habsburgs in Central Europe: The Military Confines in the Era of Ottoman Conquest* (Leiden, 2000), pp. 117–59.

28. G. Börekçi, 'A Contribution to the Military Revolution Debate: the Janissaries' Use of Volley Fire during the long Ottoman–Habsburg War

of 1593–1606 and the Problem of Origins', *Acta Orientalia Academiae Scientiarum Hungaricae*, 59 (2006), pp. 407–38.

29. G. Ágoston, *Guns for the Sultan: Military Power and the Weapons Industry in the Ottoman Empire* (Cambridge, 2005).
30. C. Finkel, *The Administration of Warfare: Ottoman Campaigns in Hungary, 1593–1606* (Vienna, 1988).
31. G. Ágoston, 'Habsburgs and Ottomans: Military Change and Shifts in Power', *Ottoman Studies Association Bulletin*, 22 (1998), pp. 126–61; R. Murphey, *Ottoman Warfare* (London, 2000).
32. R. Murphey, 'The Ottoman Resurgence in the Seventeenth-Century Mediterranean: The Gamble and Its Results', *Mediterranean Historical Review*, 8 (1993), pp. 186–200.
33. T. M. Barker, *Double Eagle and Crescent: Vienna's Second Turkish Siege* (Albany, New York, 1967) and 'New Perspectives on the Historical Significance of the "Year of the Turk"', *Austrian History Yearbook*, 19–20 (1983–4), pp. 3–14; A. Wheatcroft, *The Enemy at the Gate: Habsburgs, Ottomans and the Battle for Europe* (London, 2008).
34. G. Ágoston, 'Behind the Turkish War Machine: Gunpowder Technology and War Industry in the Ottoman Empire, 1450–1700', in B. D. Steele and T. Dorland (eds), *The Heirs of Archimedes: Science and the Art of War through the Age of Enlightenment* (Boston, Massachusetts, 2005), p. 125.
35. M. Hochedlinger, 'The Habsburg Monarchy: From "Military-Fiscal State" to "Militarisation"', in C. Storrs (ed.), *The Fiscal-Military State in Eighteenth-Century Europe* (Farnham, 2009), p. 83.
36. NA. SP. 97/20.
37. K. M. Setton, *Venice, Austria and the Turks in the Seventeenth Century* (Philadelphia, Pennsylvania, 1984).
38. A. Arkayin, 'The Second Siege of Vienna (1683) and Its Consequences', *Revue Internationale d'Histoire Militaire*, 46 (1980), pp. 114–15.

7: Conflict, 1683–1707

1. J. A. Millward, *Beyond the Pass: Economy, Ethnicity, and Empire in Qing Central Asia, 1759–1864* (Stanford, California, 1998).
2. P. Perdue, *China Marches West: The Qing Conquest of Central Eurasia* (Cambridge, Massachusetts, 2005).
3. J. Gommans, 'War-horse and Post-nomadic Empire in Asia, c.1000–1800', *Journal of Global History*, 2 (2007), p. 14.
4. J. A. Lynn, 'Forging the Western Army in Seventeenth-century France', in M. Knox and W. Murray (eds), *The Dynamic of Military Revolution, 1300–2050* (Cambridge, 2001), pp. 39–40.

5. A. Balisch, 'Infantry Battlefield Tactics in the Seventeenth and Eighteenth Centuries on the European and Turkish Theatres of War: the Austrian Response to Different Conditions', *Studies in History and Politics*, 3 (1983–4), p. 44.

6. J. A. Lynn, *Giant of the Grand Siècle: The French Army, 1610–1715* (Cambridge, 1997), p. 476.

7. P. Lenihan, *1690: Battle of the Boyne* (Stroud, 2003).

8. O. van Nimwegen, *De subsistentie van het leger: Logistiek en Strategie van het Geallierde en met name het staatse leger tijdens de spaanse successieoorlog in de Nederlanden en het Heilige Roomse Rijk, 1701–1712* (Amsterdam, 1995), with English summary.

9. For a first-hand account, G. W. Story, *An Impartial History of the Wars of Ireland* (London, 1693).

10. J. Childs, *The British Army of William III, 1689–1702* (Manchester, 1987).

11. C. Storrs, 'The Savoyard Fiscal-Military State in the Long Eighteenth Century', in Storrs (ed.), *The Fiscal-Military State in Eighteenth-Century Europe* (Farnham, 2009), p. 206.

12. C. Storrs, 'The Army of Lombardy and the Resilience of Spanish Power in Italy in the Reign of Carlos II, 1665–1700', *War in History*, 4 (1997), p. 376, and *The Resilience of the Spanish Monarchy, 1665–1700* (Oxford, 2006).

13. J. M. Stapleton, 'Forging a Coalition Army: William III, the Grand Alliance, and the Confederate Army in the Spanish Netherlands, 1688–1697' (PhD, Ohio State, 2003).

14. H. Kleinschmidt, 'Using the Gun: Manual Drill and the Proliferation of Portable Firearms', *Journal of Military History*, 63 (1999), 601–29.

15. C. Duffy, *The Military Experience in the Age of Reason* (2nd edn, London, 1998).

16. B. Davies, *Warfare, State and Society on the Black Sea Steppe, 1500–1700* (London, 2007).

17. R. Hellie, 'The Petrine Army: Continuity, Change, and Impact', *Canadian-American Slavic Studies*, 8 (1974), p. 239.

8: Naval Capability and Warfare

1. D. Lombard, *Le Sultanat d'Atjéh, au temps d'Iskandar Muda, 1607–1636* (Paris, 1967).

2. D. Trim, 'Medieval and Early Modern Inshore, Estuarine, Riverine and Lacustrine Warfare', in Trim and M. Fissel (eds), *Amphibious Warfare, 1000–1700: Commerce, State Formation and European Expansion* (Leiden, 2006), pp. 357–420.

3. E. van Veen, 'How the Dutch Ran a Seventeenth-Century Colony: The Occupation and Loss of Formosa, 1624–1662', *Itinerario*, 20 (1996), pp. 59–77.

4. J. Glete, *War and the State in Early Modern Europe: Spain, the Dutch Republic and Sweden as Fiscal-Military States, 1500–1600* (London, 2002).
5. R. D. Bathurst, 'Maritime Trade and Imamate Government: Two Principal Themes in the History of Oman to 1728', in D. Hopwood (ed.), *The Arabian Peninsula: Society and Politics* (London, 1972), pp. 89–106; G. Ames, 'The Straits of Hurmuz Fleets: Omani–Portuguese Naval Rivalry and Encounters, c.1660–1680', *Mariner's Mirror*, 83 (1997), pp. 398–409.
6. V. Ostapchuk, 'Five Documents from the Topkapi Palace Archives on the Ottoman Defence of the Black Sea against the Cossacks', *Journal of Turkish Studies*, 2 (1987), pp. 49–104, and 'The Human Landscape of the Ottoman Black Sea in the Face of Cossack Naval Raids', *Oriente Moderno*, 20 (2001), pp. 23–95.
7. T. Kirk, *Genoa and the Sea: Policy and Power in an Early Modern Maritime Republic, 1589–1684* (Baltimore, Maryland, 2005).
8. NA. SP. 84/202 fol. 121.
9. A. De Groot, 'The Ottoman Mediterranean since Lepanto: Naval Warfare during the Seventeenth and Eighteenth Centuries', *Anatolica*, 20 (1994), pp. 269–93.
10. G. D. Winius, *The Fatal History of Portuguese Ceylon: Transition to Dutch Rule* (Cambridge, Massachusetts, 1971); R. J. Barendse, *The Arabian Seas: The Indian Ocean World of the Seventeenth Century* (Armonk, New York, 2002).
11. R. Baetens, 'The Organisation and Effects of Flemish Privateering in the Seventeenth Century', *Acta Historiae Neerlandicae*, 9 (1976), pp. 48–75.
12. J. R. Jones, *The Anglo-Dutch Wars of the Seventeenth Century* (London, 1996); M. Palmer, 'The Military Revolution Afloat: The Era of the Anglo-Dutch Wars', *War in History*, 4 (1997), pp. 123–49.
13. G. Rowlands, 'The King's Two Arms: French Amphibious Warfare in the Mediterranean under Louis XIV, 1664–1697', in D. J. B. Trim and M. Fissell (eds), *Amphibious Warfare 1000–1700: Commerce, State Formation and European Expansion* (Leiden, 2006), pp. 263–314; E. Laloy, *La Révolte de Messine, l'Expédition de Sicile, et la Politique Française en Italie, 1674–1678* (Paris, 1929).
14. P. Aubrey, *The Defeat of James Stuart's Armada, 1692* (Leicester, 1979).
15. J. Glete, *Navies and Nations: Warships, Navies, and State-Building in Europe and America, 1500–1860* (Stockholm, 1993); D. Dessert, *La Royale: Vaisseaux et marins du Roi-Soleil* (Paris, 1996).
16. S. Willis, *Fighting at Sea in the Eighteenth Century: The Art of Sailing Warfare* (Woodbridge, 2008).
17. J. Israel, *The Dutch Republic and the Hispanic World, 1606–1661* (Oxford, 1982).
18. C. Boxer, *The Dutch in Brazil, 1624–1654* (Oxford, 1957).

19. S. P. Sen, *The French in India: First Establishment and Struggle* (Calcutta, 1947), pp. 321–51; G. J. Ames, 'Colbert's Grand Indian Ocean Fleet of 1670', *Mariner's Mirror*, 76 (1990), pp. 235–40.

20. K. Zandvliet, *Mapping for Money: Maps, Plans and Topographic Paintings and Their Role in Dutch Overseas Expansion during the 16th and 17th Centuries* (Amsterdam, 1998).

21. A. Gat, 'What Constituted the Military Revolution of the Early Modern Period?', in R. Chickering and S. Förster (eds), *War in an Age of Revolutions, 1775–1815* (New York, 2010), p. 46.

22. P. Bamford, *Fighting Ships and Prisons: The Mediterranean Galleys of France in the Age of Louis XIV* (Minneapolis, Minnesota, 1973).

23. G. Symcox, *The Crisis of French Naval Power, 1688–1697* (The Hague, 1974).

24. J. R. Bruijn, *The Dutch Navy of the Seventeenth and Eighteenth Centuries* (Columbia, South Carolina, 1993).

25. J. Glete, *Navies and Nations: Warships, Navies and State Building in Europe and America, 1500–1860* (2 vols, Stockholm, 1993), I, 192.

26. S. F. Gradish, 'The Establishment of British Seapower in the Mediterranean, 1689–1713', *Canadian Journal of History*, (1975), pp. 1–16.

27. T. Hale, *An Account of several New Inventions and Improvements now necessary for England* (London, 1691).

28. G. Halkos and N. Kyrazis, 'A Naval Revolution and Institutional Change: The Case of the United Provinces', *European Journal of Law and Economics*, 19 (2005), pp. 41–68.

29. J. Glete, *War and the State in Early Modern Europe: Spain, the Dutch Republic and Sweden as Fiscal-Military States, 1500–1660* (London, 2002).

9: Warfare, Social Contexts and State Development

1. C. Tilly, *Coercion, Capital, and European States, AD 990–1990* (Oxford, 1990), Tilly (ed.), *The Formation of National States in Western Europe* (Princeton, New Jersey, 1975).

2. B. Downing, *The Military Revolution and Political Change: Origins of Democracy and Autocracy in Early Modern Europe* (Princeton, New Jersey, 1990).

3. K. DeVries, 'Gunpowder Weaponry and the Rise of the Early Modern State', *War in History*, 5 (1998), pp. 127–45.

4. B. Teschke, 'Revisiting the "War-Makes-States" Thesis: War, Taxation and Social Property Relations in Early Modern Europe', in O. Asbach and P. Schröder (eds), *War, the State and International Law in Seventeenth-Century Europe* (Farnham, 2010), p. 58.

5. J. A. Brandão, *'Your Fyre Shall Burn No More': Iroquois Policy toward New France and Its Native Allies to 1701* (Lincoln, Nebraska, 1997).

6. G. Hanlon, *The Twilight of a Military Tradition: Italian Aristocrats and European Conflicts, 1560–1800* (London, 1996); M. Hochedlinger, 'Mars Ennobled: The Ascent of the Military and the Creation of a Military Nobility in Mid-Eighteenth-Century Austria', *German History*, 17 (1999), pp. 141–76.

7. D. Potter, *War and Government in the French Provinces: Picardy, 1470–1560* (Cambridge, 1993).

8. M. Gutmann, *War and Rural Life in the Early Modern Low Countries* (Princeton, New Jersey, 1980); J. Canning (ed.), *Power, Violence, and Mass Death in Pre-Modern and Modern Times* (Aldershot, 2004).

9. J. Ruff, *Violence in Early Modern Europe, 1500–1800* (Cambridge, 2001).

10. P. Brummett, 'The River Crossing: Breaking Points (Metaphorical and "Real") in Ottoman Mutiny', in J. Hathaway (ed.), *Rebellion, Repression, Reinvention: Mutiny in Comparative Perspective* (Westport, Connecticut, 2001), pp. 222–3.

11. L. M. Heywood, 'Slavery and Its Transformation in the Kingdom of Kongo, 1491–1800', *Journal of African History*, 50 (2009), p. 18.

12. J. A. Lynn, *Women, Armies, and Warfare in Early Modern Europe* (Cambridge, 2008), pp. 150–9.

13. G. J. Millar, *Tudor Mercenaries and Auxiliaries, 1485–1547* (Charlottesville, Virginia, 1980).

14. F. Redlich, *The German Military Enterpriser and His Work Force* (2 vols, Wiesbaden, 1964–51).

15. D. Kolff, *Naukar, Rajput and Sepoy: The Ethnohistory of the Military Labour Market in Hindustan, 1450–1850* (Cambridge, 1990).

16. G. Rowlands, 'Foreign Service in the Age of Absolute Monarchy: Louis XIV and his *Forces Étrangères*', *War in History*, 17 (2010), pp. 141–65.

17. C. Storrs, *War, Diplomacy and the Rise of Savoy, 1690–1720* (Cambridge, 1999), pp. 316–17.

18. P. Wilson, *Europe's Tragedy: A History of the Thirty Years War* (London, 2009), p. 828.

19. D. J. B. Trim, 'Ideology, Greek, and Social Discontent in Early Modern Europe: Mercenaries and Mutinies in the Rebellious Netherlands, 1568–1609', in J. Hathaway (ed.), *Rebellion, Repression, Reinvention: Mutiny in Comparative Perspective* (Westport, Connecticut, 2001), p. 52.

20. D. Potter, 'Les Allemands et les armées françaises au XVIe siècle. Jean-Philippe Rhingrave, chef de lansquenets: étude suivie de sa correspondance en France, 1548–1566', *Francia*, 20 (1993), pp. 1–20 and 'The International Mercenary Market in the Sixteenth-Century: Anglo-French Competition in Germany, 1543–50', *English Historical Review*, (1996), pp. 24–58.

21. J. Lindegern, 'The "Swedish Military State", 1560–1720', *Scandinavian Journal of History*, 10 (1985), pp. 305–36.

22. C. Boxer, 'Asian Potentates and European Artillery in the 16th–18th Centuries', *Journal of the Malaysian Branch of the Royal Asiatic Society*, 28 (1966), pp. 156–72; S. Subrahmanyam, 'The *Kagemusha* Effect: the Portuguese, Firearms and the State in Early Modern South Asia', *Môyen Orient et Océan Indien*, 4 (1989), pp. 97–123; G. V. Scammell, 'European Exiles, Renegades and Outlaws and the Maritime Economy of Asia, c. 1500–1700', *Modern Asian Studies*, 26 (1992), pp. 641–61.

23. L. R. García, 'Types of Armies: Early Modern Spain', in P. Contamine (ed.), *War and Competition between States* (Oxford, 2000), p. 62.

24. Y. Dai, 'To Nourish a Strong Military: Kangxi's Preferential Treatment of His Military Officials', *War and Society*, 18 (2000), pp. 90–1.

25. M. Perrie, *Pretenders and Popular Monarchism in Early Modern Russia: The False Tsars of the Time of Troubles* (Cambridge, 1995); C. Dunning, *Russia's First Civil War: The Time of Troubles and the Founding of the Romanov Dynasty* (University Park, Pennsylvania, 2001).

26. D. McKay, *The Great Elector* (London, 2001), pp. 169–78.

27. P. Sonnino, *Louis XIV and the Origins of the Dutch War* (Cambridge, 1988).

28. D. Morgan, *Medieval Persia, 1040–1797* (London, 1988), p. 105.

29. R. Hainsworth, *The Swordsmen in Power: War and Politics under the English Republic, 1649–1660* (Stroud, 1997).

30. R. E. Mayers, *1659: The Crisis of the Commonwealth* (Woodbridge, 2004).

31. NA. SP. 84/200 fol. 1.

32. NA. SP. 84/202 fol. 128.

33. J. A. Lynn, 'Forging the Western Army in Seventeenth-Century France', in M. Knox and W. Murray (eds), *The Dynamics of Military Revolution, 1300–2050* (Cambridge, 2001), pp. 52–3.

34. G. Rowlands, *The Dynastic State and the Army under Louis XIV: Royal Service and Private Interest, 1661–1701* (Cambridge, 2002), pp. 166–71; J. Chagniot, 'La rationalisation de l'armée française après 1660', in *Armées et Diplomatie dans l'Europe du XVIIe Siècle* (Paris, 1991), pp. 97–108; and H. Drévillon, *L'impôt du sang: Le métier des arms sous Louis XIV* (Paris, 2005).

35. M. Hochedlinger, 'The Habsburg Monarchy: From "Military-fiscal State" to "Militarisation"', in C. Storrs (ed.), *The Fiscal-Military State in Eighteenth-Century Europe* (Farnham, 2009), p. 82.

36. K. J. V. Jespersen, 'Social Change and Military Revolution in Early Modern Europe: Some Danish Evidence', *Historical Journal*, 26 (1983), pp. 4–13.

37. D. Dessert, *Argent, Pouvoir et Société au Grand Siècle* (Paris, 1984); J. C. Collins, *Classes, Estates, and Order in Early Modern Brittany* (Cambridge, 1994).

38. J. A. Lynn, 'The *trace italienne* and the Growth of Armies: the French Case', in C. J. Rogers (ed.), *The Military Revolution Debate* (Boulder, Colorado, 1995), pp. 169–99.

10: Conclusions: Beyond the Military Revolution

1. D. A. Neill, 'Ancestral Voices: The Influence of the Ancients on the Military Thought of the Seventeenth and Eighteenth Centuries', *Journal of Military History*, 62 (1998), pp. 487–520.

2. J. Bennett and S. Johnston, *The Geometry of War, 1500–1750* (Oxford, 1996).

3. A. W. Crosby, *The Measure of Reality: Quantification and Western Society, 1250–1600* (Cambridge, 1997).

4. J. Roberts, *The Compleat Cannoniere* (London, 1639).

5. E.g., Joseph Furttenbach, *Architectura navalis* (Frankfurt, 1629), and, far more significantly, Paul Hoste, *L'Art des armées navales* (Lyons, 1697).

6. NA. SP. 78/142 fol. 287.

7. A. E. López, 'La Historiografía Hispana Sobre la Guerra en la Época de los Austrias: Un Balance, 1991–2000', *Manuscrits*, 21 (2003), pp. 161–91.

8. P. Lorge, *The Asian Military Revolution: From Gunpowder to the Bomb* (Cambridge, 2008).

9. J. M. Hill, *Celtic Warfare* (Edinburgh, 1986) and 'The Distinctiveness of Gaelic Warfare, 1400–1750', *European History Quarterly*, 22 (1992), pp. 323–45.

10. B. Davies, *Warfare, State and Society on the Black Sea Steppe, 1500–1700* (Abingdon, 2007).

11. P. Dukes, 'The Leslie Family in the Swedish Period (1630–35) of the Thirty Years' War', *European Studies Review*, 12 (1982), pp. 401–24; S. Murdoch, *Scotland and the Thirty Years' War, 1618–1848* (Leiden, 2001); A. Grosjean, *An Unofficial Alliance: Scotland and Sweden 1569–1654* (Leiden, 2003).

12. P. Bushkovitch, 'The Romanov Transformation, 1613–1725', in F. Kagan and R. Higham (eds), *The Military History of Tsarist Russia* (Basingstoke, 2002); M. Paul, 'The Military Revolution in Russia, 1550–1682', *Journal of Military History*, 68 (2004), pp. 9–45; B. Davies, 'Military Engineers and the Rise of Imperial Russia', forthcoming essay. I would like to thank Brian Davies for letting me read and cite his paper.

13. J. Needham, *Military Technology: The Gunpowder Epic* (Cambridge, 1987), pp. 393–8; J. Waley-Cohen, 'China and Western Technology in the Late Eighteenth Century', *American Historical Review*, 98 (1993), pp. 1531–2.

14. C. Imber, *The Ottoman Empire, 1300–1650* (2nd edn, Basingstoke, 2009), p. 294.

15. W. Maltby, 'Politics, Professionalism and the Evolution of Sailing Ships Tactics', in J. A. Lynn (ed.), *Tools of War: Instruments, Ideas and Institutions of Warfare, 1445–1871* (Chicago, Illinois, 1990), pp. 53–73.
16. C. Duffy, *Through German Eyes: The British and the Somme, 1916* (London, 2006), p. 323.
17. Notably the third edition of Geoffrey Parker's *Military Revolution*; and O. van Nimwegen, *The Dutch Army and the Military Revolutions, 1588–1688* (Woodbridge, 2010).

Index